THE LONDON MISSIONARY SOCIETY IN SOUTHERN AFRICA, 1799–1999

THE LONDON MISSIONARY SOCIETY IN SOUTHERN AFRICA, 1799-1999

Historical Essays in Celebration of the Bicentenary of the LMS in Southern Africa

Edited by John de Gruchy

OHIO UNIVERSITY PRESS
Athens

Ohio University Press
Athens, Ohio 45701
© 2000 by Ohio University Press
Printed in the United States of America
All rights reserved

First published 1999 in Southern Africa by David Philip Publishers (Pty)
Ltd, 208 Werdmuller Centre, Newry Street, Claremont 7708, South Africa

First published 2000 in USA by Ohio University Press, Athens, Ohio
Ohio University Press books are printed on acid-free paper ∞ ™

09 08 07 06 05 04 03 02 01 00   5 4 3 2 1

Library of Congress Cataloging-in-Publication Data

The London Missionary Society in Southern Africa, 1799-1999: histori-
cal essays in celebration of the bicentenary of the LMS in Southern
Africa / edited by John de Gruchy.
  p. cm.
Originally published: Cape Town, South Africa : David Philip, 1999.
Includes bibliographical references and index.
  ISBN 0-8214-1349-X (pbk.)
  1. Missions—Africa, Southern—History—19th century.   2. London
Missionary Society—History—19th century.   3. Congregationalism—
History of doctrines—19th century.   4. Africa, Southern—Church
history—20th century.   6. London Missionary Society—History—20th
century.   7. Congregationalism—History of doctrines—20th century.
8. Africa, Southern—Church history—20th century.
  I. De Gruchy, John W.   II. London Missionary Society.

BV3555 .L66 2000
266'.02341068—dc21   00-036683

CONTENTS

CONTRIBUTORS

Professors Jean and John Comaroff, Department of Anthropology, University of Chicago, USA

Dr Elizabeth Elbourne, Department of History, McGill University, Quebec, Canada

Dr Natasha Erlank, Department of History, Rand Afrikaans University, Johannesburg

Professor Norman Etherington, Department of History, University of Western Australia

John de Gruchy, Robert Selby Taylor Professor of Christian Studies, Department of Religious Studies, University of Cape Town, South Africa

Dr Steve de Gruchy, Director, Moffat Mission, Kuruman, Northern Cape, South Africa

Dr Helen Ludlow, Department of History, Johannesburg College of Education, South Africa

Professor Andrew Ross, Department of Ecclesiastical History, Edinburgh University, Scotland

Dr Robert Ross, Co-ordinator of African Studies, Leiden University, The Netherlands

Professor Christopher Saunders, Department of History, University of Cape Town, South Africa

Professor Les Switzer, Department of History, University of Houston, USA

ACKNOWLEDGEMENTS

I wish to express my thanks to David Philip Publishers for their readiness to publish this volume. David Philip is a great-grandson of John Philip, the LMS Superintendent at the Cape who figures prominently in the book. I am also indebted to Russell Martin for his support, editorial skills and friendship. Gilliam Walters did sterling work as my research and editorial assistant, and the volume would not have been possible without her help. Finally, my gratitude to all the authors who so willingly contributed essays to the volume under considerable pressure.

JOHN DE GRUCHY
Cape Town

REMEMBERING A LEGACY

John W. de Gruchy

At one time the London Missionary Society (LMS) was the best known of all the Christian missions at work in South and southern Africa. The only society that had arrived earlier was the Moravian, but its founding work at Genadendal was brought to an early halt by the authorities and was only resuscitated later. LMS missionaries were not alone in pioneering missionary outreach through-out much of the Cape Colony and beyond its borders, but they were often in the forefront, and to be found in many of the far-flung corners of the region. Some, such as Robert Moffat and David Livingstone, were regarded back home in Britain as heroes and role models. Others, such as Johannes van der Kemp, James Read and John Philip were less known there but well known in the Cape Colony. The latter three were, in fact, notorious as far as the settlers and colo-nial officials were concerned because of their role in championing the rights of slaves and the indigenous people. Beyond the northern border of the colony, Moffat also gained notoriety, charged with gun-running by the Boers. But whether the missionaries of the LMS were heralded as saints or condemned as traitors or agents of European colonisation, they played an important role in shaping the social history of southern Africa during the nineteenth century.

The LMS was founded in London in 1795. Its charter made clear that the purpose of the society was 'not to send Presbyterianism, Independency, Episcopacy, or any other form of Church Order and Government' to distant lands, but to take 'the Glorious Gospel of the blessed God to the heathen'. Four years later, in 1799, Johannes van der Kemp landed in Cape Town, the first of the many LMS missionaries who would follow. This volume of essays is, there-fore, in part a contribution to the celebration of the bicentenary of that event and, as such, the beginning of the Congregational church tradition in southern Africa. Perhaps that is sufficient reason for its publication. However, I believe that there are other reasons for revisiting the legacy of the LMS at this time.

The first has to do with the contemporary status of Christianity in South and southern Africa in the light of the missionary movement, and especially its links with European colonialism and economic expansion. As already intimated, opinions on the LMS missionaries were polarised at the time between those who regarded them as heroes and those who named them demons. But the issues that divided opinion were somewhat different from those that have attracted the attention of scholars in more recent times, especially during the post-Second World War process of African decolonisation. Most historians, especially those working from a materialist perspective, have condemned the missionaries as agents of imperialism and capitalism. That there is evidence to support this judgment is undeniable. Sometimes their role was unwitting, but often it was intentional. Yet it cannot be denied that there were some missionaries who, whatever their faults, were critical of the colonial adventure and who tried to the best of their ability and insight to identify with the plight and cause of the indigenous people. At least some of the LMS missionaries can be numbered amongst the latter.

The reason for remembering their legacy, then, is not to whitewash the record and restore the missionaries to any pure and undefiled status. Those who read these essays will soon recognise that their warts are as much in evidence as any of their virtues. They were men and women of their time who believed in the Empire and the need to spread 'civilisation', but they also had a mission to 'proclaim the Glorious Gospel', and that was the primary reason why they came to our shores. These essays indicate ways in which they both failed and succeeded in that task, and, as such, are intended to contribute to an ongoing debate on the place of Christianity in the social history of southern Africa. If we cannot celebrate their sins we can and surely must celebrate their contribution to the struggle for justice.

The second reason for remembering the LMS legacy is an ecumenical one. The LMS was not founded to promote a particular denomination but to further the cause of the Christian gospel. Within a decade or so, as particular denominations in Britain and elsewhere began to establish their own missionary societies, this ecumenical ethos began to change. Very soon the dominant group left within the LMS was the Independents or, as they became better known, the Congregationalists. So the LMS, by default, became the missionary society of the Congregational churches in Britain. Yet the policy of the LMS in southern Africa was not, in the first place, to establish a Congregational denomination but self-supporting congregations and to allow them the freedom to determine their future structure. A number eventually opted for other denominations, which explains in part why, despite the fact that the LMS was the pioneer missionary society, it did not establish a large denomination. The majority of the LMS congregations did, however, associate themselves with the Evangelical Voluntary Union founded in 1859 by British settlers, which became the Congregational Union of South Africa in 1877. Much later, in 1967, the United Congregational Church of Southern Africa (UCCSA) was established, uniting the Congregational Union, the churches of the LMS in

Botswana and Zimbabwe, as well as the Bantu Congregational Church which was founded by the American Board Mission in Natal. Some of the essays recognise this latter link.

However, the salient point that needs to be made does not have to do with the denominational development of the LMS, the American Board or Congregationalism. Rather it is the sad recognition that what started out as a venture full of ecumenical promise did not achieve that goal. Instead of the creation of a united African church, denominationalism took root and flourished as each European church went its own way. European denominationalism and division has done considerable damage in southern Africa. Yet those who are true to the legacy of the LMS believe that the ecumenical vision which inspired its founders remains mandatory for the church today. How the church in South and southern Africa will express its given unity in the twenty-first century remains to be seen. That it must seek to do so is essential to its integrity and witness.

The third reason for remembering the legacy of the LMS has to do with the process of Africanisation, currently of such importance for the church in southern Africa. Like most other missionaries, those of the LMS were generally ill-equipped to understand, let alone appreciate, African culture and religion. For them, sub-Saharan Africa was the 'dark continent' plagued by ignorance, disease and heathenism. They had come to bring the truth, healing and redemption. Christianity and European civilisation were, if not coterminous, at least somehow intrinsically connected. After all, Christian norms and values had shaped European society for at least a millennium. So they had come to help Africans to enter into the modern civilised world, a world dominated by the benign rule of Britannia and its commercial expansion.

If Africans were to enter the modern world, and to benefit to their own advantage, so the missionaries argued, they needed to learn the appropriate habits, skills and work ethic. With these given assumptions the failure of the missionaries to understand and appreciate African culture and religion was inevitable. Yet they did recognise the importance of language. With little if any training, the LMS pioneers learnt the indigenous languages, created grammars, and translated the Bible. Linguists and philologists may, with justification, criticise the results of their labours, but this can in no way gainsay the remarkable achievements of the likes of Moffat. We can surely learn from their mistakes as we seek today to develop a multi-cultural society, but we can also learn much from their dedication to learn the language of others with whom we share a common land and destiny.

The fourth and final reason for remembering the legacy of the LMS has to do with the role of women within the missionary scheme of things. There can be little doubt that the leadership of the LMS, including the male missionaries who came to South Africa, were patriarchal in their views. They were men of their time. But there is plenty of evidence that, despite this, their wives and other women missionaries were often remarkable people in their own right. Jane Philip is a good example, and there were others. Moreover, many of their converts were women who became missionary pioneers themselves. Indeed, the spread of Christianity in southern Africa was largely the result of the work of indigenous converts, and the majority of these were women.

South Africa is a very different place today from what it was when Van der Kemp landed on the shores of Table Bay in 1799. Part of the reason for this can be attributed to what he and subsequent LMS missionaries achieved in the course of the nineteenth century. Much of this has been forgotten, and the memory of what they accomplished may become even more dim during the course of the next century. This would be a pity because their role needs to be remembered. As many leaders of the struggle against colonialism and apartheid in southern Africa have warmly acknowledged, they were the products of Christian missions as much as anything else.

The origin of this volume can be traced back to discussions within the United Congregational Church regarding appropriate ways to celebrate the bicentenary of Congregationalism in southern Africa. Various proposals were made and several adopted which were aimed at the constituency of the UCCSA itself. But it was also felt that more was required than basking in the glories of the past as popularly conceived. If our memories are to serve the present and future they must be chastened by critical reflection on the past. That is the purpose of this collection of essays; hence most of them have been written by professional historians. Their aim has not been to praise or damn the missionaries but to reconstruct the story as truthfully as possible using the resources of their craft.

The first of the essays, that by Christopher Saunders, provides an overview of the literature that has been written about the history of the LMS in southern Africa during the past 170 years. This gives the reader a useful guide to the way in which the story of the LMS has been told and evaluated. Saunders helps to locate the essays of this volume within a larger framework of discussion.

We then move to three essays on the best known of the patriarchs of the LMS, Robert Moffat and his son-in-law, David Livingstone. The essay on Moffat has been written by Steve de Gruchy, who is currently director of the Kuruman Moffat Mission. De Gruchy writes from the perspective of one who is an 'insider'. He is the only author, apart from the editor, who is a member of the UCCSA as well as an ordained minister and theologian. But of more significance in this case is his perspective as one who is attempting to stand in Moffat's shoes, though at a very different time in history. Andrew Ross has written widely on the LMS and on Livingstone. He is also an 'insider', though not within the UCCSA. An ordained minister of the Church of Scotland, he was a missionary in Malawi for several years, and more recently a church historian at the University of Edinburgh. The next essay, that by John and Jean Comaroff, two distinguished social anthropologists at the University of Chicago, is written from a very different perspective. The work of the Comaroffs is widely recognised as breaking new ground in interpreting the connections between the missionaries, colonialism and African culture. Readers of this essay will not be disappointed.

The next four essays are case studies of the work of the LMS in two important colonial centres, Cape Town and Grahamstown, during the period 1820–50. The initial two focus on the work of John and Jane Philip. John Philip was the first Superintendent of the LMS in southern Africa and one of the most prominent missionary leaders of the day. His role in combating slavery is well known. Less known is the work of Jane Philip, who made a major contribution to education in early Cape Town, especially amongst the underprivileged. Natasha Erlank, a history graduate of Cape Town and Cambridge, helps us to understand some of the internal dynamics within the Philip home, shedding fresh light on the role of women within the structures of the LMS at the time. In a complementary essay, Helen Ludlow, who teaches at the Johannesburg College of Education, provides new insight into the educational ministry of the LMS, and especially the Philips.

The next two essays take us to the eastern Cape frontier. Both of them focus on controversies which began to erupt during this period as missionaries sought to minister to newly established indigenous congregations while, at the same time, functioning within the framework of settler society. The basic issue had to do with whether African converts had sufficient capacity to run the affairs of their own churches. This was a particularly acute problem given the congregational polity of the LMS, which stressed the role of the local church in decision-making. Debates about such matters were to plague the emerging church in southern Africa, irrespective of denomination, for the next century. It is interesting to reflect, with hindsight, on how long it took for the church to respect the leadership of Africans. Robert Ross teaches at the Rijksuniversiteit at Leiden in the Netherlands, and Elizabeth Elbourne at McGill University, Montreal.

In the final two essays, those by Norman Etherington and Les Switzer, our attention shifts from the Cape to Natal, and from the LMS to the American Board Mission. Etherington teaches history at the University of Western Australia, Nedlands, and Switzer at the University of Houston in Texas. As already indicated, the ABM was the missionary society of Congregational churches in the United States and, as such, represented this tradition in Natal. In many respects the issues facing the two societies, ABM and LMS, were the same. However, there were also some important differences, which reflected differences of historical context and missionary style. These become evident in the essays. Etherington's deals with the living standards of the missionaries in comparison with their black colleagues and congregants. This provides an early account of a problem that is still with us, namely the division of the church along class lines. The other essay, that by Switzer, reflects the growing tensions within the emerging mission church in Natal, which resulted from the inability of the missionaries to appreciate the dynamics of African culture. Again, it is an issue that has continually affected the church in southern Africa, and one which is explored in various ways throughout this volume. It is a fitting place to end.

Looking Back: 170 years of Historical Writing on the LMS in South Africa

Christopher Saunders

That more should have been written on the LMS than on any other missionary society in South Africa is hardly surprising.[1] No other society was more important in the nineteenth century, or as controversial. Because a number of its leading members played active political roles, historians otherwise little interested in the history of missions as such devoted much attention to the LMS.[2] And in the second half of the twentieth century, the interest continued, in part because of the ways in which missionary work was linked to colonialism, but also because, as many LMS missionaries opened frontier relations with indigenous peoples, their writings constituted the single most important extant source on early contacts with those peoples. While the destruction of the papers of John Philip in a fire at the Wits Library in 1931 was an immense tragedy for later scholarship on the LMS in South Africa, the large collection of journals and correspondence between the missionaries in the field and the secretaries and directors of the Society in London not only survived, but from the 1960s became more accessible to scholars.[3] Much exciting new work, as we shall see, has been based on material in that collection.

In surveying what has been written about the LMS since the early nineteenth century – and any such survey must inevitably be highly selective – it is at once apparent that a distinction can be drawn between literature which is broadly sympathetic to the work of the Society, whether by people with links to the Society or by professional historians, and that which is, in one or other way, critical of the activities and role of the missionaries of the LMS. But to survey sympathetic and critical literature in turn would obscure the connections between them, so I shall, instead, adopt a broadly chronological approach. And in doing that one can distinguish between the scholarly work of the last thirty years, which has taken the study of the LMS into new terrain, and what went before. I shall first survey the earlier literature, whether amateur or professional, polemical or hagiographic, and then turn to this relatively recent scholarly work, to see in what ways it has advanced our knowledge. Finally, I shall point to some issues which require further research.

The first reflective accounts of LMS work came from the missionaries themselves. Snippets of history can be found in some of their reports published in the *Transactions of the London Missionary Society* and elsewhere. The first general discussion of the early work of the Society at the Cape appeared in the pages of *Researches in South Africa*, which John Philip, the single most important figure in the entire LMS story, published in 1828. His book was written to put the case for the Khoikhoi, and to rebut the many charges made against the early LMS missionaries by white farmers and colonial officials.[4] Later, other missionaries, such as John Mackenzie, published work which in part reflected on aspects of the history of the activities of the Society in the region.[5] Some of those who wrote on that history wished to explain the difficulties of the work in South Africa;[6] others, like Philip in the *Researches*, in order to challenge criticisms of the LMS in newspapers or official papers at the Cape.

The *Researches* provoked a debate about the early history of the Cape, but that debate turned on the way the white settlers had treated the Khoisan, rather than on the specific actions of the LMS missionaries.[7] It was not until thirty years after Philip's death, when the winding down of LMS work in what is now South Africa was far advanced, that a full-scale critical account of the LMS role emerged. George McCall Theal, most prolific and influential of South African historians, set out a view of the LMS which long remained the dominant one in the historical consciousness of most white South Africans. When he had worked at Lovedale mission in the early 1870s, Theal had written sympathetically of the LMS and other missionary societies,[8] but after he moved to Cape Town later in that decade, he accepted the settler view on many issues. He now elaborated the earlier critical view of the LMS, the one Philip had sought to rebut, using what evidence he could find to present Philip himself as a political busybody and naive supporter of the indigenous people, responsible for much that had, from a settler perspective, gone wrong at the Cape in the early nineteenth century. From Theal's multi-volume *History of South Africa* this critical view of the LMS found its way into much later writing, including history textbooks for schools.[9]

This critical view did not, of course, go unchallenged. Even before being sent the 'gold-mine' of the John Philip papers in 1920, the Oxford-trained William Miller Macmillan had rejected Theal's pro-settler view of South African history. Drawing on the Philip papers, Macmillan was able to provide the first detailed, analytical account of the political role of the LMS in the early nineteenth century. In his classic works, *The Cape Colour Question and Bantu, Boer, and Briton*, Macmillan presented Philip as the most knowledgeable South African of his time, and he treated sympathetically the concern of the LMS missionaries to bring about social change.[10] It was very fortunate that Macmillan used the Philip papers to good effect before they were destroyed, for a wealth of unexploited information about the Society was lost when they went up in smoke.[11] From his perspective, the early LMS missionaries were important in establishing the Cape liberal tradition, which looked to the incorporation of people of colour into a common society based on equal political rights and the gradual elimination over time of economic inequalities. In the 1920s Macmillan was concerned to reassert the importance of that tradition at a time when it was under threat from supporters of segregation.

The 'liberalism' of the early LMS missionaries, and the political role of Philip, would long continue to stimulate historical research, as we shall see, but in addition there was also work by those interested in the missionaries for their own sake. At the time of the Society's centenary, two amateur historians wrote histories to mark the event and included, from the brief published reports of the Society, much factual information about who the missionaries were and the way in which the Society's work had grown in South Africa. Such writing tended to present that growth as straightforward and unproblematic; little context was provided and, not surprisingly, the writing was reverential in tone.[12]

In 1911 Professor J. du Plessis published the first scholarly general survey of South African mission history. His book aimed to 'place the establishment and growth of Christian Missions in their true historical setting'. The chapters he devoted to the LMS constituted by far the best coherent survey then available of the history of its missions, seen within the context of all mission work in South Africa. Though the views and methods of the leading LMS missionaries had 'excited disapproval', Du Plessis added that 'none can refuse them the honour due to talent, industry and Christian character'.[13] His main interest was in the way mission work had developed, not in what message the missionaries purveyed, or how it was received by the people among whom they laboured. Useful as an overview, his book remained largely descriptive and institutional, and the 'progress' of the missionaries in spreading the Christian gospel was considered largely unproblematically.[14]

A similar approach was to be found in later works on the theme of 'the planting of Christianity in Africa'.[15] A well-written and well-ordered short history of the LMS, which moved from one area of activity to another, was contained in the pages of *The Harvest and the Hope*, which appeared with the subtitle 'The story of Congregationalism in southern Africa' in 1970. Written by D. Roy Briggs and Joseph Wing, leading ministers in the newly established United Congregational Church of Southern Africa, and published by that church, it took most of its chapter titles from hymns in *Congregational Praise*.[16] While Briggs and Wing gave coherence to the LMS story, and implicitly drew attention to the legacy of the Society's work by looking at later developments, their treatment was inevitably very superficial because they were concerned with so great a period of time, and their approach was mainly institutional. Other writers produced detailed biographies of leading figures in the LMS, drawing on new research, but they too tended to be uncritical of their subjects and to show little interest in the people among whom they worked, or the way in which the missionary message was received. They failed to see how Christianisation had helped destroy indigenous cultures.[17]

Such writing ignored a new and important critical voice that had made itself heard in 1952, the year when whites celebrated the arrival of Van Riebeeck at the Cape three hundred years before. Until then, criticism of the LMS had come from those unsympathetic to the ways in which the early LMS missionaries had championed the cause of the oppressed. The new criticism came from one who identified with the liberation of the oppressed. Dora Taylor, who wrote under the pseudonym 'Nosipho Majeke', was a member of the Unity Movement who had no time for liberals, and wished to challenge Macmillan's sympathetic view of Philip and the 'Blessed Missionaries'.[18] *The Role of the Missionaries in Conquest*, though a work of advocacy, was based on considerable research.[19] Its central argument was that the missionaries had played a key role in undermining African societies and facilitating their conquest and destruction. Though Taylor tended to lump the LMS with other missionary societies, she used Philip and the LMS as her main examples in setting out her case that missionaries were 'agents of conquest'. Philip was 'the most far-reaching representative of British Imperialism in the country at that time', and she quoted extensively from his *Researches* to try to show that he advanced the interests of Britain and capitalism.[20] Van der Kemp and the Reads were accused of furthering 'divide and rule' policies,[21] while Moffat, Livingstone and Mackenzie, in opening the 'road to the north', had acted as an advance party for Cecil Rhodes. Even those missionaries who had spoken out against colonial expansion were seen as having been, albeit unwittingly, part of the advance guard of colonialism. In somewhat similar but more scholarly vein, Jack Boas argued two decades later that the LMS missionaries were leading agents in the evolution of South Africa's modern racial policies. They had promoted the move to wage labour and encouraged other segregationist practices.[22]

Such charges against the missionaries could not be dismissed as mere polemic. Various people asked Macmillan to respond to Taylor's book, but his interests had long since moved away from Philip, and he chose not to.[23] The social anthropologist Monica Wilson, herself the daughter of a missionary, came to the defence of the missionaries by stressing their spiritual aims and how they had often opposed the settlers on the issue of colonial expansion.[24] Anthony Sillery and Anthony Dachs showed that John Mackenzie's imperialism was motivated by humanitarian concerns: he campaigned for the territory of the Tswana to be taken under British rule because he rightly saw that the alternative was Boer rule, which would be, for them, a far worse fate.[25] Others did not rebut Taylor's arguments explicitly but sought, through bringing out the complexities and ambiguities of the missionary role, to show that while her argument was not wrong, it was partial and limited. Like others before and after her, she had generalised about the missionaries and seen them out of context; even missionaries who could be said to be agents of conquest were many other things as well.[26] To the extent that LMS missionaries had accepted congregations worshipping separately, they had done so because they believed this to be in the interests of the indigenous people. Much of the work of a new generation of scholars would implicitly address issues that Taylor had raised. While most of these scholars did not study the missionaries for their own sake but for other purposes, yet they added much to our knowledge of the LMS story, and took the study of the LMS and its role in new directions.

A precursor of this new work was Donovan Williams, then head of History at the University College of Fort Hare, who in 1959 submitted a doctoral thesis to Wits University on the missionaries of the eastern Cape in the first half of the nineteenth century. He showed in detail for the first time how unsuccessful they had been in converting Africans, and analysed their cultural and social impact on the people among whom they worked. He not only was sensitive to differences between the various missionary societies, but also pointed to the striking differences within the LMS itself. From his work, as from that of many others after him, it would become apparent that few generalisations about the Society's impact would in fact hold water.[27]

From the mid-1960s an Africanist thrust developed in South African historiography. Seeking to uncover the history of African societies, scholars no longer merely used the published *Transactions* but began to make extensive use of the unpublished Council for World Mission papers, for the missionaries had been the first literate observers to reside among most African groups. The voluminous LMS archives now began to be widely recognised as one of the most important sources of information on African societies in southern Africa in the nineteenth century. Most scholars working in the Africanist tradition had as their prime focus African societies rather than the missionaries themselves, but there was now a major interest in analysing how colonial and capitalist influences on the expanding frontier had undermined African societies. As LMS missionaries had been in the vanguard in carrying such influences into the interior, they were often the subject of study. Using the LMS records – which often involved reading between the lines, literally as well as figuratively[28] – and with a new understanding of how indigenous societies worked, these scholars uncovered new information about missionary activities, which they saw within a broader context, that of the frontier as a whole, than previous writers had. This was the case, particularly, in the thesis which Martin Legassick completed in 1969 on missionary interaction with the Griqua and the Sotho–Tswana. He had set out to write about the Tswana but had found himself increasingly drawn into a study of the way in which the LMS missionaries had created and supported, as well as undermined, the Griqua polities.[29]

In the 1970s and 1980s Legassick himself and most leading historians were mainly concerned with political economy issues, such as state formation, settler rule, capitalist penetration, dispossession and proletarianisation. Such concerns did encourage work on the role of missionaries as the purveyors of capitalist norms and the market economy,[30] but the study of missionaries themselves was not fashionable. Within the Africanist paradigm, with its concern for African initiatives, there was interest in the work of 'native agents' – a sub-theme in Legassick's thesis – and it now became clear for the first time how important they had been in advancing the work of the Society. The career of the best known of these 'native evangelists', Cupido Kakkerlak, was researched in detail.[31]

But most of what was written on the missionaries in the 1970s tended to elaborate on what was known rather than explore new dimensions or raise fundamental new questions. Jane Sales wrote a narrowly focused but detailed history of the activities of the LMS among coloured communities in the east-ern Cape, and her sympathetic study was notable for including information on their role as providers of education.[32] *The Kitchingman Papers* showed James Kitchingman, who had previously been little known, to have been a key figure at Bethelsdorp. As spin-offs of work for that volume, the present writer both re-examined the career of James Read, who was almost as little researched as Kitchingman, and presented him as an early radical, and explored, in as much detail as the records allowed, the history of the 'Bushman mission' which James Read and his son founded north of the Kat River Settlement.[33] That Settlement, the relative prosperity of which had aroused white envy, and which had then been the scene of a significant rebellion against white overlordship, attracted much new attention, some of which focused on the key role of the LMS in its establishment and subsequent history.[34] With rare theological insight, Andrew Ross, who was concerned to correct what he saw as inadequacies in Macmillan's portrayal of Philip, provided new evidence on the Scottish and theological background of the Superintendent. Like Macmillan, Ross present-ed Philip as 'humanising the dislocations associated with colonisation in south-ern Africa'.[35]

Whereas in the early 1980s Norman Etherington could lament the lack of new approaches to mission history, by the early 1990s not only was there an upsurge of interest in that history but new questions were being asked of that history.[36] While previously the Cape's eastern frontier had been the prime focus of attention, major studies were now completed on the LMS elsewhere, such as the far northern frontier of Namaqualand and southern Namibia in the first decades of the nineteenth century, where LMS missionaries, many of them Germans, had worked among the Khoi, before handing over their work to the Rhenish Missionary Society.[37] Nigel Penn showed how the first LMS mission, among the San, was established in part on the initiative of a local white con-vert, but also in the context of the British wishing to see peace brought to the turbulent northern frontier.[38] Karel Schoeman, librarian at the South African Library, produced much detailed work on the history of particular LMS missionaries and mission stations. His full-scale biography of J.J. Kicherer and shorter life of Ann Hamilton, wife of the missionary artisan Robert Hamilton, were both based on a careful reading of the Society's *Transactions* and the relevant correspondence in the Council for World Mission papers.[39] Much more controversially, Julian Cobbing tried to argue that the LMS missionaries had covered up their complicity in 'slave-raiding', the capture and sale of African labour. Robert Moffat was identified as the chief culprit, being involved, according to Cobbing, in both cattle-raiding and the capture of slaves. But Cobbing could produce no substantial evidence to support his conspiracy theory, while much other evidence suggested it was nonsense. Moffat had indeed helped arm the Griqua to repel the attacking 'Mantatees' at Dithakong in 1823, but he was a man of humanity and compassion who had explicitly refused offers of cattle and had criticised his predecessors for their involvement in trade.[40]

The history of the LMS at the Cape was not neglected. A major study by Elizabeth Elbourne linked the work of the LMS in Britain to their early activities at the Cape, and explored with great sophistication their work among the Khoi, pointing out that by the time they arrived the Khoi's spiritual universe had come under threat through a long period of colonial expansion. Mission Christianity was then used by Khoi as a way to reconstruct their broken world.[41] In more orthodox vein, Noël Mostert used the LMS records to weave new detail on the missionaries into a rich tapestry of change on the eastern frontier in the early nineteenth century. He was concerned not only with the well-known figures such as Van der Kemp and Philip, but also with lesser-known ones.[42] From such work the individualism of the LMS missionaries emerged in sharper focus than before, as did the way in which rivalries between the LMS and other missionaries helped shape political struggles between and within African societies.

Following trends in international scholarship, South African historians became attracted more than before to such themes as culture, ideology and gender.[43] The missionaries were now seen, not so much as agents of conquest *per se*, but rather as agents of cultural imperialism. Following Edward Said, it was widely accepted that cultural influences were often more important than direct domination and physical force in establishing the colonial relationship. But Christian beliefs and teaching were not merely imposed by agents of cultural imperialism; Africans accepted Christianity for their own reasons, and appropriated it and turned it to their own use.[44] As the scholarly study of the missionary enterprise came back into fashion, the focus was now on the ambiguities and contradictions in the missionary 'encounter', and on the changing social, cultural and symbolic context in which that encounter took place. Scholars sought to understand what Africans had thought of the missionaries and their message, and to investigate how indigenous belief systems had inter-acted with the new ideas which the missionaries brought.[45] At the same time, missionary attitudes to aspects of traditional culture were explored, as scholars asked how those attitudes – towards, say, for the Xhosa, *intonjane* (girl's initia-tion), *ukwaluka* (circumcision), *lobola* (wrongly called 'bride price') and the drinking of *utywala* (beer) – had changed over time.[46]

Much of the new work was social history. Missionary wives, previously ignored, now became a subject of study, along with single females employed on mission stations and the type of education given to women. Historians now wished to know why women had been more receptive to the Christian mes-sage than men. It was shown how missionaries had helped to reshape gender relations in African societies, and sought to initiate women into the Victorian cult of domesticity. Women's issues, previously given hardly any attention, were now said to be 'central' to the evangelical enterprise.[47] The sexual scandals which plagued the LMS in the second decade of the nineteenth century were explored in detail, along with the way in which the missionaries had provided medical help.[48]

How the missionaries had presented their message, and how it had been received, was a major interest. There was a new concern with the language of the missionaries, as post-modernists emphasised the importance of discourse, and it was shown how the missionaries often played key roles in shaping indigenous languages by committing them to writing.[49] When he discussed the LMS and other missionaries in his magisterial history of *The Church in Africa*, Adrian Hastings ranged from where the missionaries came from and their interrelationships in the mission field to their medical skills and their influence on local languages.[50] The missionary enterprise was now seen as complex, multi-faceted and as continually contested between the evangelisers and the evangelised. And it was the work of the LMS among the Tswana which attract-ed the single most influential new study.[51] The anthropologists John and Jean Comaroff, in what they called a 'historical anthropology of cultural confronta-tion', set out with great subtlety and style the way that confrontation developed over such issues as water, language and education, or where mission stations should be sited. They saw the interaction between the missionaries and the Tswana as a kind of conversation, in which each side often misinterpreted the other. The Comaroffs showed both how the Tswana sought to use the mis-sionaries for their own purposes, and how they creatively mixed ideas of their own with those of the missionaries, to produce a new amalgam, thereby con-tributing to the Africanisation of Christianity.[52]

As Richard Elphick pointed out, the Comaroffs tended to ignore the core of the message the missionaries brought: the ideas of Christ's suffering and res-urrection, of sin and salvation, and the need for all to repent and believe the gospel.[53] Some of the new scholarship, indeed, so emphasised the social, economic and political impact of the missionaries that conversion, the central goal of the missionary enterprise, was hardly mentioned. The better scholarship did, however, try to take further Williams's probing of the reasons for the relative lack of success in conversion in the early period, and to ask why the missionaries were much more successful in the later period of their work. It was suggested that part of the reason why the LMS had attracted more converts among the Khoi, Basters and Oorlams than among Bantu-speaking Africans was that Khoi society was fragile, and so easily destroyed, which made the Khoi particularly receptive to the missionary message.[54] Khoisan preachers, argued Elizabeth Elbourne, were crucial in proclaiming that God was on the side of the oppressed, and made it possible for the Khoisan to be 'able to claim their own covenant with God'.[55] The Khoi and other converts adapted the new message, integrating it into their existing beliefs. Conversion was no longer seen as the sole result of the missionaries, but a product of the realisation that Christianity was appropriate to new conditions of life in which people found themselves.

Scholars now showed a new sensitivity to social context and to different traditions within the ranks of the LMS. Robert Ross suggested that the reason why more ex-slaves in the western Cape did not convert may have been that the missionaries there were more quietist and evangelical than those on the eastern frontier.[56] On that frontier conversions only became significant after conquest or violent dislocation, and the LMS had already withdrawn from much of its work on the Cape eastern frontier by the time the most serious disruptions occurred among the Xhosa.[57] The LMS were more successful among the Tswana in part because Khama of the Ngwato chose to give them a missionary monopoly.

At the bicentenary of the Society a rich literature exists on its work in South Africa, but much remains to be done. For all the attention paid to its early agents – an attention out of proportion to their numbers and evangelical achievement[58] – James Read sen. and jun. are among those who still await biographers. The histories of many of the smaller stations remain to be written.[59] We know little about the work of the LMS in Cape Town,[60] and neither the way in which the Society handed over its work to others over the decades, nor the history of land-holdings on its missions has been explored in depth.[61] Most interest has been paid, not surprisingly, to the early missionaries and to key figures, to the neglect of the later history of the LMS, especially from the 1880s. Only one important article treats the influence of the LMS in the South African War, crediting it with doing more to perpetuate the myth that the war was being fought in the interests of blacks than any other body. The history of the Society after the war is little researched.[62] There is no adequate survey of the contribution the LMS made to education,[63] or of the influence of the LMS on other missionary societies, though it is clear that such influence was extensive.[64]

Relatively little has been written on the theology of the LMS, which 'represented doctrinally … the least formal and the most individualistic conception of Christianity',[65] and the importance of that theology for its work.

Perhaps above all, we still await a more adequate integration of the history of the LMS – along with that of other missionary societies – into the mainstream historiography of South Africa.[66] Such an integration will have to grapple with the significance of the LMS and try to assess its legacy. Was it indeed the case, for example, that 'The liberal tradition in South Africa arose largely from the presence and works of the LMS'?[67] Attacks on Philip from a conservative perspective continued into the 1980s,[68] but are unlikely to be renewed. More significantly, Andrew Bank has argued recently that the humanitarian liberalism which Philip represented faded in importance in the late 1840s and 1850s, and that discontinuities between it and later liberalism were more important than continuities.[69] For later liberals, Philip remained an ambiguous figure, associated with external influences. That they wished to identify with an indigenous liberalism perhaps helps explain why few twentieth-century liberals saw Philip as one of 'the fathers of South African liberalism'.[70]

While mission work cannot account for 'the vast scale of twentieth-century conversions',[71] the LMS laid important seeds for the later Christianisation of South African society. The Society's legacy can most easily be seen in the Congregational and other churches which took over its work; its more diffuse legacies, such as its influence through the founding of the educational institution of Tiger Kloof, remain difficult to assess. The LMS is remembered above all for its tradition of militant social involvement: more than any other society, its missionaries worked for social justice. Though the LMS was quicker to hand over its work to others, the tradition of social concern remained alive, even if it lay fallow for long periods. In the 1970s black theologians poured scorn on, or ignored, the LMS and its liberalism, but others drew strength from the voices of conscience of Van der Kemp, Read, Philip and others, and from the tradition of fighting for social justice begun by members of the LMS who had gone out of their way to identify with the poor and oppressed. The different ways in which people have looked back at the LMS and remembered its work are not the least important of the many themes for future generations of scholars to study.

The Alleged Political Conservatism of Robert Moffat

Steve de Gruchy

There is a perception amongst missiologists and historians of South African church and culture that Robert Moffat was the archetypal politically conservative missionary.[1] It has been argued that against the likes of colleagues from the London Missionary Society (LMS) such as Johannes van der Kemp, John Philip and James Read, he stands out as one who avoided engaging in political action on behalf of the poor and oppressed and – even worse – that he was in fact rather disdainful of such involvement by these others. Thus in a recent biography of John Philip, Andrew Ross has written:

> Robert Moffat and many others of the [LMS] staff belong to that form of evangelicalism which was much more pietistic in its understanding of the Gospel than was Philip's. For them, individuals were to be converted – converted individuals, in so far as they had political power, would then begin to use it better, but it was not the primary task of the Christian to work for a more just society. Even when put as delicately as Wilberforce did by calling this zeal, the zeal for the 'reform of manners', Moffat's brand of evangelical did not accept it as a primary task, except in areas like the clothing converts ought to wear and the sexual mores of African Christians. Neither Philip nor Weld nor any other leader of their wing of evangelicalism ever demoted the preaching of the Gospel from the position of number one priority, but they insisted that the development of civilisation and good government were inextricably involved in the attempt to live out the dictates of the Gospel. As for Moffat, that form of belief, he felt, led to political involvement which in turn led to the distraction of time and effort into the spiritually and morally ambiguous sphere of political controversy, exactly what he constantly criticised Philip for doing.[2]

Ross goes on to characterise Moffat's racial attitudes thus: 'good was to be done to and for Blacks, but this had nothing to do with brotherhood or human equality'.[3]

Yet even this rather bleak picture of Moffat has been called into question in a dramatic way. Julian Cobbing alleges that Moffat was actively engaged in slavery. In a central thrust to a broader discussion on early South African history, he has argued that, together with his co-conspirators from the Cape Colony, Moffat engineered an attack on a defenceless village (Dithakong, or Old Littakoo in the missionary records) in order to secure slaves to trade for arms and ammunition.[4] Cobbing's questioning of Mfecane theory has found some degree of critical acceptance, but the rather bizarre accusation that Moffat was a slave trader has been comprehensively refuted and laid to rest by both Elizabeth Eldredge[5] and Guy Hartley.[6]

In all these debates the personality and character of Robert Moffat and the estimation of his contribution to rural South Africa take second place. Very little effort has been taken to grasp what Moffat was trying to do, the limitations that both time and space created for him, and the depth of analysis required for one who spent 53 years working in southern Africa. It may be that the location of this writer opens up some new ideas and possibilities in trying to evaluate Moffat's legacy, which the mere reading of words on paper struggles to convey. This point has been well made by John and Jean Comaroff in a 'shift of focus that requires a change of voice' occasioned by a visit to the old LMS school, Tiger Kloof. They have drawn attention to a poetic or aesthetic sense of 'knowing' in the task of social commentary, in the introduction to the first volume of their magisterial work, *Of Revelation and Revolution*.[7] Likewise, I cannot but draw into my thoughts the impressions that I have gained by being the Director of the Kuruman Moffat Mission Trust in Kuruman for the past five years, charged with overseeing its role in the post-1994 South Africa. This does not, of course, provide any epistemological privilege, but it is nonetheless a 'way of knowing', a specific collapse of the hermeneutical distance between then and now that does raise certain themes and questions to prominence which may otherwise be ignored. The chief of these is the intuitive sense that Moffat has left us a legacy that is worthy of respect for those concerned about the church's role in contemporary South African politics, a role that can now best be characterised as 'reconstruction' rather than 'resistance'.[8]

INTRODUCING ROBERT MOFFAT

Robert Moffat (1795–1883) was for many years the senior missionary in the interior of southern Africa, yet now he seems to lie in a forgotten corner of South African history, both general and ecclesiastical. His fate is similar to that of his mission station. At one time it was the nerve centre of church life, exploration, trading and communications. Then, with the discovery of diamonds and gold and the domination of the political scene by people like Rhodes and Kruger, the geo-political epicentre of southern Africa moved to the east, and the railway line bypassed Kuruman on its way from Kimberley via Mafikeng to Bulawayo. Kuruman lapsed into a backwater, and with it the memory of Robert Moffat. Perhaps the exploits and death of his more famous son-in-law, David Livingstone, even in his own lifetime also served to push his achievements from the public's consciousness.[9]

There have been some attempts at keeping Moffat's memory and work alive. Three serious biographies have been written about him by his missionary son John (1886),[10] Edwin W. Smith (1925)[11] and Cecil Northcott, a director of the LMS (1961),[12] but all three of these are dated and out of print, like all the other smaller 'biographies' of Moffat published as part of a stream of missionary literature to sustain the work of the missionary societies such as the LMS.[13]

In Moffat's own lifetime he published *Missionary Labours and Scenes in South Africa* in 1842 whilst he was in Britain overseeing the printing of the Setswana New Testament.[14] Our understanding of the early period of his work is greatly enhanced by *Apprenticeship in Kuruman*, a collection of journal entries and letters from 1820 to 1828 edited by Isaac Schapera.[15] Furthermore, the relationship with Mzilikazi and the establishing of the mission in Matabeleland (as the Ndebele kingdom was then known to whites) are well documented in Moffat's own Matabele journals and letters edited by J.P.R. Wallis.[16] Most recently – and yet still 25 years ago – Mora Dickson published *Beloved Partner: Mary Moffat of Kuruman*, a moving biography of Robert's wife Mary. Given the dates of these publications, and the fact that other than the Dickson biography of Mary Moffat they are all out of print, is it too far-fetched to suggest that very few people really have a 'feel' for Moffat or perhaps sufficient depth of appreciation for what he really stood for?

To illustrate we may rely on comments from Ross's work on John Philip mentioned above. He writes:

> Certainly Robert Moffat's career in South Africa was a distinguished one and a very long one, from 1817 to 1870. Yet, despite his massive achievement in translating the Bible into seTswana and the importance of his relations with Lobengula [*sic*] the king of the Ndebele, Moffat's role in the planting and development of Christianity in southern Africa was a limited one. As for his significance in the general history of South Africa, it cannot be estimated as anything more than marginal to that history.[17]

Apart from the fact that Ross is making this point in a polemical debate between Philip and Moffat to the detriment of the latter,[18] the reference illustrates both the factual inaccuracies that even a scholarly account can make of Moffat's life: it was Lobengula's father, Mzilikazi, with whom Moffat had a 35-

year-long relationship, as well as the rather biased opinion about Moffat's significance. Both of these points suggest that an in-depth analysis of Moffat's life on its own terms is long overdue.

Robert Moffat was one of the great South Africans of the nineteenth century. He came to this country at the age of 22, and began his work as the senior missionary amongst the Tswana near Kuruman at the age of only 25. He served his single post in the Kuruman River valley for fifty years with only one break in England (1839–43), during which time he oversaw the printing of the New Testament, translated the Psalms, went on an extended lecture tour and wrote a 600-page book. Having left school at the age of 10 and having had a father who questioned his intellectual ability,[19] he nevertheless learnt Dutch at the Cape – which he used throughout his life – and then Setswana at the Kuruman. He more or less created the orthography for Setswana, translated the entire Bible into this language, and then had the gall to print it – on the edge of the Kalahari Desert – making it the first Bible printed on the African continent. He also wrote and published a range of Setswana hymns, which are still in regular use. His vision and passion oversaw the building of the first school room and 'square' houses north of the Orange River – as well as the aesthetically pleasing church (which he called a chapel) and which remained the largest building in the interior of South Africa until Johannesburg became a city.

He was a charismatic man who had the uncanny ability to build relationships of mutual respect with a wide range of people and numbered amongst his personal friends chiefs such as Afrikaner of the Nama, Waterboer of the Griqua, Mothibi of the Tlhaping, Makaba of the Ngwaketse, Sechele of the Kwena, Mzilikazi of the Ndebele, and Sir George Grey of the Cape Colony. He fathered ten children, five of whom died before him, three as infants in heartbreaking conditions. He was the father of one missionary (John Smith Moffat) and the father-in-law of three others (David Livingstone, Jean Fredoux and Roger Price). His domestic relations were such that, Scottish patriarch that he undoubtedly was, he yet created the space in which his wife Mary emerged as a strong and powerful frontier-woman in her own right, even to the extent of locking him out of his study when she considered it important.[20] Their letters tell of a deep love and affection for each other, a dependability and a faithfulness that many great men (and I do mean *men*) struggle to achieve even momentarily in their lives of fame.[21]

Moffat lived on the edge of the Kalahari for fifty years and it showed. He was a large man with a great beard, and was more hardy and tough than many of the great Voortrekker leaders we once learnt about in school. He was a hunter, a horseman, an explorer, a strategist and a frontiersman who knew the African bush from first-hand and at very close quarters. He was a blacksmith who could set up a forge almost anywhere and fix any part of an oxwagon, spending days at the furnace if need be. He was a farmer who established the first use of irrigation in the interior of the sub-continent when he dammed the famous 'Eye' of Kuruman and dug irrigation channels for five kilometres to carry water to his gardens.[22] He was a miller who built a corn-mill using the power of the water in his furrow (and once damaged his hand in it). He knew thirst, hunger and the uncertainty of almost everything he set out to accomplish, and yet he never gave up and was always willing to take the risk.

The irony is that all of this meant very little to Moffat, at least in terms of his own self-understanding. He was so certain of his own calling as an apostle of God, and of what he liked to call the 'spiritual' task he was to fulfil as a missionary, that he discounted all of these 'temporal' things and downplayed them whenever he could. This is what confuses the surface reader and possibly leads to the accusation of his being pietistic and 'other-worldly' and to the allegations of his holding to a conservative political position. Yet these accusations and allegations do not do justice to Moffat, and we need to correct them if we are to evaluate his legacy in this generation.

DISCERNING PRIORITIES, DEFINING POLITICS

Moffat was a man of many talents and gifts yet he constantly underplayed their importance and focused upon his role as a missionary, evangelist and teacher of the faith. This he understood to be his priority, against which all else faded into insignificance, and it was this strict sense of his role as a Christian missionary rather than a private commercial trader or government official that shaped many of his concerns and thoughts. Nevertheless, the job description of a frontier missionary was a broad and general one, and many things could and did fall within the tasks and duties of 'teaching the faith'. With the benefit of hindsight we may identify the three major achievements of Moffat in his fifty-year sojourn at Kuruman: firstly, the building of the infrastructure of the mission in the Kuruman valley; secondly, the translation and printing of the Setswana Bible; and thirdly, the pushing of the mission frontier northwards through what is today Botswana into Mzilikazi's Matabeleland.

Discerning priorities

The first crucial area in which Moffat concentrated his energies was the development of the mission infrastructure in the Kuruman River valley. When he arrived at the LMS mission to the Tswana in 1821,[23] it was situated at the village of Maruping (New Littakoo), about ten kilometres further down the valley from its present site.[24] Various factors influenced him to persuade Chief Mothibi of the Tlhaping to grant him land closer to the Eye, the most important of which was the greater possibility of the intensive use of irrigation for agriculture. Much time was spent in the next six years establishing the gardens and homesteads.

21

This early period of settling in (from 1820 to 1828) has been characterised by Schapera as the 'apprenticeship at Kuruman' for both Robert and Mary, and his edited collection of journal entries and letters from this period covers the key and foundational events of the first decade amongst the Tswana. Even a cursory appraisal of these journals and letters will make clear how difficult it was for the mission to establish its infrastructure in the face of raiding bandits, warring parties and rumours of attacks. This is the period during which the Battle of Dithakong took place, and on a number of other occasions the Moffats and their colleagues had to retreat to Griquatown for refuge. This was also the period in which the Moffats buried their first son in the new grave-yard, and Robert visited Cape Town with Peclo (Mothibi's son) as well as taking a retreat to finally master Setswana.

The year 1829 was something of a watershed for the Moffats at Kuruman. In that year the first converts were baptised, the school room was built, the translation of the first book of the Bible (Luke) was completed, work on the church building commenced, and Moffat undertook his first of five visits to Mzilikazi. By the start of the 1830s the infrastructure of the mission as we know it today was well established, apart from the church, which was begun in 1829 and completed in 1838. It is well to note and consider that all of the materials involved in this building were either made or prepared at Kuruman, or – as in the case of the roofing beams in the church – were brought over a great distance by oxwagon. The sheer expense of time and energy involved in such an undertaking was tremendous, given these limitations.

The second achievement of Robert Moffat, the translation and printing of the Setswana Bible, is perhaps his most astonishing. Having only one year of formal education, not only did Moffat become comfortable in Dutch,[25] but he also learnt Setswana, reduced the language to writing, developed the orthography and then set about translating the Bible into it. The work that he and his helpers, especially William Ashton, did between 1830, when he completed the first book, the Gospel of Luke, and 1857, when the final pages of the Old Testament were translated, has had a dramatic impact on the growth of the Christian church in the Setswana-speaking region of southern Africa.

Having done all of this, he then undertook to print the Bible on his press on the edge of the Kalahari. The full story of this press is told in Frank Bradlow's *Printing for Africa*,[26] so here we need just to sketch its broad outlines. Whilst Moffat was in Cape Town to have the Gospel of Luke printed, the press arrived for use by the LMS. John Philip gave it to Moffat and it was brought back to Kuruman on oxwagon. Moffat and his colleague Roger Edwards learnt the trade whilst in Cape Town, and then undertook small printing jobs such as Scripture selections, school readers and Setswana grammars. Moffat did not intend to print the Bible in Kuruman, but after the lengthy stay in England to have the New Testament (and then the Psalms) printed there he decided that it would in fact be easier to both translate and print in Kuruman, thus enabling him to continue with other work of the mission. By means of the press, the Old Testament was translated and printed by 1857 and a revision of the New Testament by 1867.

The mission today has the privilege of printing on this press and can attest to the fact that it is a painstaking and slow task to print each page. The point for us to note here is that Moffat persevered at this task precisely because the translation and printing of the Bible in Setswana was a priority for him. Indeed he considered himself responsible to two societies whilst at Kuruman, the LMS and the British and Foreign Bible Society,[27] and his energy and commitment are recognised by the latter in a memorial window in the library at the Bible Society House in London.[28]

Moffat's third major achievement was the opening of the frontier between Kuruman and Mzilikazi's Matabeleland via what is today eastern Botswana. Moffat made five visits to Mzilikazi in all, and the published journals and letters from these journeys form one of the best sources for understanding Moffat's unfolding perspectives. The journeys were undertaken in November 1829–January 1830; May–August 1835; May–December 1854[29]; July 1857–February 1858; and July 1859–August, 1860.[30] The first two were to Mzilikazi's capital near to what is today Pretoria, and the last three, undertaken after a 19-year hiatus, were near to what is today the city of Bulawayo in Zimbabwe.

Although Mzilikazi's capital was the goal of all five visits, these journeys afforded Moffat with a unique perspective on the drama of southern Africa. In the first two visits he was able to experience, at first hand, the social dislocation later historians were to call the Mfecane, and in the later three visits he could record the social, cultural and political effects of white encroachment on land that was previously held by Africans. The trips also enabled Moffat to visit and explore the situation amongst the Tswana to the north of Kuruman, and he spent time with the Ngwaketse, Kwena and Rolong en route.

The trips accomplished a number of things that were of general importance to the mission and wider community, including finding timber for the roof of the large church at the Kuruman, assisting a scientific exploration, support and follow-up of the work of what were called 'native teachers' amongst the Tswana tribes, confirmation of the bona fides of the Lutheran Hermannsburg missionaries with the Kwena of Sechele, freeing of numerous captives taken by the Ndebele such as the young Hurutshe boy,[31] the Griqua 'princess' Troey[32] and the recognised 'chief' of the Ngwato, Macheng,[33] introduction of British traders to Mzilikazi, and delivery of supplies to David Livingstone further north on the Zambezi. However, from the perspective of the LMS, the key achievement of Moffat's relationship with Mzilikazi was the establishment of a permanent mission station amongst the Ndebele at Inyati near Bulawayo, a mission station that continues to this day. Moffat accompanied this group, which included his son John Smith Moffat, on his third visit to Matabeleland (1859–60) and spent a good deal of time with them helping to establish the station in the same practical way that he had set about at Kuruman 35 years earlier.

Moffat's three key achievements should help us understand the priorities that he had as a missionary, and to recognise the fundamental demand of *time*. People are not able to accomplish all that they want to or all that they believe they should, and the discerning of priorities and effective time-management in the light of those priorities are a key task for anyone in a leadership role. It does not take a genius to recognise that Moffat had priorities that were to a large extent different from those of missionaries further south who resided and worked in the Cape Colony, and that this had an impact upon their different uses of time and energy. It is also clear that these priorities were not used as an excuse for not doing other things but were indeed real and worthy pursuits.

Moffat discerned that a clear priority for him was making the Bible available to the Batswana, and he focused much of his energy on this, even to the point of undermining his health. It was, moreover, a priority that was recognised by John Philip when he assigned the press to Kuruman. Mary Moffat was conscious of the priority of the translating and printing of the Bible, writing that 'I can, however, call to mind how we have been sustained and strengthened for the last forty years, and our lives preserved, till we have seen the whole of the precious volume in print in this language.'[34] David Livingstone in a letter also reveals how others in the field viewed Moffat's vital work at translation when, writing as a doctor after his father-in-law had injured an arm in his mill, he said: 'You will be obliged to spend your time in better work than roofing and other manual labours, the which although all very necessary are not to be compared with the effects of translations, for these will be known when our stations are swept away and we are all dead and rotten.'[35] All of this meant that Moffat did not have the time or energy to be active in the kind of work that Philip and Van der Kemp were involved in.

In terms of establishing the infrastructure at the Kuruman and then pursing the relationship with Mzilikazi, we can recognise the same issues at play. Running not just a mission station, but the mission base for the LMS in the interior, was a full-time occupation. If we add to this the fact that Moffat had to oversee its building in the first place, and the development of its gardens for the provision of basic foodstuffs, whilst translating and printing the Bible and setting off on long journeys into the interior, with almost no infrastructural support, then we must recognise that being a missionary was a full-time occupation and, from Moffat's perspective at least, a priority that would be undermined if one took on a formal political responsibility in the way that he perceived Philip and Van der Kemp to do.

Defining politics

Moffat had a very clear understanding of his role as a missionary and expressed his concern that the involvement of missionaries in formal politics was likely to detract from the many other important responsibilities they had. Yet this was not from a particular opposition to political engagement, for Moffat felt the same concern with regard to confusing the role of a missionary with that of a trader,[36] and went to great lengths to ensure that he was not considered one of the latter.[37] This clear role definition also meant that whilst he would offer his services as an interpreter, he would refuse to represent the British government to the chiefs as this was contrary to the missionary's role.[38]

In his book *Missionary Labours and Scenes*, Moffat deals with the question of roles in an honest and open way, and not (as has been inferred) in a pietistic manner. In much the same way that Archbishop Desmond Tutu in 1994 called on priests in the Church of the Province of Southern Africa (Anglican) not to join political parties lest their role be confused, and in the same way that the successor body to the LMS in southern Africa, the UCCSA, has disciplined ministers for holding political office because of the confusion of roles and authority, so Moffat felt after clear personal experience at Griquatown with Anderson and later with Peter Wright, whose work as missionaries was severely undermined by their appointment as government agents,[39] that 'more than twenty years' experience among aborigines beyond the boundary of the colony has convinced the writer that the two offices ought not to be held by the same person'.[40] Nevertheless, even in the light of this statement, Moffat went on immediately to say:

> No missionary, however, can with any show of Scripture or reason, refuse his pacific counsel and advice, when those among whom he labours require it, nor decline to become interpreter or translator to any foreign power, or to be the medium of hushing the din of war arising either from family interests or national claims; nor is it inconsistent with his character to become a mediator or intercessor where life is at stake, whether arising from ignorance, despotism, or revenge …
>
> A missionary may do all this, and more than this, without endangering his character, and what is of infinitely more importance, the character of the gospel he proclaims; but his entering into diplomatic engagements places himself as well as the great object of his life in jeopardy.[41]

For Moffat the concern had to do with the role of missionary rather than the message of the missionary. He knew that if missionaries became involved in political tasks, they did not have the authority and power to ensure that things happened. Interestingly, the Comaroffs in their critique of the missionaries' politics recognise the 'impotence of the evangelists in the political arena',[42] though it does not seem to have occurred to them that Moffat himself may have recognised this and that this was his main concern in advocating a distance between the missionary and the government agent.

The third of Moffat's main achievements, namely the visits to the Batswana in the north and to Mzilikazi both south of, and then north of, the Limpopo, raises the issue of how we define politics. Those who have considered Moffat to be 'apolitical' either have not explored Moffat's interaction with the Tswana and Ndebele chiefs, or have a very Western understanding of what constitutes politics. As at Kuruman with chief Mothibi and the Tlhaping, on his journeys north Moffat spent time with a number of Batswana chiefs such as Sechele and Sekhomi, and especially with Mzilikazi. His role here was both religious, in the sense that he was concerned to deal with issues such as preaching, conversion and Bible reading, and also political, in the sense that he was concerned about issues of human abuse, honesty, forgiveness, integrity and honour. Moffat always felt slightly awkward in getting involved in these issues lest his role be confused with that of a government agent, but he did nevertheless take on specific issues, the most notable being his participation in the Macheng affair, which undermines any attempt to call Moffat 'apolitical'.[43]

There is another sense in which Moffat's priorities disclose a political concern, namely his incarnational approach to mission. Both the effort he spent on translating the Bible into Setswana and that on establishing the mission infrastructure need to be understood from this perspective. In his essay 'The Translation Principle in Christian History', Andrew Walls has written:

> Bible translation as a process is thus both a reflection of the central act on which the Christian faith depends and a concretization of the commission which Christ gave his disciples. Perhaps no other specific activity more clearly represents the mission of the Church.
>
> The parallel of Scripture and Incarnation is suggested in the opening words of the Epistle to the Hebrews in the relation between the partial, episodic, occasional words of God spoken through the prophets and the complete and integrated Word spoken all at once in the Son (Heb. 1:1–4). The issues and problems of Bible translation are the issues and problems of Incarnation. The struggle to present writings embedded in languages and cultures alien to the present situation of every people is validated by the act which translated God into a medium of humanity. As the Incarnation took place in the terms of a particular social context, so translation uses the terms and relations of a specific context. Bible translation aims at releasing the word about Christ so that it can reach all aspects of a specific linguistic and cultural context, so that Christ can live within that context in the persons of his followers, as thoroughly at home as he once did in the culture of first-century Jewish Palestine.[44]

The desire to incarnate the gospel into the lives of ordinary Batswana, and in so doing to introduce the great themes of the Bible to the people of the region, clearly held some dangers and problems. Yet from a perspective that can define politics in a broader sense than just elections, public protest and the making of laws, we can recognise that the desire to translate and make the Bible available in the language of the common people was a political task given the Bible's clear stance on justice, freedom and peace.[45] Two other options existed, of course, both having valued traditions in the church. Considering that the Batswana had to learn to read and write Setswana anyway, why not just use the English Bible and teach Christians to be fluent in English in a way that Latin was used in the medieval church, or that Arabic is used for the Koran in Islam? If the goal of the missionaries was to create 'civilised Englishmen' out of the heathen, then creating a class of people who used English would have gone a long way towards that goal.

The second option was to simply not translate the Bible and give the 'poor natives' only what they thought they should hear. Moffat and his fellow translators could have done either of these things, but they did not. This decision, to make the Bible available in Setswana, both through translation and printing, was a political decision to incarnate the Word of God within the lives of ordinary people. This is not to say that Moffat understood it in these terms. But somewhere beyond the motives that historians of culture believe they are able to identify, there was a concern on the part of Moffat to be involved in something bigger than just his own agenda, and the translation of the Bible goes beyond the categories that the social sciences may wish to use. Once it was done and given over to the Batswana it would set in motion impulses that would go much further and deeper than Moffat could have imagined.

This concern – through Bible translation – to incarnate the gospel in the interior of southern Africa was made real in another way as well, namely, the establishment of the mission infrastructure at Kuruman. The missionaries were not the first white Europeans with whom the Batswana had contact, for they had experience of hunters, traders and explorers, all of whom were transitory and predatory in the sense that they took from the land and the people and did not give back. The missionaries signalled their different intentions in three ways. The first was by arriving with their wives and children, and thus by showing the desire to live for the long term amongst the Tswana, a desire that often went to tragic lengths as the Makololo Expedition would show. The second was to learn the language of the local people, rather than to follow the classic colonial pattern of expecting the colonised to learn the colonisers' language. The third pointer to their incarnational intention was to build an extensive infrastructure, as Moffat did at Kuruman. This approach to mission was recognised in Moffat by others, particularly by one who was closest to him, his missionary son John. The latter noted in respect of his freedom of movement amongst the Tswana and the Ndebele that 'the principle upon which his whole life among natives was based was that of implicit mutual confidence. It was the secret of much of his success.'[46] It was no doubt this sense of confidence that led the chief Sechele to send his children to Kuruman to be in safe keeping during the period of violent attack from the Boers.[47]

Moffat gave expression to this incarnational desire to be amongst the people when he wrote in the foreword to his book of 1842, that amongst the Tswana 'he hopes to live, labour and die',[48] and then to the LMS directors describing his return to Kuruman after being in England in the following way: 'still one thing lacked. It was once more to be with the people who had been for many long years the objects of our most anxious solicitude, again to gaze on their well known faces, and to mingle with them once more in their solemn feasts, and to tell them again the tale of Divine love'.[49] Thus, upon his retirement John Smith Moffat could make the telling comment that 'in one sense it was not a question of going home, but of leaving it'.[50]

The mission infrastructure signals an incarnational intention, both then and now. Here is a physical reminder of God's presence amongst people, and though, as a good Nonconformist, Moffat would not like to think of places being holy, one LMS representative did get as close as a Congregationalist could by calling it 'this *almost* holy place'. You cannot have that experience if you do not have the infrastructure, just as you cannot teach literacy and agriculture without the physical structures to enable it. Places like Fort Hare, Lovedale and Tiger Kloof were politically important precisely because they were places. And so today, whilst Van der Kemp and Philip may have left a testimony on paper, it is Moffat who has left a testimony in stone and can best share a legacy with a new generation using the infrastructure for good.

CONTEXT AND PROPHETIC PROTEST

The Comaroffs point out that their account of the Nonconformist mission in southern Africa 'is not written as a chronology of events or processes',[51] and later they restate this, saying that 'in order to analyse the politics of the mission, we do not offer a chronicle of events'.[52] There are benefits in this approach – as the Comaroffs' work amply demonstrates – but it does fall into the trap of writing about the characters and views of the missionaries in such a way that individual role players are reduced to ideal types in which their own narrative, biography and chronology and the linear development of their own thoughts are dispensed with.[53] Thus, what Moffat wrote in England in 1842 is taken to be 'Moffat's point of view' for all time, and little attention is paid to his thought in dialectic tension with the changing political circumstances in which he found himself.

What makes Moffat a difficult person to deal with in this manner is that he lived a long and eventful life. Coming to Africa at the age of 22 he left at the ripe age of 75. Is it possible to assert that he held exactly the same ideas and understanding of the relationship between the gospel and society throughout the entire 53-year period? This question seems to be an important one and yet, as we have seen, is overlooked by everyone who writes about Moffat, both his detractors and his supporters. None of the three serious biographies of Moffat[54] even begin to ask the question about the development of his personality, and the role that outside forces and events might have had upon his ideas and perspectives. Given the hermeneutic circularity between consciousness and social events it is difficult to believe that the ideas of the young, naïve bachelor of 1817 were the same as those of the senior missionary and grandfather of 1870.

One of the key issues in which Moffat's perspective experienced a natural development was his growing political concern, in the light of the changing socio-political environment, between his first period at Kuruman up to and including his sojourn in Britain (1820–43) and his second period (1844–70). In the first of these periods, the Kuruman valley was beyond both the colonial frontier and the trekboer frontier, so Moffat had very little to do with the impact of colonial administration or the political implications of white settlers. As his social location *vis-à-vis* colonial government was very different from that of Van der Kemp and Philip, it could be expected that he had little to say about colonial authorities, and it is thus no surprise that they differed in the realm of political perspective. Philip's struggles were not those of Kuruman, where the Colony was experienced as a benign help to which appeals for assistance could be directed in the face of repeated attacks from brigands, rather than as a governing authority to whom one addressed a prophetic message about justice and human rights. The colonial authority, it must also be remembered, was the institution which taught Moffat how to use a printing press, and which kindly printed the Gospel of Luke in 1830. This kind of relationship – which was not experienced by Moffat as unjust or oppressive towards his own people – forms the backdrop to his political views in the first period,[55] the period from which almost all commentators draw their conclusions about Moffat's political views.[56]

For example, based purely on a study of Moffat's first eight years in Kuruman, Schapera passes the all-encompassing remark that 'To Moffat, the missionary had only one important task: the conversion of the heathen to Christianity. He was completely opposed to the idea, so firmly held and applied by Philip, that it was also the duty of the true Christian, including of course the missionary, to champion the lot of the oppressed Native peoples and to strive for legal and political equality between them and white colonists.'[57]

We shall have cause to abandon this perspective as we consider Moffat's life as a whole and not just in fragments, for there was a marked change in the environment in which Moffat worked in the period after his 'apprenticeship' from 1820 to 1829. Towards the end of this first period at Kuruman in 1838 and just before he left for England, the impact of the Voortrekkers was beginning to be felt in the interior. Moffat had worked hard at establishing some American colleagues at Mzilikazi's kraal at Mosega, near modern-day Zeerust. The Boers attacked the Ndebele at this place, extracted much booty and destroyed the possibilities of a mission station. Not long after this, Mzilikazi retired north of the Limpopo.[58] Moffat's distrust of the intentions of the Boers becomes evident in letters and journals dating from the late 1830s.

Upon his return to Kuruman in 1843 there was, then, a decisive shift in the political environment in which Moffat worked, and there is a clear development of his thought and political concerns in the light of new circumstances. The Voortrekkers, or Boers as they were known, now well established in the interior of southern Africa, had changed the political dynamics in which Moffat worked, and drew him into a relationship with the Colony that he previously did not have. In this period, also, he was influenced by the views and experiences of his younger colleague and son-in-law, David Livingstone. For the first time Moffat had the kind of experiences that Van der Kemp, Read and Philip had had with settlers and colonial authorities and it drew forth a similar kind of political response. Once again we must note that in Moffat's life time the Voortrekkers, Tswana, Sotho and Ndebele were not citizens of the Colony, and therefore the direct approach to the Colony was of little influence.

Matters came to a head with the Sand River and Bloemfontein Conventions. Here the British government gave to the newly declared Boer republics a free hand to control the interior of southern Africa between the Orange River and the Limpopo. It was a remarkable act of political arrogance by the British in that the land was never theirs to give away in the first place, and it entrenched the oppressive racist policies of the Boer republics in the interior. Neither Moffat nor his colleagues in the LMS were silent. Without seemingly being aware of the wonderful irony of their comment the Comaroffs have written:

> Some of the Christians, moreover, resuscitating the spirit of John Philip, had campaigned loudly to have the British Administration protect the chiefdoms against settler predations. Matters first came to a head in the early 1850s when, by the Sand River and Bloemfontein Conventions, the overextended colonial government gave up all effort to control the Boers and recognised the independence of their republics across the Orange and Vaal Rivers.[59]

The irony is that it was Moffat – who allegedly had a very different political position from that of Philip – who became the leader of the group charged with 'resuscitating the spirit of John Philip'. For it was he who was elected chairperson at a meeting convened by the LMS missionaries in July 1853 to discuss the crisis, and it was he who then led a delegation to Bloemfontein to protest against both the implications of the Conventions and the Boer ill-treatment of the 'natives' in a way that would have made Read and Philip proud. Quoting from a letter from Moffat to the directors of the LMS, Northcott summarises the memorial to Sir George Clerk:

It conveyed the general impression 'made upon the native mind that the white man is combining for the destruction of the black' and that the 'emigrant farmers have always entertained very low views of the rights and privileges of the aborigines' and had destroyed six mission stations. 'The British Government is beginning to be regarded by the natives', continues the memorial, 'with distrust and suspicion, since they look upon it as combined with the Boers' and the result is 'that a general combination is now being formed among the natives in order to resist encroachment of the Boers'. The memorial looks to a 'dark, gloomy prospect and bloody war' chiefly because of 'the lure of plunder and lust of power and the desire of obtaining constrained and not paid labour on the part of the Boers'.[60]

The memorial fell on deaf ears. Clerk was there to ensure that the British withdrew from governing the Orange River Sovereignty and to persuade the Boer and English farmers to accept independence. He was not at all interested in listening to the moral concerns of the missionaries, and took no account of their insights and concerns. Moffat was extremely disappointed. He wrote to the LMS directors, 'If the Transvaal Boers are not arrested in their careers of extermination either by British power, or by the vengeance of the combined tribes, the tens of thousands of the Bechuanas will be doomed.' He also wrote to the *British Banner* that the Bloemfontein Convention 'soured the natives against the English as well as against the Boers', who now went 'hand in hand in the work of plunder, slavery and extermination'.[61] He describes the situation:

The state of the country is such as it has not been since I entered the field. The violent opposition of the tribes to the introduction of the gospel during the early years of the mission, the threatened destruction by the hordes of Mantatees, and the successful and devastating inroads made by the mixed freebooters, Korannas, Griquas and Bushmen appear now in our eyes as mere gusts compared to the storm which threatens to sweep away all the labours of missionaries and philanthropists to save the aborigines from annihilation. This is the time when all the wisdom, caution, and firmness that can be called into action are required.[62]

As the implications of the Conventions became apparent in the interior,

Moffat began to note the effects upon the Tswana and Ndebele. In a letter to the LMS designed to communicate some of this sense of injustice to the British public Moffat quoted Mzilikazi as asking, 'Do the English not trade with the Boers who ran away from their Government, and do not the English supply them with guns and ammunition, while they know the Boers use it to destroy the natives, that they may take their country?' Moffat continues:

> This was a question I felt some reluctance to answer, for it was impossible for me to deny the fact that the English did enter into a treaty to supply those very Boers with arms and ammunition. I was only glad that he appeared not yet to have heard of the law promulgated by our Government – the iniquity of which law the English language would fail to describe, though the consequences it may one day repent – that the native tribes north of the Vaal River be not allowed to purchase a single ounce of ammunition. Let anyone capable of looking this fact in the face deduce anything else than that it is the deliberate purpose of such law-givers to approve, sanction and encourage the utter extermination of the aborigines before the very men who rebelled against their Queen and shot her noble soldiers, while the man has yet to be found in these in-terior regions north of the Vaal, who has intentionally shed the blood of an Englishman.[63]

As the Boers became more entrenched in the republics north of the Orange River, they put more and more pressure on the LMS, and other, missionaries working amongst the Batswana. Moffat's son-in-law, Jean Fredoux of the Paris Evangelical Missionary Society, was ordered not to preach to the Tswana, and Walter Inglis and Rogers Edwards were ordered out of the Transvaal Republic. The nadir was the destruction of Livingstone's mission station at Kolobeng by a Boer commando that was seeking to defeat Sechele of the Kwena. These events have no precursor in the first period (1817–43), and Moffat's own expression of political concern developed in order to respond to these changed circumstances.

What is also crucial to recognise is that on his travels north to Mzilikazi passing through many Tswana tribes Moffat, through his personality and grasp of the language, was able to meet with and hear the concerns of the Tswana and Ndebele in the face of the Boer invasion. He was not unmoved by such testimony, and as a pastor and teacher he was able to express these concerns to a wider audience. Once again in his letter to the LMS directors he quotes a Motswana, Khosilintse:

> You have spoken about what the word of God says. Have not the English the word of God, and have not the Boers the word of God? Do their

teachers teach them with the same book? – (pointing to a New Testament). Are we only to obey the word of God because we are black? Are white people not to obey the word of God, because they are white? We know much of what the word of God teaches, but we are not allowed time to think about our souls while the Boers are seeking to kill us. You tell us that God may yet punish us and the Bakhatla more than he has done, for having rejected the Gospel. Did those tribes which the Boers have destroyed and made their slaves, reject the Gospel? Did those tribes, the remnants of which have fled to Sechele, reject the Gospel? Had they ever a teacher? Martinus [Commandant Pretorius] is now gone with a commando to destroy the Bamapela tribe. Have they rejected the Gospel? What has Mangkopane, their chief, done? I will tell you and why. He has killed nine Boers; I shall tell you that too. The Boers have for a long time been robbing and oppressing him and his people. When the Boers returned from Moselekatse a long time since, when they went to try to take his cattle – did not Moselekatse tell you? – they returned by the Bamapela tribe, fired on them and took many waggon loads of their children on the day. Mangkopane, their chief, got a present from another chief of a few guns and horses. As soon as the Boers heard this, they took them because a kaffir [*sic*] must not have a gun or a horse. Ask Mangkopane how many of his own children and theirs have been taken and made slaves, how many of his people have been murdered![64]

Three things are important here. The first is that Moffat chose to reproduce a long speech from a Motswana in a letter to the directors of the LMS. There is a conscious choice here to make known the concerns of those who were the victims of political injustice and to do so in their own voice without diminishing or toning down the directness of their accusations. Moffat was not only the translator of the Bible and interpreter of Christianity to the Tswana, he was also the translator of Setswana and the interpreter of black political concerns to the British public. There was no need for Moffat to include this long extract unless he sympathised with what was being said and understood the importance of sharing this view with a wider public.

The second thing to note is Moffat's own response, which is humble and accepting. Having chosen to give Khosilintse a voice, Moffat does not excuse or explain away the convictions as those on the lunatic fringe. He concludes the speech by saying to the LMS directors, 'I was right thankful to depart, for though I had many tough bones to pick in my missionary career, I never was in my life so completely floored … His eloquence was not that of fine language or modulated voice, but it was the deep tones of a stricken soul.' The third thing to note here is the implied criticism of a pietistic and 'otherworldly' spirituality ('we are not allowed time to think about our souls while the Boers are killing us'), which clearly Moffat is aware of, able to articulate, and yet not feel in any way driven to defend. In other words his political theology was deep and critical enough to sustain the wisdom of what Khosilintse was saying.

Moffat remained concerned and committed to justice and peace in southern Africa even after his retirement in England. In contrast with his first period of home leave during which time he wrote *Missionary Labours and Scenes*, Moffat did not write a full autobiography or update his first book. Much of his time was spent addressing people in Britain about the work of missions and about the political situation in southern Africa, in terms that makes the alleged distinction between him and Philip fade away. A colleague wrote to his son John Smith Moffat after the death of his father:

> His [Moffat's] views as to the native policy of the Boers in the Transvaal, and as to the duty of the Imperial Government to secure adequate protection to the loyal tribes within and near the borders of that country were equally emphatic. I well remember the speech he made on this subject at the residence of Mr W.H. James, M.P. when on Lord Shaftesbury's invitation, he gave, from personal knowledge, a vivid description of the cruel and oppressive treatment which the natives had received at the hands of the Boers during his long residence in South Africa.[65]

Until the final hours of his life Moffat remained passionately concerned about issues of justice and peace for the black inhabitants of southern Africa. His daughter Jane described how, upon hearing the news of the retrocession of the Transvaal to the Boers after the first Anglo-Boer War, he was a 'picture of sadness'. She went on to add, 'For days he was as though he had received a death-blow, nor to his dying hour did it cease to be to him a bitter sorrow.'[66] In a letter written just three weeks before his death he continued to express his concerns: 'I have oft felt much pressed in mind from the reported sufferings of the Bechwanas, robbed and trodden down by the Transvaal Boers.'[67]

These references from the second period of Moffat's work at Kuruman and his retirement to Britain are a far cry from the all-encompassing statement of the Comaroffs: 'For all his own ambiguous statements and equivocal actions in this respect, Robert Moffat was much less ready to indulge his moral conscience in the political domain.'[68]

It is clear to the reader that in its unchronological generalisations, this picture of Robert Moffat, like that of Ross quoted above, is off target. Certainly in his second period at the Kuruman valley we have seen that the changed political dynamics drew forth political protest from Robert Moffat that was neither conservative nor of a pietistic 'otherworldly' spirituality, but rather one that enabled Moffat to take part in political discussions in the public arena and to express a concern for justice, peace and human freedom.

CONCLUDING THOUGHTS

The Comaroffs have noted that the LMS missionaries had little impact in the formal world of politics because they really had no access to political power. They make the point about Philip: 'It is no surprise, then, that even the most "political" of missionaries tended to lose their secular influence long before their energies ran out. As Davies (1951:16) notes, John Philip's career ended in a long period of "political quietude." It was a pattern often to be repeated.'[69] But it was not a pattern repeated by Moffat, for unlike Philip's his career did not end in political quietude. It seems probable that like the Comaroffs, Moffat was aware of the implications of a lack of political power, and thus shaped his work accordingly. He sought to avoid short-term politics, aware of the long-term implications, and it was this which enabled his own perseverance in the face of tremendous odds. His son John, who was both a missionary and a political official, noted in the introduction to his biography of his parents that 'speaking as an official himself, he is bound to confess that political intervention on behalf of the natives has mostly ended in failure', but that this frustration was not experienced by his father.

Owing to his clear focus on the human relationship to both God and neighbour, Moffat practised what I would call a political theology of 'creative detachment', one in which the expectation of disillusionment was calculated in at the beginning rather than experienced at the end. It may just be that it is precisely this disinterestedness[70] that created the space in which he could be an effective agent of construction in a society awash with full-scale transformation. This gave him the energy and vision to sustain his work until the end, to focus on long-term objectives which were within his power to achieve, and to relate to a range of people without unrealistic expectations as to what could be achieved. Moffat knew that the missionaries were not politicians – not because they were uninterested in political matters – but because they simply did not have the access to political power to achieve what they wanted to do. They had rather to work with and amongst people, sharing with them the tools that might one day enable them to become shapers of their own destiny and creating both the hope and discomfort arising from the eschatological promise of the Kingdom of God. (Is this perhaps what the Comaroffs misunderstand as the 'seductive promises of the Church'?)[71]

Though like their teacher, Schapera, the Comaroffs have pointed to the rural–urban tension between the political choices of Moffat and Philip,[72] they have not really taken this into account as a crucial issue in political options, and reflect thus possibly the urban and urbane social location of most commentators. As those in rural development know only too well, it is easy to come in with guns blazing for a few years, full of political theories and rhetoric, and then to leave disillusioned. The long-term effects of this are that the 'recipients' are left worse off than at the start. It is more difficult to settle in for the long term, to learn the language, to leave the formal politics to those who hold political leadership in the community, and to focus instead on the long-range work of human development. It is more difficult, but it is also more empowering and more necessary. Fifty years working slowly in one rural community is more likely to lead to long-term human and socio-political development than five years of feverish agitation.

It is here that the contemporary concerns of the mission for rural advancement and political development find a creative and appreciative dialogue with the work of Moffat. For if Moffat had a word for today, then I sense that he would encourage us to take the options that would build up community life, invest time and energy in long-term, people-based projects and – in the name of good politics – remain suspicious of all politics and politicians.

DAVID LIVINGSTONE:
THE MAN BEHIND THE MASK

Andrew Ross

William Monk, editor of David Livingstone's Cambridge Lectures, headed a subsection of the appendix he wrote for the second edition, 'The unity of the human race further proved by Dr Livingstone's researches in South Africa.' In this section he declared

> Differences in colour, speech, natural characteristics, religious belief, moral, social and intellectual condition, may stagger some about the unity of the race; but be it remembered that these diversities are mostly refer-able to external circumstances ... The same pleasures, anxieties, crimes, virtues, vices, noble or mean actions and influences, affect alike in many instances the soul of the most cultivated philosopher and of the most uncivilised savage.[1]

Dr Monk asserted the oneness of humanity so firmly because it was being denied by so many of the thinkers of his day; thinkers who saw themselves as on the cutting edge of modernity. He was asserting human unity in what was becoming a losing battle in the English-speaking intellectual world against the rising tide of the complex of ideas that came to be called, depending on the perspective, scientific racism or Anglo-Saxonism. The profound difference between Monk and David Livingstone was that Livingstone was unshakeably rooted in the same intellectual tradition as the early leaders of the London Missionary Society (LMS) in the Cape, Van der Kemp, James Read and John Philip. What Monk had to assert, they had taken for granted.

Even as Livingstone arrived in the Cape in 1841 the ideas of Carlyle and the Scottish anatomist and popular science lecturer, Robert Knox, were beginning already to influence the history of Africa. Their influence upon the 1820 Settler community of the eastern Cape is clear, witness J.M. Bowker's famous 'Springbok' speech at Gert Else's farm in July 1841. This well-known leader of the 1820 Settlers, second only in authority within that community to Godlonton, the editor of the *Grahamstown Journal*, said:

Colonise Kafirland, and the whole of the fertile and de-populated tracts between here and Natal; millions of the pale yellow-coloured could find food and a home there ... The day was when our plains were covered with tens of thousands of springboks; they are gone and who regrets it? ... yet I must own when I see two or three of them on the wide plains, and know that they are the last of their race my heart yearns towards them, and I regret that so much innocent beauty, elegance and agility must needs be swept from the earth.

My feeling toward the Kafir are not of that stamp ... I know him to be the great bar to all improvement among us. I know that rapine and murder are in all his thoughts, and I see them in his looks and hate him accordingly ... Is it just that a few thousands of ruthless, worthless savages are to sit like a nightmare upon a land that would support millions of civilised men happily?[2]

The 'pale yellow-coloured' was not a reference to the importation of Chinese labourers, but to the poorest sections of the British working class. Carlyle coined this phrase to describe them in his infamous essay *On the Nigger Question*. The idea that humanity was not one but was divided into a number of mutually exclusive groups arranged on an ascending scale of moral as well as intellectual ability with, at the top, the fair-haired and fair-skinned European, the Anglo-Saxon (the darker Europeans, particularly those of Celtic origin, were on an inferior level), was becoming a widely held idea in the English-speaking world. In addition it was becoming commonplace to see destiny as willing the removal of inferior groups if they stood in the way of progress.

Already, in 1852, the intellectual climate was such that *The Times* was able to publish an editorial that took for granted the division of humanity into superior and inferior races. This editorial also presumed without question that the survival of the strongest was an immutable law of nature with which humankind simply had to learn to live. This editorial in *The Times* of 17 March 1852 was concerned with Mlanjeni's War, as the Xhosa called the eighth frontier war between them and the Cape Colony. The editorial complained that yet again the Xhosa had, in modern soccer parlance, forced a draw. The writer contrasts the last three Xhosa wars fought by British forces with a massacre of well over a thousand African men, women and children by a Transvaal commando under Andries Pretorius, a Transvaal commandant whom Livingstone had met when attempting to expand his mission into the western Transvaal.

We doubt very much if as many Kafirs [Xhosa] have fallen by the bullets or bayonets of our troops in the last three wars, as were destroyed in this single expedition of Pretorius. It would be hard indeed to argue that such an example should be followed; but of this we are convinced, if the colonisation of South Africa is to be continued, the savage tribes of our frontier can only successfully be countered, like the savages of all other regions, by acts resembling their own. The backwoodsmen of Kentucky pursued the Red Indian as the Red Indian pursued them, and the victory in the end fell to the superior race.

In 1963 Philip Curtin wrote his incisive *The Image of Africa* in which he described the revolution in British attitudes to Africa that took place in the middle decades of the nineteenth century. In the first decades of the century the attitude toward humanity that inspired Van der Kemp, Read, Philip, Fairbairn, Livingstone and others was a very influential one, although there were rival understandings in the English-speaking world. This view was culturally arrogant but it took for granted the oneness of humanity. It was a viewpoint particularly strong among evangelical Protestants. In the United States it was basic to the thinking of the leadership of the Second Awakening and the revival campaigns of Charles Finney, whose books were avidly read by Livingstone. This non-racial philosophy profoundly shaped the new American Antislavery Society whose 1833 constitution laid down as a fundamental plank in its platform that the slaves should be freed and immediately receive equal civil rights with their white fellow Americans.[3]

The non-racial, low-qualification franchise of 1852 for the new Assembly for the Cape Colony and the brief and unsuccessful attempt at the 'Reconstruction' of the defeated Confederate States in the United States were the last flings of the oneness of humanity philosophy influencing government policy in the English-speaking world. Within missionary circles it lived longer but even there it had given way by the end of the century.

The period when the belief in one humanity was the dominant, though never universal, attitude was called by Curtin 'the Era of Conversionism'. Conversionism held that Christianity, education and legitimate commerce, if allowed to operate freely among African people, would free them from the power of their fallen and degraded cultures and let them become equal members of civilised society. This attitude produced Fourah Bay College and the Lovedale Institution, the Rev. Tiyo Soga and Bishop Samuel Adjai Crowther. This understanding was produced by a powerful combination of evangelical and Enlightenment thought articulated so clearly in John Wesley's *Thoughts on Slavery* of 1774 or again in John Philip's preface to his *Researches*. Both these doughty evangelicals took for granted the fundamental Enlightenment concept of inalienable human rights, which every human being possessed simply by virtue of being alive.

Of course there had been opposition to this idea articulated in a literary form as early as Edward Long's *History of Jamaica* but the oneness of humanity was the dominant attitude till the middle of the century. However, the scholarly consensus of Gossett, Curtin, Bolt, Lorimer and Malik is that the 1850s saw the beginning of a massive change in the intellectual climate of the English-speaking world. Robert Knox's lectures, which he gave all over the United Kingdom in the 1840s, were published in 1850. In these lectures he insisted that race was the key to every aspect of human history and culture. It was the scientific study of race that was essential for an understanding of human reality. 'Race is everything, literature, art, science, in a word civilisation, depend on it' was the core of Knox's message. Increasingly scientific thought was moving in the direction Knox pioneered and this movement tied in with the Anglo-Saxon or Teutonic interpretation of history that scholars of Harvard, Columbia and Oxford universities propounded in the last decades of the nineteenth century. The so-called Anglo-Saxon or Teutonic peoples were the pinnacle of human development, of the evolutionary process. Democracy grew out of Germanic tribal traditions and their descendants alone could be trusted with democratic rights. Knox had already preached this historical doctrine along with his scientific assertion that race was all, but its academic authenticity was apparently verified by the wide-ranging and impressive consensus of Bishop Stubbs, E.A. Freeman and J.R.Green at Oxford, A.B. Hart and Henry Cabot Lodge at Harvard, H.B.Adams at Johns Hopkins, and J.G. Burgess at Columbia.

This racial understanding of human reality that came to dominate the English-speaking world took two forms. The first was that implied in *The Times* editorial to which we have referred and was made explicit by Bowker. This attitude saw 'backward' or 'savage' peoples as destined to be swept aside by the superior race in the inexorable march of progress. It was ferociously expressed by Knox himself: 'What signify these dark races to us? Who cares particularly for the Negro, or the Hottentot or the Kaffir? These latter have proved a very troublesome race, and the sooner they are put out of the way the better.'[4] This was the frame of mind that produced dreadful results like the deliberate genocide of the Tasmanian Aborigines and of some Native American groups in parts of the United States.

Among many people, particularly those in government as well as the majority of missionaries (a minority, like David Clement Scott of Blantyre, held on to a one-humanity position), the impact of race thinking took a different practical direction. This was an attitude of responsible and caring superiority, which led Curtin to refer to the decades from the 1860s up to the First World War as the 'Era of Trusteeism'. However, it can be argued that trusteeism lasted much longer than suggested by Curtin, not being effectively dispelled until after the Second World War.

Trusteeism accepted that other peoples were inferior to the Anglo-Saxon but did not accept that the inferior people should be treated cruelly, let alone their eradication. It was the duty of the superior race to care for the inferior races, to ensure they were treated with justice and helped to develop as far as their limited abilities could go. It was this attitude that informed Kipling's 'The Whiteman's Burden' and the compassionate but thoroughly Anglo-Saxonist *Our Country* by the leading proponent in America of the social gospel, Josiah Strong. Believers in 'trusteeism' sought to prevent ill-treatment like that perpetrated in the Congo Free State but in their view the idea that the inferior races could be entrusted with leadership roles or with the vote was clearly mistaken. Trusteeism was the conviction of the leadership of the English-speaking world in the first decades of the twentieth century and it shaped, with regard to Africa, the actions of the radical Liberal government of Great Britain, which first came to power in 1906. That administration laid the first bricks in the foundations of the welfare state but it also enacted that the new Union of South Africa would have universal white male suffrage over the protests of those who believed in the non-racialism of the old Cape constitution. Asquith and Lloyd George were happy to leave the future of the 'natives' of South Africa in the hands of Jan Smuts, a worthy trustee, and no one of any consequence demurred.

This profound change in the intellectual climate of the English-speaking world has shaped the way in which David Livingstone has been understood since this national hero's funeral in Westminster Abbey in April 1874. Livingstone was a product of the 'Era of Conversionism', indeed it can be argued that he was one of the greatest proponents of its ideas. However, after his death he was taken up by an army of writers who made him into an icon of the 'Era of Trusteeism'. A classic example is the *Life* by Edward Hume, commissioned and published in 1910 by the Sunday School Union. The author ends his preface with these words:

it is not too much to say that the work of exploration and development carried on by his successors has been made easier by the perfect frankness with which he dealt with the coloured races of Africa.

In such a sense, therefore, Livingstone still lives. And as confidence in the honesty of purpose of the governing race will need to be the foundation of British rule in South and Central Africa, as it has been in India, so the man whose labours resulted in strengthening this reputation for fairness has a claim on Anglo-Saxon gratitude which each year should see deepened and extended.[5]

The years after 1874 saw the emergence of a Livingstone publishing industry. When I gave up counting the books on Livingstone in the library system of Yale University I had reached seventy, and then I discovered that there were still more in the Day Missions Library which had not yet been put onto the computerised catalogue. Between 1890 and 1960 hardly a child who attended a Protestant Sunday school in the English-speaking world could have escaped receiving, as a prize, a book on Livingstone.

Of course the vast majority of these publications were derivative. They were based on a handful of major studies: those of Blaikie, Roberts, Hughes, Sir Harry Johnston and Campbell were probably the most important. However, this myriad of derivative studies must not be underestimated. They had a massive impact on the popular image of Livingstone; books like Hume's for the Sunday School Union reached a very wide audience indeed. The liberal imperialist image of Livingstone they created has lasted for about a hundred years, but it is an image that has hidden Livingstone from people, an image that has acted as a mask.

The body of writers who have taken up Livingstone since the mid-1950s beginning with Gelfand in 1956 and Seaver in 1957 have not shaken free of the liberal imperialist image. It set their agenda and some have simply represented it in a modified and modernised form. A striking example of this was Northcott's *David Livingstone* of 1973 in which Livingstone is set alongside Albert Schweitzer as a typical benevolent paternalist. The object of this exercise is to show that whatever David Livingstone was, he was not a benevolent paternalist.

Who then was David Livingstone? A satisfactory answer to that question will need a full-scale biography. This biography will have to leap over the barrier of Curtin's 'Age of Trusteeism' and start with Livingstone firmly in his setting of evangelical 'conversionism' alongside John Philip and James Read, Theodore Weld and Charles Finney. Timothy Holmes's *Journey to Livingstone,* which, unfortunately, has not been widely distributed, is the first and only study to make this attempt.

What can be done in the space available is to highlight certain areas of Livingstone's thought and work which have been either misunderstood, omitted or underplayed by his biographers. We will focus on some of the key areas that need revision in order to begin to set Livingstone free from the shackles of 'trusteeism'.

However, I first need to make clear what will not be considered. Livingstone's relationship with Mary Moffat, his wife, and their children present complex problems that will not be discussed. One thing, however, must be said of this; it was not cold indifference on the part of Livingstone that led to their being sent to Britain in 1852. Livingstone was deeply torn by the move he felt he had to make. Why Mary and the children did not simply go to stay with the Moffats at Kuruman may have more to do with Mary's relations with her mother than has been considered heretofore. One need only read Livingstone's letter on the death of their daughter at Kolobeng to realise his capacity for love.[6]

The first and fundamental point to make in any new approach to Livingstone is that he is a prime example of Curtin's 'conversionist' attitude to Africans. He was not another benevolent paternalist like Schweitzer.

Schweitzer, with his belief in the essential inferiority of the African people for whom he had come to do good, is a perfect example of Curtin's 'trusteeism'. Livingstone lived on into the new era of the 'scientific' study of race and of Anglo-Saxonism but he was never part of it. He saw Africans as human beings with unlimited potential that could only be fulfilled through Christianity and civilisation. Africans were not cut off from people of European stock by genetic, biological or evolutionary barriers. In the classic 'conversionist' mode, Livingstone believed that it was their culture that was degraded and that held Africans down but they were as fully human as any white person. The point is that to Livingstone whites could be equally degraded; the issue was not a matter of biological determinism.

> Sechele asked the Boers on commando not to fight on Sunday. The former beat the Bakwains hollow in lying and meanness, and it would be an insult to compare the honesty of the Bakwains with the dishonesty of the Boers … I bear the poor wretched Boers in the Interior no malice. I never did, but I pitied their ignorance and wickedness. Although I were a Boer myself I could not help saying, as they do, that in morality they are decidedly inferior to the Bakwains, and considerably worse indeed than the heathen who have had no advantages.[7]

His attitude to Africans and their potential is made very clear at the beginning of his *Missionary Travels and Researches in South Africa*. 'Our great-grandfather fell at the battle of Culloden, fighting for the old line of kings; and our grandfather was a small farmer in Ulva, where my father was born.' He goes on, when discussing stories about his grandfather, to say: 'This event took place at a time when the Highlanders, according to Macaulay, were very much like the Cape Caffres, and anyone could escape punishment for cattle-stealing by presenting a share of the plunder to his chieftain.'[8] This attitude, which sees his grandfather and great-grandfather to have been as the Xhosa were in his time, is in startling contrast to the attitude of Bowker, the editorial writer in *The Times* or Dr Schweitzer. In some ways his attitude is made even more explicit in his lament in a letter to a friend about the Boer raid on his old mission among the Kwena at Kolobeng.

> They went the whole hog – attended church on Sunday, hearing Mebaloe preach, and then made the parson flee for his life on Monday. He ran the gauntlet … He has lost all he had, viz. 27 head of cattle and his furniture, etc. His house was burned by the Christians. He it was who stood by me when bitten by the lion, and got bit himself … Some fine young men whom I knew and loved have fallen. My heart is sore when I think of them.[9]

These last two sentences presume a common humanity in a form that challenges even the most beneficent form of Curtin's 'trusteeism'. In his last years he became aware of the new scientific ideas of race that were being propagated. Leading members of the Anthropological Society of London had attacked him and his ideas. In their view his was a sentimental attitude toward Africans, seeking to educate and Christianise those who were incapable of either because of their essential inferiority. This did not provoke any particular reply in his public writing. However, towards the end of his life, while reflecting on cannibalism among the Manyema, Livingstone wrote: 'And yet they are a fine looking race; I would back a company of Manyuema men to be far superior in shape of head and generally in physical form too against the whole Anthropological Society.'[10]

Perhaps even more striking as an example of his assumption of a common humanity is his insistence on the right of Africans to defend themselves by force against aggression by whites. Some of his biographers have discussed this only with reference to the Kwena of Sechele defending themselves against the Boers. Most modern biographers are still apologetic about this, like Seaver,[11] who asserts vehemently, 'There is no foundation whatever in the assertion, which has sometimes been made, that Livingstone was guilty of "arming the natives."' Whatever the technical details of who gave whom what, when and where, which cannot now be certainly discerned, it was through Livingstone's contacts with European hunters, travellers and traders that Sechele and his people got their guns and ammunition. It is also clear, according to Seaver and other apologists, that Livingstone gloried in their ability to defend themselves against the power of the white man which was transforming so many of their neighbours into squatters on their own land.[12]

So many biographers have treated this incident as a special case since these same Boers were enemies of British authority in the Cape. Even the more modern of his biographers, other than Holmes, have either skipped over in an aside or ignored entirely Livingstone's defence of the Xhosas' right to defend their homeland against the British. While in Cape Town to see Mary and the children off to Britain preparatory to his going north to the Kololo of Sebituane, he wrote of the War of Mlanjeni:

By the same post I send a letter to my brother containing Sandillah's [Sandile's] speech to Renton, to be printed in America. All we learn of the Caffre war is one-sided. We must hear both sides. It is well Sandillah speaks out so nobly. Bringing out converts to assist the English is infamous. We must preach passive resistance or fighting for one's own countrymen.[13]

Indeed he went further and defended what was to most whites at that time the indefensible, the Cape coloured rebellion against the British in that same war. In a number of letters to Thompson of the LMS and to family and friends he denounced the whole British colonial set-up in the Cape Colony, including what he called the 'Mobocracy of that cesspool called Grahamstown'.[14] This sustained critical attack is fundamental to understanding Livingstone but it is passed over with no or only brief comment: Blaikie gave it nineteen lines; Jeal, who tries hard at a new approach, does not see its significance. However, he did not simply write letters but, as we have seen, sent Sandile's speech to be published in America.

More importantly he composed a long considered piece for the *British Quarterly*, which had readily published an earlier essay by him critical of the policy of the LMS within the Colony. This new piece, however, was not published. In the Zimbabwe National Archives there is a 78-page essay by him that would appear to be either what he sent to the *British Quarterly* or a development of it. One quotation from it to be found in Holmes is enough once and for all to set apart Livingstone from the attitude towards Africa and Africans of the English-speaking world in the 'Era of Trusteeism': 'but we would prefer perpetual war to perpetual slavery. No nation ever secured liberty without fighting for it. And every nation on earth worthy of freedom is ready to shed blood in its defence. We sympathize with the Caffres, we side with the weak against the strong.'[15]

Perhaps more telling, because they come in a context when he is not discussing race relations nor is involved in any conflict, are his remarks in a letter to his daughter Agnes. He is describing his situation of being a curiosity among the Manyema and so having difficulty in obtaining any privacy:

The door is shut, all save a space to admit light … eager heads sometimes crowd the open space, and crash goes the thin door, landing a Manyuema beauty on the floor. 'It was not I,' she gasps out. 'It was Bessie Bell and Jeanie Gray that shoved me in, and — ', as she scrambles out the lion's den, 'see they're laughing'; and fairly out, she joins in the merry giggles too.[16]

This simple human relationship between Livingstone and Africans towards the end of his life is paralleled by incidents in his first years in Africa, described in a letter to his sister Agnes:

I was at this interrupted by one of Bubi's wives bringing me some beans and a draught of curious sort of beer … I gave her a string of amber beads and two rings, I believe given me by your companions. In giving them I called her 'sister', which pleased her so very much she is determined to act the part of one. Every evening since she sends me a huge bowl of sour porridge or beans or some sweet reeds with the message, 'Sister sends you this as she ought to take good care of her brother.'[17]

To sum up, Africans could be heroes, young men whom he loved, 'very pretty' Manyema girls or they could be, as he termed the Batoka, 'savage and cruel under success, but easily cowed and devoid of moral courage'.[18] In other words they were simply people.

The next element in the Livingstone story that needs reconsideration is why he went north from his mission at Kolobeng and then left missionary employment forever? The question, perhaps, should rather be asked the other way round. How was it that he stayed so long in the conventional set-up of the LMS Bechuana mission?

From the very beginning of his stay in Africa, indeed while he was still in Dr Philip's house in Cape Town, he displayed a serious desire to be some kind of pioneer, going beyond where anyone else had gone, never building on another man's foundations. In a number of these early letters he writes as though he felt this as a calling and that any time spent on a mission station was only some kind of preparation for his real task. On 30 March 1841 he wrote to his sisters Janet and Agnes about Dr Philip's suggestion that either he or the other new missionary, William Ross, should stay in Cape Town and look after his local congregation while he went up-country: 'I would not for a moment think of remaining. I shall go immediately when I get the opportunity. I would never build on another man's foundation. I shall preach the gospel beyond every other man's line of things.'[19] This is a recurring theme in his letters from then on.

On arrival at Kuruman what he finds there only encourages his feeling of the need to move on. As he writes to his parents in September 1842, 'The population in this country is very thin indeed … I don't know what the new missionaries will make of it when they come.'[20] When Moffat arrived back from Britain, Livingstone and the veteran Roger Edwards founded a new mission to the north at Mabotsa. Livingstone then moved on to work with the Kwena people of Sechele, first at Chonwane, then at Kolobeng. These two sites had been chosen as a result of two long treks that Livingstone had made, the first with Edwards, the second, very significantly, only with some Tswana companions. This latter trip was aimed at immersing himself in the language and culture of the Tswana people. Already the north and stories of a lake beyond the Kalahari that no European had seen were attracting him. However, lake or no lake, Livingstone has consistent criticism to make of the activities of the LMS in southern Africa.

First there are too many missionaries in what were essentially pastoral roles in the Colony itself, and north of the Orange there are far too many missionaries for the very thin population of the area. 'The smoke of a thousand villages' story of Moffat's might have been true of somewhere but not of the semi-desert where the LMS mission was at work north of the Orange.

At Kolobeng, where Livingstone had set up the furthest inland station of the

Society, he became very aware of the threat from the Boers to any expansion of missionary activity and so he decided to trek eastwards and meet up with them. This did not bring about any change in Transvaal policy but it did open Livingstone's eyes. He wrote of the treks to the east that he had made with only Tswana companions. 'Have been engaged in itinerancy much of late among the tribes living Eastwards of Chonuane. The number of the inhabitants is prodigious as we approach the coast. There the population of the Bechuana country chiefly resides.'[21] The country and people to the east did attract him because here at last was the dense population, the existence of which had first drawn him to Africa. The problem was the intransigent opposition of the Boers to the LMS and to his ideals. So it was back to the north to which he constantly referred in his letters to family and to the LMS officials.

In 1849 he went north in the company of two British 'sportsmen', W.C. Oswell and Mungo Murray, and they were the first Europeans to see Lake Ngami whose existence had fascinated Europeans for some time. This brought Livingstone fame but what was much more important was that through his contacts with Sekhomi of the Ngwato (father of the great Seretse Khama) he learned on this journey of the existence of the powerful and populous Kololo kingdom of Sebituane further to the north. A vast new densely populated area now appeared to lie open to Christian mission unhindered by the threat of Boer or other (in Livingstone's view) degrading European influences. Here was an area where the Christian gospel and honest trading could together trigger off the upward rise of the people to play their part in the modern world. It would be a new day dawning for Africa, a phrase he would use again and again, even at times in the last despairing wanderings amid scenes of horror created by the East Coast slave trade.

In 1850 and again in 1851 Livingstone went north, each time with Mary and the children. This horrified his mother-in-law and most other observers. On the second journey Oswell came along; without the aid of Oswell, who became his lifelong friend, the journeys could never have taken place. On the second journey they met Sebituane, who made them welcome and set aside a 'garden' for Livingstone so that he would have his own food when he came back. Sebituane died but his heirs continued the policy of friendship to their visitor. Livingstone was now determined that this was where his future lay. However, he was also clear that a new route to Kololo country had to be found, since the journey from the Cape was far too arduous. So, having taken the family to Cape Town to see them off, he embarked in 1852 on his astonishing journey up to the Kololo kingdom, from there to Loanda, then back across Africa via the Kololo kingdom to the east coast. This *viagem contra costa* in a sense determined the rest of his life. He had found his dense population, he had found healthy highlands for European missionaries and traders, and he had found rich soils and local cotton production that, if opened to the world, could bring prosperity to these lands and provide an alternative for British industry to the slave-produced cotton of America which he so abhorred.

This optimistic picture was, however, threatened by a dark shadow that was tragically to grow and dominate his life: the Portuguese and Swahili slave trades. On the subsequent Zambezi Expedition financed by the government in order to open up the Zambezi Basin, Livingstone discovered that the East Coast slave trade was expanding rapidly and much of the economy and social structure of east central Africa was being destroyed by it. During these years, 1858 to 1864, his high hopes raised during the *viagem contra costa* seemed to be disappearing before his eyes. It was to open up East Africa to the world and to expose to the world the horrors being perpetrated by the slave trade that he returned to Africa on his third and last 'journey'. Wherever he went in those last years there were the Swahili slavers, with the occasional Portuguese in the south. At times, to his despair, he was so short of resources that he was dependent on Swahili slavers simply to stay alive. Yet he struggled on, calling down the blessing of God on anyone who would end this terrible trade. Livingstone was always going to go north; once he had, he was sucked into a lifelong struggle with the forces that were destroying his dream.

This brings us to another area of Livingstone's life in need of revision. For how long was Livingstone a missionary? The astonishing journey across Africa brought him great fame and ended his employment by the LMS. Did it mark a change in his life from missionary to explorer? In one sense it clearly did. He was never thereafter employed as a Christian missionary. Admittedly the Zambezi Expedition was related formally to two missionary ventures, the LMS to the Kololo and the inaugural UMCA mission to Malawi. However, giving assistance to them was only a marginal part of Livingstone's duties as a government servant. His last journey had no formal institutional relationship to any missionary society or church.

Yet in another more fundamental way Livingstone has to be seen as still the same man with the same interests and motivation at the end as at the beginning of his life in Africa. As early as 1841, as we have seen, he was talking of being a pioneer, of not building on other men's foundations. He had always understood the task of the missionary very individualistically. Despite his close personal relations with Robert Moffat, he never accepted Moffat's and the LMS's insistence on teamwork supervised by committee. What few biographers have noted is that on this issue he was much closer to John Philip, who opposed the development of district committees. Livingstone also said that Dr Philip believed in letting the individual missionary seek out and do that which he was best at. Livingstone felt that the committee system of running the work of the LMS was falling away from the true spirit of 'independency'. In addition, no biographer has noted the influence of Charles Finney upon him. The liberal evangelicalism of Finney had little regard either for 'old school' Calvinism or for the institutional church and denominational loyalties. All of this fitted well with the old tradition of 'independency' and helped shape Livingstone's theology and his understanding of the missionary task.

Livingstone's apprenticeship in southern Africa enabled him to reshape Philip's famous definition of the missionary task as Christianity and Civilisation, to include Commerce as the third 'C'. So when he took off to the north in 1852, he arranged that George Fleming, a trader, should go with him. It was legitimate commerce and Christianity that were going to save Africa's peoples both from their degraded and degrading cultures and from the even more destructive power of the slave trade. For in Livingstone's eyes even degraded African traditional culture had some virtues that the slave trade and slavery threatened to destroy. In 1869 among the Manyema, who were cannibals, he insisted that they were morally superior to those people touched by slavery.[22] If Christianity and legitimate commerce were the key to the uplifting of Africa's peoples, then central Africa with its dense population had to be opened up to them — all the more urgently because of the threat of the Portuguese and Swahili slave trades. The need to bring this about dominated the rest of his life and cannot be separated from his deep Christian faith. As he understood it Christian mission could not be limited to the work done by missionary societies. Would anyone in the long history of Christianity before the rise of the Protestant missionary societies in the last decade of the eighteenth century ever have thought so anyway?

There is one apparent contradiction in his policy for central Africa as we have attempted to portray it. While in Britain preparing for the Zambezi Expedition Livingstone explicitly discussed the idea of setting up a white 'colony' in central Africa to speed the transforming process. This appears to contradict his bitter condemnation of the bad effect on African society of white colonists, whether the Boers or the English variety of Grahamstown and the eastern Cape. Livingstone mentioned this idea to the Duke of Argyll and to Professor Sedgwick,[23] apparently intending it to be confidential, though Sedgwick refers to the idea in the introduction to the published version of Livingstone's Cambridge Lectures. What he meant is still a matter of dispute. Debenham insisted that he was already advocating British imperial expansion into the area.[24] I believe it is clear that he did not mean British imperial rule over Africa. It appears rather that he was using the word 'colony' to mean a settlement of outsiders, like an ancient Greek 'colony', though that analogy cannot be taken very far. Livingstone did explicitly describe it as a settlement of carefully selected virtuous Christian men and women whose lifestyle, Christian witness and stimulation of the local economy would be a transforming influence on the surrounding villages. Timothy Holmes suggests that perhaps what he intended was something like the Jesuit Paraguayan 'Reductions',[25] but this does not quite fit. Certainly Livingstone's intention was similar to that of the

Jesuits in that each sought to save traditional communities from foreign slave raiders. However, nothing Livingstone says suggests anything on the scale of the 'Reductions'. He appeared to be contemplating only one community that would act as a catalyst among the African societies and also, because of the colony's outside connections, act as a deterrent to the slavers. This is a topic that needs further investigation though it was not an idea that Livingstone appears to have followed up.

Livingstone was an avid and accurate recorder of Africa's fauna and flora. Of this there is no dispute, as also with his abilities as a mapper of the terrain through which he passed. This is no surprise given his initial studies at Anderson's College (now Strathclyde University), which was a pioneering scientific institution in the 1830s. What is much more surprising in view of the normal attitude of the time towards the 'degraded cultures' of Africa was Livingstone's interest in the traditional culture of the people among whom he lived. This began with the treks he made while still at Kuruman, waiting for Moffat to return from Britain. He used these journeys to immerse himself in the Tswana language and culture. As he said, this was essential if the gospel was to be effectively transmitted. This intimacy with Tswana people enabled him to reach the conclusion that the idea of a single creator God was not absent from Tswana culture in the way that Moffat had said it was. Livingstone discussed this problem with his brother Charles in a letter of March 1847.[26] In the same letter he weakens the impact of the evidence he presents by complaining that no Tswana was able to pull it all together in order to give a rational account of God!

Livingstone's mastery of Setswana was the basis of his development of theories about the African languages. His achievement in this area has been widely acknowledged but there is one idea upon which he focused in his thoughts on language of which only Holmes among his biographers sees the significance. This is Livingstone's persistent assertion of the relationship between what became known as the Bantu family of languages and the Coptic of Ancient Egypt. Others have, of course, noticed his suggestion but only Holmes[27] insists on its significance as indicating Livingstone's view of Ancient Egypt as an African culture. I agree with Holmes, and this is Livingstone again challenging the consensus of academic opinion in Europe and the United States that Ancient Egypt was an essentially Mediterranean culture and the product of a race higher on the evolutionary ladder than Africans.

What is striking about his interest in African cultures was the seriousness with which he treated the traditional healer, the *sing'anga* or *nganga* in so many different languages of southeastern Africa. Livingstone had penetrated the people's understanding of reality deeply enough to distinguish this kind of practitioner from the witchfinder, both lumped together as 'witchdoctors' in so much European writing. As late as the second half of the twentieth century many Western-trained doctors in Africa were still scorning the traditional healer. Livingstone did not. In his instructions to Dr (later Sir) John Kirk he wrote:

> One especial means of gaining their favour will be by giving them the benefit of your medical skill and remedial aid. They possess medical men among themselves who are generally the most observant people to be met with; it is desirable at all times to be on good terms with them. In order to this [sic] slight complaints, except among the very poor, ought to be referred to their care, and severe cases, before being undertaken, should be enquired with the doctor himself and no disparaging remark ever made on the previous treatment in the presence of the patient.[28]

At other times he took the *sing'anga* remedies seriously enough to try them on himself. This openness towards African medicine came from his openness to African culture, an openness extraordinary in someone so devoted to the 'conversionist' commitment to Christianity, civilisation and commerce, whose flipside was usually a complete rejection of any interest in African culture except as an enemy to be overcome. His ability to take African medicine seriously was not a result of the limits of the medical science of the time. His medical education in Glasgow and London was firmly based on the approach of modern science. His training enabled him to make at least two important medical-scientific discoveries. The first was to relate an almost exclusively cereal-based diet to the loss of vision he found among people he examined. Second, he was the first scientist to see the usefulness of treating tripanosiomiasis with arsenic. What enabled him to be open to the value of African traditional medicine was the genuine scientific open-mindedness he had gained from his university education in Scotland at the end of what has often been termed its Golden Age. He was truly open-minded in a way Western medicine was ceasing to be because of the growth of a kind of scientific dogmatism in the Western world.

Livingstone's disastrously bad relations with Edwards, Inglis and other LMS colleagues in southern Africa, relations that were matched in their unpleasantness by those with so many members of the Zambezi Expedition, are well documented. They are not to be discussed directly here. However, in attempting to discuss Livingstone as an African traveller some light can be cast on this problem. The Zambezi Expedition was a failure because of Livingstone's misjudgement of the possibilities of navigating the Kebrabassa gorge, and because the rapidly growing impact of the Portuguese and Swahili slavers was totally transforming the societies he had come to 'uplift'. Holmes is correct in insisting that the expedition also had achievements to its credit.[29] However, it was seen at the time as a failure and one which reflected badly on Livingstone, particularly because of his bad relations with almost all the European members of the expedition and his unsympathetic handling of the UMCA mission. Because this seems such a contrast with the cross-Africa journey it has been, and still is, suggested that Livingstone was only an effective leader of an expedition when it was made up of Africans who treated him as a 'master'. This judgement pays no attention to his last expedition. It had no Europeans and he was clearly the *baas* yet it was also a disaster in terms of his leadership. He had to get rid of the sepoys which the Governor of Bombay had sent to accompany him, various troops of paid porters were recruited to work for him and he had bad trouble with them all. Sir Harry Johnston, somewhat bewildered by this, wrote: 'The admirable manner in which he handled his Makololo in his former expeditions seems to have deserted him.'[30]

This is just the point: on his early treks among the Tswana he travelled with people from the mission or sent with him by a local chief. They were not professional porters, they were in some sense his comrades. On the truly magnificent *viagem contra costa* he was with a group of Kololo sent by the chief Sekeletu, who basically was the sponsor of the whole 'expedition'. In contrast with so much that has been written, Livingstone knew that his great achievement was also an African achievement, an achievement of the Kololo people as much as his own.

Livingstone made this very clear himself in *Missionary Travels and Researches,* where he wrote:

> While at Shesheke, Sekeletu supplied me with twelve oxen – three of which were accustomed to be ridden upon – hoes, and beads to purchase a canoe, when we should strike the Leeambye beyond the falls. He likewise presented abundance of good fresh butter and honey, and did everything in his power to make me comfortable for the journey. I was entirely dependent on his generosity, for the goods I originally brought from the Cape, were all expended by the time I set off from Linyanti to the west coast. I there drew £70 of my salary, paid my men with it, and purchased goods for the return to Linyanti. These being now all expended, the Makololo again fitted me out, and sent me to the east coast. I was thus dependent on their bounty, and that of other Africans, for the means of going from Linyanti to Loanda, and again from Linyanti to the east coast; and I feel deeply grateful to them.[31]

The one period when things went well in those last years was when he was stationary for many months among the Manyembe in 1872. There Chuma, Susi, Amoda and the two women Ntaoeka and Halima, wives of Amoda and Chuma, were with him in what was a surprisingly happy period for him. They, with a handful of the men sent up from Zanzibar led by Jacob Wainwright,[32] went with him to the south on those last agonisingly painful wanderings till he died at Chitambo's. Then they embarked on one of the most astonishing of nineteenth-century journeys in Africa, taking his mummified body to the British authorities on the coast.

It was not that Livingstone could not command Europeans but only Africans, rather that Livingstone simply was not able to command organised expeditions, never mind who made up the team. His extraordinary successes were always with people who had a special relationship to him and when the journey was, or became, something personal to him, like the treks in present-day Botswana and Transvaal, the cross-Africa journey and the last wandering journey from Unyanyembe to Chitambo's. He could charm and gain the life-long affection of Europeans, such as Thomas M. Steele, William Oswell, Sir John Kirk and Horace Waller of the original ill-fated UMCA mission as well as many Africans – Sechele, Sebituane, Mamochisane, Sekeletu, those who carried him to the coast and others whose names we simply do not know, like his 'sister' in Bubi's village among the Kwena. However, to play the disciplined role of leader in the formally organised social structure of an expedition was beyond him. It caught him up in a mass of problems that frustrated and angered him because they got in the way of whatever he held to be his purpose, which he followed with a commitment that many have called obsessive. Johnston summed up this weakness succinctly: 'Little effort seems to have been made to keep the men together on the march, and although Livingstone complains bitterly of the mal-treatment of the animals, he apparently took no measures to prevent it, but was content to push on along the road in feverish haste.'[33]

This is the 'feverish' obsession with what he wanted to do, with what he so often felt called to do, that, when taken together with his very individual and 'independent' understanding of Christianity, made him a hopeless team player in the 'committee-ocracy' of the LMS in southern Africa in the 1840s as well as on formal 'expeditions'. As Tim Jeal has pointed out, anyone who achieved university entrance level by going to night school from 8 p.m. to 10 p.m. after an 8 a.m. to 8 p.m. day at the mill, as Livingstone did, must have had a ruthless obsessiveness in his character.[34] This obsessiveness also led Livingstone to turn on those who stood in his way or distracted him from what he saw as the real job in hand. He often treated such people with gross unfairness, as can be seen in any study of his relations with some colleagues in the south or on the Zambezi Expedition.

This anger has also got to be seen as part of his background. The working class population of the industrial west of Scotland, of which the Livingstones were typical, was made up of thousands of displaced Gaels, both Irish and Scottish. If there is anything they shared it was an extreme touchiness about their personal dignity and the disconcerting ability to switch almost instantly from good humour to anger and back again.[35] Slights were seen where none might be intended, and provoked what others, from outside that milieu, saw as a bewildering over-reaction. This attitude, which is also entwined with class consciousness, was clearly an element in Livingstone's relations with so many of the whites with whom he clashed. Oliver Ransford, who cannot have known many working-class Scots, decided on the basis of these characteristics that Livingstone was a congenital manic-depressive.[36]

New studies of Livingstone's life and work are much needed since he is central to so much missionary activity and concern in the late Victorian and Edwardian periods. He links the social, political and religious history of southern, central and eastern Africa and his life overlaps two very different eras in the European approach to Africa. In one dramatic moment the two eras meet at Ujiji when Stanley 'finds' Livingstone: on the one hand Livingstone, who talked his way through so many crises, and on the other Stanley, who, backed by his well-armed African mercenaries, was to shoot his way through all difficulties on his Congo Expedition.

The new studies must also attempt to understand the theological influences that helped shape Livingstone's faith. These cannot be simply passed over as Scottish Calvinism. This is a mistake that Timothy Holmes makes in what is possibly the best modern biography yet. Above all the new studies must not begin with Victorian Britain and its empire but with a thorough delve into Scottish history. They must start with a family that was part of the massive Gaelic immigration into the industrial heartland of Scotland. They must start with a young man who was a member of only the second generation of his family to speak English, whose great-grandfather died a tribal warrior at Culloden in 1746. It was after their victory at Culloden that the British government began its rapid and ruthless destruction of the last armed tribal society in Western Europe, which led to that Gaelic diaspora. It was into Scotland in the aftermath of these changes that David Livingstone was born and in which he grew up. By beginning there some help may be found to resolve the conflicts this man still provokes among historians.

CULTIVATION, CHRISTIANITY & COLONIALISM: TOWARDS A NEW AFRICAN GENESIS

John L. Comaroff and Jean Comaroff

Civilization ... must originate and depend on the culture of the ground.[1]

Two things stand out clearly in the archives of the early LMS mission to the Southern Tswana, two motifs in the encounter between Europeans and Africans along this colonial frontier. The first was the evangelists' realisation that, if they were to 'civilise' and convert 'the Bechuana', they would have to begin on the terrain of everyday life.[2] In so far as it became evident that this 'native' world was not to be remade simply by smashing its idols and icons, or by means of theological argument, the civilising mission could not depend on didactic means to achieve its ends; Moffat, Livingstone and their brethren might have preached and prayed but, in the pragmatic matter of re-forming Southern Tswana, they vested most of their hope in a prosaic theatre of Protestant industry which set forth the mundane signs and practices of European modernity.[3] This show-and-tell was based on the faith that the Africans would be unable to resist the temporal benefits of civilisation;[4] being childlike and impressionable, they would learn readily by imitation.[5]

The second recurring motif in the encounter was the stress of the first generation of LMS emissaries on things material. For evangelists and abolitionists everywhere, as has often been remarked, commerce was the very antithesis of, and an antidote to, both slavery and primitive communism. In this regard, the missionaries took for granted that consumption and production were all of a piece;[6] that, tied together by the market, they were indissolubly bound up in the workings of advanced capitalist economy and society. If Tswana were to gain entry into the modern Christian commonwealth, therefore, both − production and consumption − would have to be recast, each in relation to the other and both from the ground up. Hence Moffat's insistence that civilisation originated in 'the culture of the ground',[7] that civility had its genesis in the soil. Hence, also, Campbell's

Till the present system shall undergo a complete revolution, [the Tswana]

can never abound in grain, nor can it become an article of trade. The land that may be fairly claimed by each nation is capable of supporting more than twenty times the population, if the ground were to be cultivated ...[8]

The 'complete revolution' was meant to be at once conceptual and concrete: a matter of culture and agriculture, of moral and material economics. In this essay, then, we look at the campaign of the colonial evangelists to revolutionise patterns of production among Southern Tswana, a campaign that shaped a new field of social and cultural distinction, a field of classes-in-formation. We trace out both the short-term impact of the mission outreach and the historical processes of the long run – sometimes surprising, often ambiguous, inevitably complex – which it unleashed.

THE CIVILISING MISSION AND THE CULTURE OF THE GROUND

> *There, on their pious toils their Master, smil'd*
> *And prosper'd them, unknown or scorn'd of men,*
> *Till in the satyr's haunt and dragon's den*
> *A garden bloom'd, and savage hordes grew mild.*[9]

The centrality of agriculture to colonial evangelism owed much to the close ties, sociological and imaginative alike, that bound the LMS missionaries to the displaced peasantry at home. In their theology, too, cultivation and salvation were explicitly associated[10] – *vide* Mark 4:3–32 – so that agrarian labours-and-scenes saturated spiritual discourses and vice versa. Thus, for example, Robert Moffat, professional gardener and farmer's son, told his readers how he and his brethren 'put their hand to the plough', preparing the arid African earth for a 'rich harvest of immortal souls'.[11]

But cultivation was not linked only to salvation. In the culture whence the missionaries came, it was connected to colonialism[12] and civilisation as well. Hear, again, Moffat: 'Let missionaries and schoolmasters, the plough and the spade, go together, and agriculture will flourish, the avenues of legitimate commerce will be opened ... whilst civilisation will advance as the natural effect, and Christianity operate as the proximate cause of the happy change.'[13] Nor was this a fleeting vision. If anything, it grew more elaborate over time. At his ordination in Edinburgh in 1858, John Mackenzie, an LMS evangelist of the next generation, said: 'As to civilisation and the temporal interests of the people, I conceive that I am furthering both when I preach the Gospel ... In order to complete the work of elevating the people, we must teach them the arts of civilized life ... We must teach them to till their own land, sow and reap their own crops, build their own barns ...'[14]

Given the African concern with cattle, it may seem odd that the early LMS missionaries seldom included pastoralism in their plans; indeed, they were notably silent on the salience of livestock in the Kingdom of Christ. This did not arise from an ignorance of the value of animals to Southern Tswana. Quite the contrary. The stress on the civilising role of cultivation, rather, flowed from an axiom as old as English colonialism itself: that sedentary agriculture was both a cause and an effect of civility and advancement.[15] 'The way to increase the productivity of both land and people in Africa', the Rev. W.C. Willoughby was to say in the 1920s, 'is to cultivate each by means of the other.'[16] Cattle and culture, ranching and refinement, on the other hand, seemed almost inimical. As long as it had no fixed abode, or did not accompany settled tillage, pastoralism excited visions of shiftless, shifty people wandering about sans property, propriety or a proper place in the body politic.

At the turn of the seventeenth century, Edmund Spenser had blamed the barbarity and belligerence of the 'wild Irish' on their semi-nomadic, pastoral pursuits.[17] In order to allay the threat they posed to England, and to bring them within the compass of its civilisation, they had to be made to live settled agrarian lives. The Bible might have spoken of a chosen people who herded at least as much as they tilled − a point not lost on Tswana − but, to the modernist imagination, evolution depended on cultivation. Like their contemporaries in England, the evangelists absorbed the axiom that agriculture made men peaceful, law-abiding and amenable to education. At once civil and servile. To wit, Livingstone blamed the lawlessness of 'the Boers' on the fact that they 'were more a pastoral than an agricultural race'.[18] Not for naught had Spenser warned an imperially minded England that all who live 'by [the] kepinge of cattel ... are both very barbarous and uncivill, and greatly given to warr'.[19] From a purely evangelical perspective, too, mobile populations posed problems: Philip is reputed to have told his colleagues that, as long as people had 'no settled homes ... it was easy for them to desert the means of instruction'.[20]

If the rude savage was to be refined, then, it would be tillage that would do it. As he sowed, nurtured and harvested his crop − all with enlightened techniques and tools − the Tswana yeoman would make himself anew. This agrarian revolution, as was often said, was intended to enable African converts to yield enough of a surplus to tie them through trade to Christian Europe.[21] The dark continent would become a 'fruitful field', a rich rural periphery of the metropolitan centres of civilisation abroad.[22] No more would it call forth the 'agonizing tears of bereaved mothers', the 'orphan's cry, the widow's wail'.[23] Not, that is, if their menfolk were restored to them as true husbandmen. Even in its most materialist moments, *circa* 1820–50, the civilising mission continued to ring, not merely of biblical pastorale, but also of romantic naturalism and abolitionist moralism. It also invoked many of the old tropes: Africa, savage and infantilised, devastated by bondage, its women dispossessed and its men laid low − all awaiting the white saviour to regenerate them so that they might once more harvest their own crops and 'sit under their own vine and fig-tree'.[24]

No matter that Tswana had never suffered slavery. In Nonconformist narratives of South Africa, *difaqane* served much the same imaginative function as did the slave trade further north. This period of upheaval in the 1820s, usually ascribed to the rise of the Zulu state and the subsequent predations of displaced warrior peoples,[25] had ostensibly robbed 'the native population' of its moral manhood and its capacity for self-determination – and had left it 'unprotected … without missionaries'.[26] Some of the peoples of the interior were badly disrupted by the turmoil of the times, yet most Southern Tswana had managed to grow some crops in temporary places of refuge, to recoup their herds, and to keep intact their political communities. But such subtleties went largely unspecified in the stark stories penned by the Christians. These told of soil strewn with blood and bones by 'warlike, wild tribes', of a wake of women and children left to wander about, barely surviving on wild fruit, locusts, and 'garbage'; even, added the horrified evangelists, on human flesh.[27] Here too we detect traces of the vision of Africa-the-Fallen, of its children as foundlings.

Such accounts did more than merely confirm the pained portraits of darkness and degeneracy circulated by philanthropists. They also justified the resolve of the clerics to 'train [the Bechuana] up in the habits of civilized life';[28] in particular, to teach them how to farm productively in the fields of God.[29] Hence the essential gesture in the imagery of colonial evangelism, one to which we keep returning:[30] the missionary, a black male convert at his back, tending an 'abandoned mother' in the bush. In most versions she is being handed the 'bread of life', long a European symbol of cultivated food – and, not coincidentally, the stuff of the sacrament and icon of the gospel.[31]

AFRICAN AGRICULTURE: SEEING, SEEDING, SOWING, REAPING

Superstition, socialism and agrarian aesthetics

The civilising mission might have portrayed Africa as uncultivated, even empty. But the early evangelists nonetheless expatiated on Tswana economy, taking care to underscore how much had to be erased or remade. Much of their commentary was a discourse of absence: it focused on the lack of ways and means taken for granted in European culture. Most notable were references to the want of money, itself assumed to be indispensable to an advanced economy; of markets or anything beyond rude barter;[32] of civilised crops, especially refined species of maize, corn or vegetables;[33] of irrigation[34] and all but the simplest implements and technologies;[35] of privately owned land;[36] and of any capacity for invention or self-improvement by the exercise of reason.

Still more striking than this discourse of absence, however, was the discourse of irrationalities that permeated mission texts and conversations: Tswana economy was portrayed as a repertoire of illogical, impractical, improvident means and ends. A noteworthy feature of this discourse was its obsession with the aesthetics of agrarian production and material life. Some evangelists were quite open in their disapproval of the 'disorderly' way in which Tswana put nature to use 'without regard to scenery or economy',[37] destroying the 'park-like appearance of the landscape'.[38] Many of them harped on the preference, in cultivation and construction, for the 'sinuous' and 'arc-shaped' over neat rectangular forms. Philip once likened Dithakong and its environs to an 'ant-hill',[39] but Mackenzie was most direct: '[Tswana] gardens and arable land', he lamented, 'are laid out in a manner which offends the eye of a European.'[40] Even as late as 1899, Willoughby claimed that Africans could not plough a linear furrow.[41] At issue here was not merely taste violated. Beauty, after all, was truth. And truth – in the form of rational, universal knowledge – opened the path from savagery to civility.

Again, the idea that civilisation expressed itself in squares and straight lines ran to the core of contemporary British culture. In *The Return of the Native*, for instance, Thomas Hardy contrasted the wildness of Egdon Heath, *circa* 1840–50 ('an uncouth … obsolete thing') to the 'modern' countryside 'of square fields, plashed hedges, and meadows watered on a plan so rectangular that on a fine day they look like silver gridirons'.[42] No wonder that Philip, in praising the progress of the Kuruman mission (*circa* 1825), chose to stress the 'taste' with which its rigidly rectilinear garden had been laid out. There was, he stated, 'something very … pleasing' in this place of 'rising beauty'.[43] By contrast, Tswana terrain was much less attractive, much less productive, much more like farmstead Ireland, *circa* 1815, which Halévy was to dismiss, stereotypically, as 'a disgusting sight … [there being] no vestige of a garden'.[44] But the putative irrationalities of Tswana economy were described in terms that went far beyond the aesthetic. Among the things most commonly remarked by the missionaries were (i) the prevailing politics of production; (ii) the unenlightened 'selfishness' of Africans; (iii) the savage 'superstition' and 'enchantments' said to saturate their material lives; and (iv) their 'unnaturally' gendered division of labor.

The Nonconformists regarded it as utterly beyond reason that chiefs should orchestrate the rhythms of agrarian production; that the annual cycle should be punctuated by collective rites; that cultivation should be seen to depend on a ruler providing spring rains to inseminate the land; that women should not be permitted to plant before the sovereign 'gave out the seed-time'; that each activity, from sowing to harvest, should begin with tributary toil on royal fields.[45] The evangelists might have asserted, throughout the century, that 'traditional' authority was on the wane, but they continued to complain about it. As late as 1900, Brown was to write, from Taung, that the local chief was still the channel 'through which the rain flows to the people. He still exercises the right of saying when the ploughing shall begin … Corn in some gardens may be fully ripe, and even wasting from ripeness; but the owners of these gardens dare not reap till the chief has given permission …'[46]

Another obstacle, equally irrational in the eyes of the Europeans, was summed up by Willoughby: 'The African', he declared, 'lives a simple socialistic life, subordinating his individuality to the necessities of the tribe.'[47] Hence his antipathy to 'healthy, individualistic competition', to the maximisation of time and effort, and to self-possessed industry.[48] Tswana might have been crafty and duplicitous,[49] suspicious and jealous of each other.[50] And they might have been 'keenly alive to their own interests';[51] 'under the influence', Hodgson put it, 'of [the] selfish principle'.[52] But this was quite different from the kind of rational individualism that persuaded people to 'submit to the labour of cultivating the ground'.[53]

The allusion to rationality here picks up another theme in the discourse. Many of the evangelists spoke of the need to rouse the Tswana capacity for 'reason', thereby to counter 'savage superstition'. The latter, held Philip, flowed 'from confused ideas of invisible agency'.[54] These led the Africans to believe that successful cultivation depended on the observance of taboos; that female pollution could cause the clouds or the crops to abort; that the fertility of fields might be increased by the ministrations of medicine men.[55] Much to the annoyance of the missionaries, moreover, such beliefs had been placed as impediments in their way: 'Till lately, the missionaries have not been allowed to use manure for their gardens. It was formerly universally believed that if the manure were removed from the cattle-kraals, the cattle would die …'[56] From the standpoint of the LMS, the enchantments of savagery had yet another insidious side to them: they encouraged an irrational conservatism in the face of challenge and change, making Tswana reluctant to accept the most obvious proof of the superiority of civilised practices. Added Philip: 'it was against their practice to deviate from the customs of their ancestors. When urged to plant corn, &c., they used to reply that their fathers were wiser than themselves, and yet were content to do as they did: they also regarded every innovation as an insult to the memory of their ancestors.'[57]

But it was the division of labour – in particular, gendered relations of production – for which most opprobrium was reserved. Lichtenstein might have likened Tswana agriculture to that of the 'Mosaic forefathers'.[58] But the evangelists found the comparison altogether less happy. To them, African economy was 'topsy-turvy'.[59] The men, whose herds were tended by youths and serfs, looked to be lazy 'lords of creation':[60] their political and ritual activities were mostly invisible to the European eye, their leather work did not appear to be work at all, and their exertions as smiths went largely unremarked. Women, on the other hand, seemed to have been forced into what was properly male labour, building and thatching, digging and 'scratching' on the face of the earth like 'beasts of burden'.[61] Missionary accounts of women's toil were always tinged with disgust, and were often highly emotive. Mary Moffat observed that

The women cultivate all the land, build the houses [and so on] ... while the men ... never condescend to lend a helping hand to them. Picture to yourself tender and gentle women ... bending their delicate forms, tearing the rugged earth ... dragging immense loads of wood over the burning plains, wherewith to erect their houses, thus bearing the double weight of the curse on both sexes.[62]

What is more, rather than till lands tied to the family home, they were sent to far-off fields for weeks on end, where they remained beyond the reach of the mission. Occasionally, too, existing relations of production sparked conflicts between the sexes that discomforted the Nonconformists and gave the lie to patronising talk of 'tender and gentle women'. Speaking of Batlharo, Wookey wrote, in 1873:

the gardens belong to [females]. The cattle, sheep and goats belong to the men. Well, amongst the Batlaro it seems some of the cattle had been troublesome in wandering into the gardens and destroying the women's corn. Accordingly, they determined to kill everything found in their lands. In doing this they were following a law to that effect made by a Batlaro chief; and for which also some women were cut off the church by Mr. Moffat. Numbers of cattle were hacked and killed in a most horrible manner, the women of the church taking a prominent part in the work.[63]

It is obvious why such incidents should have distressed the evangelists: hacking beasts to death, like toil far from home, was not their idea of a proper feminine activity. No wonder that the emissaries of LMS, like their Wesleyan counterparts, were so intent on confining Tswana women to house and hearth; on domesticating them, that is, within a world divided – socially and sexually – into public and private domains, sites of production and reproduction.

The missionaries were under no illusions that this would be easy. One had already learned as much at the turn of the nineteenth century, when he tried to set up a station along the Kuruman River. His request met with resistance from the local chief who, having heard news of Khoi converts to the south, feared the civilising lessons of the LMS.[64] Why? Because, the ruler insisted, they led to indigence. Twenty years on, Broadbent reported that Tswana listened to much of what he had to say but not to his advocacy of European agriculture: its division of labour 'opposed their ideas and habits'.[65] He might have added that, to the Africans, European practices appeared as 'topsy-turvy' as did theirs to the evangelists.

The missionaries did not always see quite how unreasonable was their own discourse of irrationalities; quite how full it was of counter-examples which gave a very different impression of Tswana economy. For instance, Campbell recalled that, while travelling across Rolong country in 1820, he came upon 'several hundred acres of Caffre corn; many of the stalks were eight and nine feet high, and had a fine appearance'.[66] Earlier, he and his companions had passed 'extensive corn-fields on both sides of the road'. Giving voice to the observation of one group of Africans by another, the evangelist said that the Khoi in his party, themselves familiar with agriculture in the Cape Colony, 'were amazed at the extent of the land under cultivation, having never seen so much before in one place'. Moffat also offered counter-evidence, albeit of a different sort. The Kuruman station, he noted, was situated on 'light sandy soil, where no kind of vegetables would grow without constant irrigation'. By contrast, he added, 'native grain … supports amazing drought'.[67] In this light, claims for the superiority and rationality of European techniques must have puzzled Southern Tswana. All the more so since whites from the Colony kept entering their territory to purchase their surplus cattle and, later, crops. But their discourse of irrationalities is largely irrecoverable, save, as we have said before, from traces scattered inchoately between the lines of colonial texts – and from a variety of practical reactions, some of which we shall come upon as our account unfolds.

Metamorphosis and disenchantment

Livingstone once wrote of a young chief who, eager for the benefits of civilisation, wanted him 'forthwith to commence the work of metamorphosis by means of enchantments'.[68] In fact, the first generation of evangelists did resort to a technology of enchantment – involving, among other things, their almost magical gardens – to impress the power of their presence on the Africans. But when it came to reconstructing Tswana life over the longer run, the LMS missionaries were to speak repeatedly of disenchantment. They would advocate the 'rational' expenditure of effort, introduce such 'scientific' instruments as the plough, and try to replace the 'superstitious' practices of the vernacular ritual calendar with the secular logic of commodity cultivation.[69]

Given the recent misfortunes of British agriculture, the LMS might have given careful thought to its export to Africa. According to Lord Ernle, 1815–37 was 'one of the blackest periods' in the history of English farming.[70] Some have questioned Ernle's now dated account,[71] but it is clear that the state of the rural economy was highly (if variably) precarious, the condition of small farmers being the most disastrous of all.[72] And this notwithstanding the profitable years of the Napoleonic Wars, the zeal of the king and aristocracy for agriculture,[73] the modernist rhetoric of enclosure, growing mechanisation, and the rise of High Farming.[74] Goldsmith had been prescient – unwittingly, no doubt – when, in 1770, he had rhymed: 'But a bold peasantry, their country's pride/When once destroy'd, can never be supplied.'[75] Perhaps it was this sense of loss, this nostalgia for the British yeomanry on the part of the missionaries,[76] that fuelled the horticultural dreams and schemes for Bechuanaland. Like some clergymen at home,[77] they had great faith in the capacity of a garden allotment and hard work to raise up the rude.

The agrarian revolution began modestly, centring itself on the mission garden, that master symbol of civilisation and Britishness.[78] For a while this square of red earth stood between the evangelists and hunger.[79] More than merely a source of food, it was also an exemplary appropriation of space[80] and an icon of colonial evangelism. Represented as a triumph over rank nature, it usually began as a vegetable patch, grew to include an orchard, and was expanded by the addition of fields of wheat and other crops; in short, not exactly a garden at all in contemporary English terms, but paradise to those who saw, in the creation of the first mission stations, a new African Genesis.[81]

In the ideal scenario, this Act of Creation was played out, from the first, on land bought from Africans. The gesture of purchase was itself meant to have two effects: (i) to establish missionary agriculture on a bedrock of civilised practices, thereby (ii) to make it a palpable example to the Tswana of those very practices. In an optimistically spirited letter, dated 21 November 1823, Mary Moffat wrote: 'each individual is to purchase his own ground, the missionaries having set the example.'[82] While some chiefs agreed to 'sell' plots, the evidence suggests that they made little sense of this kind of transaction. 'The particulars of … sale', Livingstone confessed, 'sounded strangely in the ears of the tribe[s].'[83] As Archbell implies, the major effect of such 'particulars' seems to have been reflexive:[84] they persuaded the Europeans, who sometimes feared for the security of their venture, that the mission was firmly implanted on soil it actually owned.

Aside from being vital to the self-sufficiency of mission stations and households, the cultivation of the garden enacted the first scenes in the narrative of reconstruction. On this ground, the evangelists performed the principles of material individualism: the creation of value by means of self-possessed labour and scientific technique, the conversion of nature into private property, and the accumulation of surplus through virtuous toil. Robert Moffat's son John makes it clear that his father spent a good part of his daily round as a 'farmer'.[85] The point, he implied, was to provide a visible model for Tswana to mimic. No wonder that Edwin Smith was to describe Moffat sen. as 'one of God's gardeners'.[86] Or that George Thompson, a Cape merchant who spent time at Kuruman in 1823, should have admired 'the example [the LMS had] set before the natives of industry in cultivating the ground'.[87]

Perhaps the most vivid insight into this didactic spirit is provided by Samuel Broadbent, a Wesleyan whose agrarian pursuits paralleled closely those of the LMS missionaries:

I and my colleagues had each enclosed a plot of ground, which we had, of course, in English fashion, broken up and cleared of the roots of weeds, and then sown with Kaffir corn, which we had obtained from the natives, and with sweet cane and various kinds of beans, also melons and pump-kins ... What became the subject of wonder and remark was the notori-ous fact that these and other vegetables grew much more luxuriantly, and were more productive, in our grounds than theirs. One day a number of respectable natives came to ask the reason of this difference ...

My first answer was, 'Your idleness.' 'How so?' they inquired. I said, 'You have seen that we have dug the soil ourselves; you leave it to your women. We dig deep into the soil; they only scratch the surface ... Our seed, therefore, is protected from the sun and nourished by the moisture in the ground; but yours is parched with the heat of the sun, and, there-fore, not so productive as ours.' I added, 'Work yourselves, as you see we do, and dig the ground properly, and your seed will flourish as well as ours.[88]

Here, in sum, were the four crucial lessons of the sacred garden. The first pre-sented itself as purely technical: that successful cultivation required digging 'deep into the soil'. This was only possible with the plough – not with the hoe, which the Europeans saw as exotic and primitive.[89] As we have said, the fabri-cation of 'refined' implements, in public at times, was an essential piece of the evangelical drama everywhere in Bechuanaland.[90] These objects became iconic of Christian cultivation at large, at once instruments and symbols.[91] Thus S.M. Molema, Tswana historian and a devout Methodist, was to write that 'no single machine ... [did] so much for the civilisation of the Bantu than the plough'.[92] Like the irrigation ditch and the well, agrarian appliances were as vital to the realisation of the Nonconformist worldview as they were to the material basis of the mission.

The second lesson lay in enclosure after the 'English fashion'. As Broadbent intimates, everything began with the founding of a fenced plot, itself the core of the imagined African farmstead of the future.[93] Within its rectangular con-fines lay the promise of great productivity, which is why Moffat was so delight-ed, in the late 1820s, to report that Kuruman – where 500 acres were brought under irrigation and neat smallholdings began to appear – had become an exemplary 'Goshen to the surrounding country'.[94]

The third lesson involved the contrast between idleness and labour. The evangelists sought by their own efforts to show that self-possessed toil was the key to a decent life. Profitable agriculture, connoting the cultivation of 'civilised' crops for both home consumption and the market, depended upon it. The essence of this lesson was to be found in the Letter of Paul to the Thessalonians 3:9–10, often invoked in mission preaching: '[We] give you in our conduct an example to imitate ... If any one will not work, let him not eat.' And in Timothy 2:2–6: 'It is the hard-working farmer who ought to have the first share of the crops.' This celebration of labour, as we shall see, was integral to the practical theology, and to the theology of practice, at the core of colonial evangelism: 'Work, the gospel of work, the sanctity of work, *laborare est orare*', to work is to pray, as Aldous Huxley would put it at a later date and in a quite different connection.[95]

But, and here was the fourth lesson, not all toil was the same. The world of work envisaged by the missionaries entailed an entirely new division of labour. The relative value of male and female exertions could not have been more clearly stated. 'Luxuriant' productivity, proclaimed Broadbent, demanded mastery over field and furrow, not scratchings on the soil. Like all the evangelists, he believed it 'of great importance ... to lead the minds of the Bechuana men to agricultural pursuits'.[96] The corollary: that, while their husbands became breadwinners, housewives ought to be confined to such 'homely' tasks as cleaning, childcare, cooking and sewing. This invoked the same ideal of gentility that had enclosed bourgeois European women in the domestic domain. And, in so doing, it revealed a contradiction in the objectives of the civilising mission. On one hand, the clergymen dreamed of a free and prosperous African peasantry. On the other, their values, firmly rooted in the age of revolution in Britain, presupposed the social order of industrial capitalism centred on the urban, middle-class household. Few Tswana women were to be embourgeoised, of course. Quite the contrary. Many had eventually to earn their livelihood as domestic workers in European settler homes, their servitude offering a bitterly ironic commentary on the evangelical model for the African family. Others were compelled to seek employment in the colonial economy, or were forced back into the arid fields of subsistence agriculture. But this was still a long way off.

Re-actions of the short run: from mockery to mimesis

What were the first reactions of Southern Tswana to the evangelical onslaught on their material practices? It is clear that they did not immediately take the lesson which the LMS and the Wesleyans alike tried to convey; namely, that the abundant yields of 'modern' agriculture were the product of a particular regime of hard labour and enlightened technique. One early response, it seems, was to conclude that the bounty of the mission garden flowed from the innate potency of the whites themselves. Thus, for example, Seleka-Rolong men vied to have their wives sow fields beside those of the Methodists[97] because, we are told, they believed that the fertility of these fields would overflow into their own, that sheer proximity to the Europeans might afford access to their agrarian powers. Given time to observe British horticulture, however, and the tenacity of the Nonconformists in essaying their methods, Southern Tswana soon began to differentiate the alien means of production from the personal capacities of their owners.

A second reaction to the agrarian challenge of the mission issued mainly from Tswana women. As some of the implications of European practices became discernible, they began to resist them by interrupting irrigation routines, damaging dams and stealing the fruits of the garden.[98] Patently, if men took to the fields, it followed that their wives would lose control over agriculture and its harvest, the very things upon which rested the well-being of their houses. The evangelists might have regarded the lot of African females as unduly arduous, their productive labours as 'unnatural'. But there is no reason to expect that these women would have seen matters in the same light. From their perspective, the horticultural innovations of the LMS gave plenty cause for fear. With some justification, as it would turn out.

Pragmatic though this response might have been, it was also shaped by a cultural vision, by a sense of the proper connections among production, gender and human capacity.[99] For a start, intensive agriculture involved hitching the ox to the plough, bridging the gendered gulf between cows and cultivation – marked by a taboo against women handling beasts – that ran to the very core of the Southern Tswana world, *circa* 1820. Yet Tswana were remarkably open to innovation and the exchange of cultural knowledge, and so it is not surprising that the evangelists' methods should have elicited their attention. Or that some people would have begun to experiment with them. In August 1821, Moffat recorded 'Queen' Mahutu's efforts to expropriate a valley that he and his brethren had sown with corn.[100] True, he would have preferred her husband, Chief Mothibi of the Tlhaping, to take over the operation; and he was quick to complain that she misused the land, watering it in the heat of midsummer when moisture was scarce. Also, as we observed a moment ago, her actions might have had more to do with the effort of women to sustain control over cultivation than with a desire to become a progressive farmer, European-style. Still, for the LMS this was one of the first signs of success.

More were to come. Philip, who always took care to describe 'the progress which rational ideas had made', tells how Tlhaping cynicism gave way to comprehension. When, in the early days at Kuruman, his brethren began to cut their irrigation channel, the Africans were unimpressed:

> Until they saw the water running into the ditch, they deemed it impossible, and treated the attempt with ridicule. But, when they saw it completed, their surprise was as great as their former scepticism ... The Bechuanas are, however, now convinced of their error; and some of them are leading out the water to make gardens and corn-fields on an inclined plane ...

On his next visit, in the mid-1820s, Philip 'had the satisfaction to see [the chief], with his people, and other Bechuanas, applying to the missionaries for seed-corn to sow on the lands then under irrigation. In reference, also, to a promise of the missionaries to plough some land, and train a span of bullocks for him, he manifested considerable pleasure.'[101] This, for the LMS, was a break-through: men, including a chief, were evincing interest in animal-driven plough cultivation. Soon after, the Seleka-Rolong leader, Sefunelo, approached the Wesleyans working among his people for seeds, 'which he promised to sow'.[102]

Once the sparks of an agrarian revolution had been kindled, thought the evangelists, there was nothing to stop its catching fire. Or so it seemed in the late 1820s and 1830s. Thus, in 1828, Mary Moffat commented that 'nearly all our poor people have reaped good crops of wheat ... and some maize ... They also grow much tobacco, which they exchange for cattle, karosses, &c.' 'I am astonished', she added, 'to see what the willing earth yields in so short a time.'[103] Her sanguine husband, in a letter written on the same day, predicted that 'Next year the crop will be much extended, [and] the station will rise to some impor-tance in a temporal as well as a spiritual point of view';[104] note, again here, the insistence on the simultaneity of the secular and the sacred. Equally auspicious reports came from the Wesleyans a few years on. In 1842, at Platberg, Cameron observed that 'numerous gardens ... have lately been walled in', and brought under cultivation; at Lishuani, 'sixty large gardens [had] been enclosed, and upward of two thousand trees planted.'[105]

The economic revolution was further off than the Europeans suspected, however, and it was not to take the course they anticipated. Sites of agrarian 'progress' were very restricted at the time, being confined to the immediate sur-rounds of the mission stations – and to those Southern Tswana who fell with-in their sphere of influence. Also, as Shillington has noted, not all Bechuanaland was ecologically amenable to agricultural intensification.[106] Especially towards the arid west, people had little option but to rely throughout the century on their herds (and, to a decreasing extent, on hunting). And the region had yet to feel the full impact of settler expansion, of unsettled subcontinental conditions and of a mineral revolution.

CULTIVATION AND CLASS: TRANSFORMATIONS OF THE LONG RUN

There was a sustained ambiguity in mid-nineteenth century accounts of Southern Tswana reactions to mission agriculture: the evangelists spoke of a tendency to cling to custom and resist enlightened self-improvement, but they also suggested that the techniques of modern farming were making rapid inroads, that an agrarian revolution was imminent. This counterpoint was not born of witting misrepresentation. Some features of the Tswana world did not give way easily: the gendered division of labour, the separation of herding from cultivation, the polluting effect of women on animals, and the difficulties this raised for hitching the beast to the plough. Also, some people were less disposed or able to experiment with European technologies: only those with sufficient livestock could use ploughs, or profit from taking surpluses and trade goods to distant markets. In short, the immediate impact of colonial evangelism on Tswana agriculture was highly variable, and it was the extremes of this variability that are reflected in the ambiguities of mission texts. This, in turn, raises the obvious question: was there any pattern at all in the way in which European means of production took root and worked their social effects? The answer, we suggest, is to be found in complex processes of class formation and cultural distinction. Before we explore these processes, however, let us lay out a brief *histoire événementielle* of agrarian change during the middle and late nineteenth century. It will serve to demonstrate the variabilities of which we speak, and prepare the ground for an analysis of social and material reconstruction.

Passing seasons, eventful years

As we have said, the evangelists saw the reconstruction of Tswana material life to depend on the entry of men into plough cultivation: from this was supposed to follow the privatisation of the soil, the emergence of the nuclear family 'farmstead', the ascendance of cropping over pastoralism; in sum, the rise of a 'true farming class'.[107] Despite early mission reports of the adoption of European techniques, however, this transformation did not occur at once. It was only after *difaqane* had disrupted production, and the viability of hunting and foraging had begun to decline, that males began to take to the fields in earnest.[108]

Eventually the plough would displace the hoe everywhere, save *in extremis*. According to Mackenzie, this was owed entirely to the LMS evangelists at Kuruman: 'Under the supervision of the missionaries, the natives learned a higher agriculture, and exchanged the hoe of their own ruder garden work for the plough and the spade. What had been done at Kuruman was imitated by the natives elsewhere.'[109] In fact, it was not so much imitation as culturally tooled pragmatism that commended the plough to Southern Tswana. Its capacity to enlarge the scale and yield of farming in this dryland, unreliable ecology was soon noted.[110] Among Tlhaping, for example, the harvests of those who went in for intensive agriculture grew markedly in the late 1830s; before that, there had been only three ploughs in the Kuruman valley. After 1838, when a trader settled on the station to cater to the demand for British goods, there was a steady increase in the ownership of implements and wagons,[111] most of them bought from the proceeds of grain sales.[112]

As productivity rose, some Tswana communities became regular exporters of European cereals. In 1844 the Rev. J. Ayliff wrote that Dutch farmers near the Orange River were 'passing out of the colony with wagons … to purchase wheat of the Bechuanas'.[113] Local produce was also finding its way to more distant markets. We cannot know, of course, what precise proportion of Southern

Tswana men actually moved into plough cultivation at this time. Many did not, or could not, and among those who did the size and success of farming enterprises was uneven. As far as can be told, many women continued, in the 1850s, to sow and reap as they had long done. According to Mackenzie, 'two styles of agriculture' prevailed in the region: the 'old' and the 'higher'.[114] Even as late as 1865, he said, few ploughs were to be found in many parts of the country. Most gardens were 'being cultivated in the old way by women with the hoe'.

When men did invest in intensive cultivation, they soon seized control over the crop. Women, however, were not banished to the domestic domain. Prosperous farmers might have had male servants and clients take over activities involving animals, but they left the rest of the burden to females. Even those who planted limited acreages, sometimes with borrowed beasts, relied on their wives, daughters and unmarried sisters for crucial tasks – and then sold the harvest on their own account. In short, to the degree that males entered the arable sector, the gendered politics of production were radically altered. What is more, distinctions of wealth and status greatly widened. Because it was only stock owners who could plough extensively, and because the plough yielded the largest returns, the rich became steadily richer. If they did not immediately become poorer, others benefited little from agrarian innovations.

If the uneven impact of European agriculture was already discernible in the 1840s, subsequent reports disclose its ever more equivocal effect. On one hand they spoke of the 'improvement' of farming in many areas. Mackenzie, for example, observed that, at Taung as at Kuruman, irrigated crops were being grown and sold with success.[115] 'Bechuana', he complained, could still not make a straight fence or furrow, but they had taken great strides in adopting modern means.[116] This had subverted the hold of custom: old forms of 'vassalage' were now disappearing, abetted by the breakdown of royal trade monopolies, and the authority of retrogressive rulers was on the wane.[117] But Mackenzie also recorded unhappier corollaries of reform[118] – among them, that the widespread use of guns, purchased from the proceeds of cropping, had so depleted the game population that hunting yielded almost nothing to those who still needed it; that, when drought and disease threatened the livestock economy, on which tillage increasingly relied, many people were forced to survive by 'picking' at the ground; that, with more pasturage being brought under cultivation, powerful families were gaining control of a disproportionate amount of land. Mackenzie might also have noted the first signs of the erosion caused by ploughs to earth whose shallow fertility was not everywhere well suited to them.[119] The material bases of both poverty and inequality were being reconstructed under the impact of European commodity agriculture.

By the 1870s, the decade that saw the onset of the mineral revolution and the growth of the diamond fields around Kimberley, the local agrarian economy had become even more polarised. Some Tswana were well placed to supply the Kimberley market with fruits, vegetables and cereals, and wagon owners also profited from selling wood to the diggings.[120] Of those who expanded their ventures during these years, most were royals who had adopted the techniques of cultivation and accumulation taught by the evangelists.[121] Others were commoners who, on becoming monogamous[122] and entering the church, had been given irrigable mission land. They procured the necessary tools, used 'modern' methods and reinvested their income in their farming enterprises. But the ideal of advancement through commodity production was realised by relatively few. Travelling in the back reaches of Tlhaping territory in 1873, Holub discovered that a 'good, useful plough' was a 'rarity', and that only a handful of families raised cereals or had 'any transactions at the Kimberley market'.[123]

Those who could not buy ploughs or irrigate their fields were steadily reduced to dependency. Many lost all access to productive land, which was taken over by their wealthier compatriots.[124] The latter set about indebting their less fortunate kin and neighbours;[125] so much so that, among Tlhaping, 'roughly two thirds of the formerly free, town dwelling population … succumbed to a clientship status' in the years after the discovery of diamonds.[126] Those in the middle made a sustained effort to continue farming on their own account, supplementing their incomes if necessary by hiring themselves out.[127] But drought and the destruction of natural resources were driving more and more people into the labour market by the late 1870s. While Southern Tswana were attracted to urban centres for many reasons, the flow was accelerated by the annexation of Griqualand West to the Cape Colony, which led settlers, speculators and administrators to disempower chiefs and dispossess their followers of land and stock.[128] Not all the LMS missionaries were upset that Tswana were being drawn into wage employment. A few even took pride in the fact that they had been so well prepared to enter the workforce, especially as skilled farmhands.[129]

Some chiefdoms were less fractured and straitened by agrarian transformations. For example, the Hurutshe at Dinokana, who retained only a small territory after Boers had expropriated their land, raised some 800 (200 lb) sacks of wheat in 1875. Having benefited from the extraordinary system of irrigation canals dug many years before by David Livingstone, they grew more maize, sorghum, melons and tobacco each year, and sold all surpluses 'in the markets of the Transvaal and the diamondfields';[130] their success, moreover, seems to have been spread evenly across the population. But this was an exception rather than the general pattern. More typical was the case of the Tshidi-Rolong, among whom it was the industrious Christian community at Mafikeng, established in 1857, that made most use of the methods of intensive cultivation. By contrast to the rest of the chiefdom, its citizenry prospered, largely from the introduction of European cereals and from marketing semi-irrigated maize to the Transvaal.[131] By 1877, this town, with its 'farmsteads' and 'enclosures', supported considerable plough agriculture, and the spacious, colonial-style houses of its richer residents signalled a level of wealth very different from that of the general populace.[132]

This process of polarisation was accelerated by external events. In the late 1870s, the Tshidi chief, Montshiwa, ousted the neighbouring Ratlou from lands that blocked his way to the diamond fields, declaring that he now grew 'corn for the markets to get money'.[133] The Ratlou, joined by Boer freebooters with designs on Tswana terrain, responded by driving Montshiwa out of Sehuba, then his capital. Retreating to Mafikeng,[134] he and his followers had their herds and crops looted, to the extent that the Tshidi came close to mass starvation.[135] In time the town recovered, but it never regained its past affluence – that much was assured by further territorial wrangling and settler violence, followed by British annexation (1885) and the imposition of taxes; by a series of ecological reverses; and by the shift of the industrial centre to the Transvaal goldfields. While the local economy did not collapse, most families had become dependent on the labour market by the early years of the new century. Only the wealthiest survived the crises with fortunes intact.

Elsewhere, too, the 1880s and 1890s were times of transition in Tswana communities. Surveying Southern Bechuanaland from the Kuruman station, the Rev. A.J. Wookey confirmed that there was little hoe cultivation any more, and that some of those who farmed commercially were doing very well. All this, he added, had positive implications: chiefs no longer enjoyed 'despotic' power; 'bushmen' serfs had largely disappeared; and women, servants and other bondsmen, like the poor and aged, '[held] a far higher position' than before.[136] Crisp agreed that the burden of a Tswana wife had been eased. But, he added, 'she has also lost her perquisite. The husband now apportions to her so much as is required for food; the rest is his to sell.'[137] Freed from the communal obligations and arrangements that surrounded female cultivation in the past, most husbands marketed as much as they could. Men of lesser means often sold small amounts to meet immediate needs and to invest in cattle and other capital goods, only to find themselves short of food and funds later. Hunger became so rife in many places that some rulers decided to regulate vending, as they were to do in the Bechuanaland Protectorate.[138]

Wookey, who did not mention the rampant marketing of crops, discussed other developments that obviously worried him. Due to the sale of wood the country had been denuded, worsening soil erosion. And, as noted earlier, wild beasts had disappeared. But, most of all:

Work amongst the men has become more general; in fact, with many, it is the only means of subsistence ... The land question has become the pressing one of the day here, and some of the chiefs, in order to get out of their difficulties, have been giving away land to Europeans to such an extent that it is a serious question whether there will be any land left for the natives to live upon ... The country itself is capable of producing far more than it does at present. There are many fountains lying unused; and all are capable of doing very much more than they are at present ...[139]

Two forms of pressure were working away at the infrastructure of local economies: the seizure of territory by settlers and the concentration of fertile land in the hands of ever fewer families. For most Southern Tswana, the conditions of production were not promising, and increasing numbers ended up labouring for wealthier neighbours, for whites, or as self-employed artisans.[140] A handful took refuge around the LMS missions, which rented plots to 'tenants',[141] and others managed to scratch out a subsistence. But many were dispossessed of the means of an independent livelihood. Matters took a general turn for the worse in 1896 with the rinderpest pandemic that decimated herds across much of southern Africa. In its wake followed famine and illness, not helped by the fact that, in the hope of containing infection, the government prevented 'the natives of Bechuanaland' from selling poultry and firewood at the diamond fields and from shooting game.[142] Both pastoral pursuits and cultivation would recuperate in time, but not fast and never fully.

The dawn of the new century, then, saw most Southern Tswana well on the road to poverty and dependency. Their reverses had not occurred *in vacuo*, of course, but were part of a broader process in which black South Africans were drawn into the dominion of colonial South Africa; converted, in large part, into what Parson has called a 'peasantariat'.[143] The story is familiar: how colonial capitalists and Christians, settlers and statesmen, despite differences among themselves, found common cause in inducing large numbers of Africans into wage labour; how tax Britannica, the seizure of property, the manipulation of agricultural prices and other blunt fiscal instruments combined to make them reliant on supplementary cash incomes; how all but the wealthy had to subsist on an uneasy mix of female peasant production and the income of low-paid male jobs, both being necessary, but not sufficient, to nurture a family; how a regulated labour force was reproduced by women 'at home', the countryside being made to bear the cost of sustaining a rising proletariat; how, in all this, the political economy of black and white, rich and poor, agrarian and industrial South Africa was integrated into a single, tightly knit structure.

CLASS FORMATION, POLITICAL TRANSFORMATION, SOCIAL DISTINCTION

At first blush, the agrarian history of the long run here seems to echo Bundy's account of the 'rise and fall' of a South African peasantry.[144] For ordinary Tswana, the early successes achieved through a selective adoption of European ways, imported mainly by the LMS, were tangible reward for their openness to alien forms of cultural knowledge – and evidence of the dynamism of their economies. But, over time, the rank-and-file experienced ever more difficulty in making a living, and found themselves less a sturdy yeomanry than a population of partly proletarianised workers, partly subsistence farmers. For most, incorporation into the political economy of colonial South Africa marked an end to their lives as autonomous producers: their 'fall', not just into poverty but also into dependency on forces beyond their control.

But this master narrative had another side to it as well. In so far as the colonisation of agriculture altered patterns of production and differentiation, it also evokes Lenin's story of the Russian peasantry under capitalism.[145] According to this story – we phrase it in its generic, not its concrete historical form – the growth of commodity production in the countryside leads initially to a general rise in output as people avail themselves of new technologies and markets. Soon, however, unequal circumstances lead to the emergence of three rural 'subclasses', each with very different social and economic means and ends: a petite bourgeoisie composed of those who, able to accumulate land and capital, become commercial farmers and exploit wage labour while diversifying their enterprises out of agriculture; a poor peasantry, including small-scale producers and landless proletarians compelled to sell their labour power either locally or at distant centres; and a middle peasantry, engaging both in subsistence cultivation and, wherever possible, in the raising of marketable surpluses, but which does not depend for its income on the exploitation of others.

Of these 'subclasses', goes the argument, the lower remains most dependent on reciprocities among kin. Its members are typically coerced either into leaving the land or into the classical 'peasant-proletarian' predicament of having to survive from a combination of subsistence gardening and wage labour, neither yielding sufficient to support the household. Middle peasants, while not in the same straits, are also in an unstable position. Unable to purchase the most efficient means of production, they cannot grow enough to protect themselves entirely from disaster. Only the upper peasantry is (more or less) secure. Free of the uncertainties of agriculture, it gradually takes on bourgeois characteristics – although its collective consciousness, like its economic strategies, is shaped by virtue of its relations and struggles with the other two fractions. In this sense, all three are classes-in-the-making, not simply socioeconomic categories.

Such a process of fragmentation occurred in British Bechuanaland from the mid-nineteenth century onwards. Three broadly discernible fractions took form, each with its own social practices and productive relations, stylistic preferences, religious and ideological proclivities. Much continued to be shared, of course: *setswana* (African ways) itself defined a common, if not uncontested or unchanging, cultural field. As Volosinov puts it, classes always share common signs; indeed, these often become an object of conflict among them.[146] Yet they speak with very 'differently oriented [and empowered] accents'. So too with class fractions. Their emergence here laid a basis for future patterns of social distinction and ideological struggle, and gave shape to the disparate ways in which colonialism worked its effects on Tswana economy and society. To that extent, the Leninist model, like Bundy's paradigm, is highly suggestive. The two, in fact, complement each other: the latter pays attention to the broad lines of domination and dependency suffered by African populations at the hands of Europeans; the former, to the modes of differentiation that took root within their societies under agrarian capitalism. Neither, it is true, addresses the capacity of indigenous people to affect their own destinies. Nor, for obvious reasons, does either describe the minutiae or indeterminacies of local processes. But they do frame the terms in which global forces entered upon Tswana terrain, there to play into a world with its own orders of value, its own social topographies and its own intractable realities.

One thing should be said immediately, though. No Southern Tswana ever lived an agrarian life anything like the ideal envisaged for them by the colonial evangelists; none simply embraced the ways and means of European agriculture. To whatever degree Tswana took over the forms of modernist horticulture, they adapted rather than adopted them, inserting them into social relations, residential patterns, tenurial arrangements, timetables and rituals of their own. Even the LMS missionaries' most purely technical truth – that advanced agriculture depended on rational procedures, hard work and scientific methods – was never passively received. The Africans saw the production of crops and cattle as a far more complicated, less neutral affair. For them, it involved social considerations, invisible forces, the intervention of ancestors and the insidious actions of enemies. Theirs, after all, was a fraught world of agnatic conflict and inter-personal rivalry.[147] Thus, in Z.K. Matthews's fieldnotes[148] on farming in predominantly Christian Mafikeng, *circa* 1938, we are told that 'every man' doctored his seed – this 'being designed not only to enhance his own opportunities of making a decent living but also at hindering the progress of his neighbours' – and that success or failure was attributed 'to the practices of magic'. The 'individual system of agricultural production' had also exacerbated 'private interest and competition', and with it the incentive to deploy *setswana* to get ahead. An economy of ancestral protection might have given way to an economy of limited good, but it was an enchanted economy nevertheless. As this suggests, European methods were absorbed into a local moral order. More than just a matter of material techniques, agriculture here was part of the politics of everyday life.

If Southern Tswana were not passive in the face of the assault of the civilising mission on their material lives, none were untouched by it either. Self-evidently, it was the most affluent sector of the population that came closest to the mission ideal in embracing agrarian capitalism. This fraction was scattered thinly, but it wielded influence far in excess of its size. It was made up, as we have intimated, of two segments: the Christian elite, and those (non- or nominal Christians) of the ruling cadres who combined advanced agricultural techniques with resources gained by 'traditional' means.[149] As Lenin's portrait of upper peasantries would have us expect, these wealthy families farmed on an ever larger scale, almost entirely for the market, and with more and more advanced implements and methods. It was they who appropriated the best land and sought to gain control of water sources; who invested their profits most determinedly in their farms; who enlarged their herds and 'modernised' their ranching techniques; who recruited as much non-family labour as possible, thereby allowing their womenfolk to become 'housewives' rather than producers, and their offspring to enter the salariat and even the professions; who acquired a monopoly over carriage by wagon and later by motorised vehicles; and who, as the century advanced, bought mechanised means of production to increase their own operations and to rent out as a source of low-risk income. It was by diversifying their interests that this fraction managed to survive the rinderpest; some did so well, in fact, that they eventually scaled down their dryland cultivation, the most fragile of their enterprises.

Where they took an active part in the life of their communities, which many did, members of the upper peasantry tended to associate themselves with the modernist ideals of the civilising mission. In their view, those who invested capital in their arable lands and their animals, who were successful in commerce and did 'great works', were the source of the commonweal. In short, the upper peasantry became the prime conduit of Protestant values. This is not to say that there were no disagreements among them. Apart from power struggles in their ranks, there were clear differences of opinion over the degree to which the adoption of *sekgoa* (European) ways should be tempered by *setswana*, particularly in respect of *mekgwa le melao* ('law and custom'). Still, these were differences of degree, not kind.

As the upper peasantry set itself apart, as it diversified its livelihood and lifestyle, it slowly took on the shape of a local bourgeoisie. At first, though, a very local one. And, in the sense of keeping close to its agnatic roots, a virilocal one too. For, despite the enthusiasm with which it opened itself up to the ways of *sekgoa*, this fraction did not repudiate *setswana*, but persisted in – indeed, initially built its fortunes on – received practices: a reliance on vernacular ritual in pursuing agricultural and social ends; the founding of capitalist enterprises on fields and cattle-posts allocated under 'communal' land-tenure provisions; the recruitment of a workforce, by and large, through 'customary' forms of servitude and clientage. In many cases, moreover, their wealth depended on access to constituted positions of authority and, via them, to human and material resources. And that, in turn, necessitated dealing with agnates, and mobilising matrikin, to negotiate genealogical rank. While several erected well-appointed residences, and others lived in scattered communities or at their farms, a good number kept their homesteads in the wards of their fathers and paternal grandfathers, not departing from the spatial and political arrangements of their world. Far from sloughing off those arrangements, many went out of their way to sustain the centralisation of their towns even when pressures towards dispersal grew.[150]

At the other end of the spectrum, the lower peasantry, which made up the majority of the population, was at once most and least affected by the impact of the civilising mission on the local economy. Most, because it suffered the greatest poverty and disempowerment. Least, because the technical 'improvements' wrought by the evangelists reached it hardly at all. Very few of the men were orthodox Christians; more of the women joined churches, but they found their way increasingly into the charismatic independent congregations which stressed pragmatic ritual, healing and material well-being, and which formed close-knit social communities.[151] These peasants did not farm for the market, though they might sell a little grain or an animal *in extremis*. As they lost access to fertile land they curtailed their agrarian enterprises or toiled either in servitude or as wage labourers. When they did cultivate they did so with crude implements and whatever beasts they could mobilise. In such circumstances, taboos against females tilling the fields with bovines gave way. As males tended to be the ones to seek employment and to be recruited by labour agencies – women were also discouraged by statute from leaving their rural homes – their wives had to take responsibility for horticulture again.[152]

Once restored to the fields, women depended on their matrikin for support and on cooperative labour arrangements to perform large tasks. Reciprocities were widely attenuated as these people were thrown back repeatedly on their social resources and on the familiar practices of *setswana*. In the process, as we have said, they turned less to the alms of the missions than to the more intimate embrace of an Africanised Christianity. Thus it is that they appeared, to Europeans, to sustain a strongly 'collectivist' ethos, to be wedded to 'traditional' forms of exchange, to be enmeshed in 'socialistic' webs of relations. And, hence, to be innately conservative and unenlightened. But, however elaborate their communal arrangements, however hard they worked together, families of the lower peasantry inevitably came to rely on at least some earned income. Always strapped, they were unable to fashion the material existence urged on them by the evangelists and the local bourgeoisie. It is not, we stress again, that they lacked the desire. Many acquired more 'advanced' means of production, engaged in commerce and bought European commodities when they could, using them to invent distinctive styles of self-presentation. But their predicament was not a matter of volition. It derived, rather, from their location in a world of patently unequal social and political relations.

Unlike the upper peasantry, the lowly favoured dispersed living arrangements. Elsewhere we have shown that Southern Tswana polities displayed opposing tendencies;[153] on one hand, a centripetal push towards aggregation at large, concentrated centres; on the other, a centrifugal pull away toward scattered agricultural peripheries. There is no need here to recapitulate their complex workings, save to say that, while ruling elites fought to sustain a pattern of centralised settlement – it facilitated their control over their subjects – poorer people saw two advantages in moving off to the countryside: autonomy from those who would subserviate them; and an opportunity, far from chiefly oversight, to maximise their harvests under ecological conditions in which the timing of arable operations was crucial. Given this predisposition, they seem to have taken little part in the public sphere unless coerced into it, which only a strong ruler could do. Hence they did not, by and large, offer an articulate countervoice to the ideology of the upper peasantry in local politics; but there is evidence that they resented those who had enriched themselves by seizing lands and forcing others into servitude.[154] Even when they did attend assemblies, they seem rarely to have spoken up,[155] although they expressed themselves volubly in other registers.

Just as the upper peasantry became a bourgeoisie, so the poorest segment of the populace became a class of peasant-proletarians. Occupying the space in-between, if somewhat uneasily, was a middle peasantry. Of the three fractions, this last is the most difficult to characterise. Its membership was unstable, consisting, in the main, of people who aspired upward but, as the Leninist model suggested, often found themselves pushed in the opposite direction. Its life-ways and material practices were also inconstant, responding to contingencies of one kind or another. Being interstitial, it was largely defined by what it was not. And yet, as the evidence indicates, the existence of a substantial middle peasantry, with its own discernible profile, is undeniable.[156]

What, then, were its distinguishing features? As we might expect, middle peasants tended, more than anyone else, to navigate the spaces between *setswana* and *sekgoa*,[157] drawing from both in constructing their ever more hybrid lifeways. On one hand, they were quick to adopt European agrarian techniques, investing in intensive agriculture and commodity production to the extent that their means allowed. Many joined the mission churches early on, were members of voluntary associations and 'improvement' societies, and took an active part in the public sphere. Yet they faced real constraints in building up their enterprises. First, they found it hard to obtain sufficient high-quality, well-watered land. Some of them, in fact, had to leave their towns and villages to pursue their economic objectives. Plaatje, for example, tells of a number who rented land on white farms in return for cash, produce and labour;[158] on these holdings, he says, they did well until the Natives Land Act of 1913 altered the terms of their tenancies. Second, because most of them were not from prominent families, they were unlikely to have 'traditional' clients or servants, and so had to recruit labour either by paying for it or by entering exchange arrangements. Three more factors added to the precariousness of their situation: (i) their business interests seldom extended beyond agriculture; (ii) they rarely had the most advanced implements, so that (iii) they had to hire them from wealthier farmers. These considerations made them especially vulnerable to stock disease, drought and personal misfortune. Not surprisingly, it was they who found it hardest to regain their former position after the rinderpest pandemic.

If middle peasants shared an ideology and some material practices with the upper peasantry, they had two things in common with those below them. One was a tendency to depend on reciprocities in the received manner of *setswana*; indeed, commercial farming practices were often accompanied by a reliance on communal work parties arranged by women. The other was a preference for living away from the capital. Middle peasants took pains to avoid being 'eaten' and to retain control over their own activities. Where men of this category ascended into the upper peasantry, they might convert wealth into political capital, vying for positions and even persuading rulers to create new offices for them.[159] If successful, they were likely to re-centre themselves at the capital – but along the way, of course, they had left the middle peasantry.

As all this suggests, middle peasants were a classical intercalary bloc. In their religious practices, for example, they frequently chose a middle way, finding the larger, more orthodox African independent churches most congenial: although they had joined the mission church early on, many of them came to resent the dominance of its established elites; but they were equally uncomfortable with the charismatic Christianity of the lowly and illiterate. They also tended to respond to economic insecurities by investing wherever possible in education. One practice, among many, demonstrates the degree to which they straddled the gulf between the other fractions, partaking of the values of each simultaneously. Like both the rich and the poor, they placed enormous value on cattle. In common with the former, they sometimes treated beasts as capital, buying and selling them for profit or using them as a means to political ends. But, like the latter, they named their animals, parted with them reluctantly and saw them as a social resource, as a mark of personal identity and as an insurance against disaster.

The fact that the middle peasantry shared so much with each of the other fractions highlights the complexities of class formation here. Relations among these classes-in-formation were often ambiguous, rendered more so by (i) the intricate lines of kinship, affinity, and political affiliation that cross-cut them; (ii) uneasy relations between the new, self-made elite and poorer, more conservative royals; and (iii) increasingly ambivalent attitudes towards indigenous ruling cadres.[160] But these were not the only sources of ambiguity. To the lower peasantry, both wealthier fractions represented a threat. Apart from having seized communal resources and put the autonomy of their compatriots at risk, they were bending the local world out of its recognisable shape in the name of their own interests. And yet they were a source of employment and aid – however costly in social terms – much closer to home than the alternatives. For middle peasants, the upper peasantry were those from whom they might purchase the means to enrich themselves, but also competitors and creditors who could preside over their ruin. And the lower peasantry, while a reservoir of labour, were those into whose ranks they might so easily fall. For the upper peasantry, both the middling and the poor were a fund of wealth: the former as a market for their agrarian services; the latter as recruits to their workforce; both as a pool of potential clients. But both also evinced a strong will to independence and dispersal, and hence resisted their machinations whenever possible.

This returns us to the broader impact of the agrarian revolution, that crucial part of the legacy of the LMS, on the internal dynamics of Southern Tswana polities. As we have said, new elites tended to favour centralisation, against the counter-pressures of the lower and middle peasantries. And they often bolstered chiefships in order to create an environment conducive to their material interests and their social values. Many, it is true, had extensive holdings scattered far and wide. But even then, as Shillington notes, they sustained a presence in the capital.[161] In the final quarter of the century, however, rulers came under increasing challenge: they lost their trade monopolies; saw swathes of territory seized, water sources expropriated and herds diminish; lost whatever military might they had had; and, with overrule, relinquished a great deal of their authority. In the upshot, as they told Mackenzie, they found it difficult to hold the centre: 'Our people are now scattered over the country like the white men.'[162] Among the southern branches of the Tlhaping, for example – annexed to the Cape Colony in the late 1870s and dispossessed of much of their land – *merafe* ('nations') were quick to disperse altogether as their sovereigns were disempowered. The Tshidi and Seleka-Rolong chiefs sustained more centralised polities, although their fortunes ebbed and flowed and, at times, their chiefdoms showed signs of fragmenting. The Ratlou, Rapulana-Rolong and more northerly Tlhaping fell somewhere between, also fluctuating considerably – and veering, in the longer run, towards the decentralised mode.[163] In sum, the period witnessed major changes in the Southern Tswana universe, many communities coming to look more like scattered peasantries elsewhere than like 'traditional' chiefdoms. Where political centres collapsed, bourgeoisies eventually gave up on them and, often, moved away. And so parts of the terrain held populations of all class fractions bound loosely, if at all, to established structures of rule. This while, not fifty miles away, there might be a *morafe* with an elaborate political order and a highly concentrated capital; with a ruler who regulated the seasons, who could fine those who took to their fields without permission, and for whom tributary fields were ploughed each year; whose wealthier subjects remained invested in sustaining the polity against the centripetal tendencies of the lower and middle peasantry.

CODA

This returns us, full circle, to the role of the LMS. It will be clear that there lay a contradiction in the efforts of its emissaries to recast the spatial coordinates of Southern Tswana life; an unwitting contradiction, it is true, but a contradiction nonetheless. On one hand, the evangelists found large towns attractive: their existence promised to make conversion easier than would have been the case with dispersed peoples. The building of churches and founding of schools also presumed centralisation, as did irrigated agriculture in this ecology. Also, at the turn of the century, the core of 'London' congregations was composed largely of upper peasants, many of whom were invested in the survival of densely populated capitals. And yet, on the other hand, the Southern Tswana future-world, as both the LMS and Wesleyans envisaged it, consisted in scattered, loosely articulated communities of individuated farmsteads, each on its enclosed lands; the preferred mode, that is, of the lower and middle peasantries. But it was the lower peasantry that was least drawn to orthodox Christianity. And, anyway, it lacked the means to live the kind of rural life of which the missionaries dreamed. Contradictions notwithstanding, the LMS encouraged decentralisation with some vigour, if often indirectly. For at issue here was the fundamental disposition – and regulation – of people in space. The evangelists had long sought to unhitch Tswana from the yoke of chiefly control, so to draw them towards the church. Ironically, from the late nineteenth century onwards, independent Christian leaders tried to detach their own followers from the orbit of the missions. The term they used for these men and women was *boikgololo*, those outspanned, unyoked.

Of course, it was not just the agrarian revolution set in motion by the missions that transformed the Southern Tswana world, though this is where some disempowered sovereigns put the blame. One told Mackenzie as much, adding: 'We accepted the Word of God in our youth, but did not know what was coming behind it.'[164] From a different vantage, it is clear that a broad confluence of historical forces was converging on this world: among others, a mineral revolution, with its insatiable demand for cheap industrial labour; overrule by two separate colonial states, each with its own apparatuses of governance; and further territorial expansion on the part of settler populations. Still, the chiefs were not entirely incorrect either. The missions, as a cultural vanguard, did prepare the way for what 'came behind'. As S.M. Molema was to put it, from the perspective of the Tshidi-Rolong Christian elite:

> There has been a complete revolution from the abject condition of existence [of earlier times] ... A new way of life, with new deeds, new thoughts, new vision, and new orientations, new physical, mental and spiritual possibilities and capacities has been revealed to the African ...

This complete revolution has, in the first place, been due to the quiet, patient unobtrusive missionary, the mainspring of African evolution.[165]

The missions, to be sure, insinuated new forms of individualism, new regimes of value, new kinds of wealth, new means and relations of production, new religious practices. And they set in train processes of class formation. All of which could not but alter, for good or ill, the internal workings of Southern Tswana economy and society – and the way in which black South Africans embraced the European presence.

In conclusion, while the agrarian revolution gave rise to an assertive class of commercial farmers, for many it brought a harvest of hunger. And a world of very different social, material and spatial forms. Having come to recreate the lost British yeomanry, the missions had contributed to making not an independent peasantry but an army of wage workers; or, rather, a population of peasant-proletarians caught up in a cycle of economic dependency. Reciprocally, white colonial society had itself become reliant on peoples like the Southern Tswana: on their bodies and their buying power, their human capital and their crops. Some evangelists, recall, saw this as an achievement on their part, though none took pleasure in the racist excesses of the colonial state or the conditions of the workplace. The claim had merit, even if it was sometimes exaggerated. For, as we said at the outset, their agrarian 'revolution' did have a palpable impact on the way in which Southern Tswana oriented themselves towards the world of markets, money and modernity.

JANE & JOHN PHILIP:
PARTNERSHIP, USEFULNESS & SEXUALITY
IN THE SERVICE OF GOD

Natasha Erlank

Dr John Philip has always proved a fertile subject for historical investigation. Almost every historian of European colonialism in Southern Africa has had occasion to mention him.[1] Treatments of him and his work are to be found within the research produced by every major historiographical trend since the nineteenth century. More recently, to take just two examples, Dr Philip has been the subject of a biography by Andrew Ross and is also featured in work by Andrew Bank on the construction of fields of debate in South African history.[2] The former uses Philip's background and evangelical affiliation to situate Philip's efforts and achievements in South Africa, stressing Philip's Scottish background and radical evangelicism. Andrew Bank is interested in the way in which Philip's views provided a catalyst for the beginning of a South African historiographical tradition. He suggests that the writing of South African history began with Dr Philip's *Researches in South Africa* (1828), which established a benchmark and precedent for liberal and conservative constructions of history throughout the nineteenth century. The debate that ensued around Philip's version of South African history has defined most subsequent issues debated in South African history.[3]

Most of the researchers writing about John Philip have concentrated on his public efforts – as missionary society director, historical writer and political agitator.[4] It seems churlish to cavil at work which is well researched, historically nuanced and productive of further debate, but on one level at least this work only reproduces the same arguments. The implicit question behind this and other work on Philip turns on his liberal status – 'native' friend or foe – and his motivation for becoming involved in the racial politics of the Cape in the early nineteenth century. Some work, either the response of historians wanting to 'affect the South Africa of their own day' or the response of an intellectual solipsism, goes as far as to suggest that Dr Philip was South Africa's first non-racial academic.[5] Other work, notably that of Dora Taylor, explicitly rejects that assumption.[6]

The subjects covered by examining these facets of Philip's life perpetuate the dominance of kinds of history which give precedence to attitudes and relationships that have to do with public 'political' issues, mediated in public spaces. This kind of history privileges political and public events and in doing so dismisses the importance of events and relationships that occur in more private arenas, including the home. 'The public sphere is assumed to be capable of being understood on its own, as if it existed *sui generis*, independently of private sexual relations and domestic life.'[7] The private sphere and its impact on the public are disregarded.[8] In this case I am referring to the need for gendered analyses of history (gendered histories, the histories of women and histories of sexuality), in order to examine both people's personal lives in their own right and the ubiquitous, though overlooked, importance of those lives to the canons of 'proper' history.[9] This is particularly important in South Africa, where the nature of racial oppression and its very public exercise have tended to overshadow other kinds of oppression, which are exercised in private as well as public spaces. Gender does not detract from analyses which wish to examine the working of race.[10] In this way struggles for power may be about race but may be phrased in gendered terms, because gender provides a convenient metaphor for describing and legitimising unequal relations.

> To ignore women is not simply to ignore a significant subgroup within the social structure. It is to misunderstand and distort the entire organization of that society. Incorporating women's experiences into our social analysis involves far more than adding another factor to our interpretation and thus correcting an admittedly glaring oversight. It forces us to reconsider our understanding of the most fundamental ordering of social relations, institutions and power arrangements within the society we study.[11]

I am not going to rewrite South African history, as the above paragraph might seem to presage, but I would like to see how a focus on gender and sexuality changes our understanding of John Philip. With respect to Dr Philip an emphasis on his attitude to race, and his entanglements with the Colonial Office, the eastern Cape Settlers and fellow missionaries in the London Missionary Society (LMS), have over-shadowed other not so public concerns in his life. These alternative concerns are not inaccessible – rather they have been overlooked. In this chapter I shall be touching on Dr Philip's relationship with his wife Jane, the sexual drive which affected his vision of marriage and structured his partnership with Jane, as well as her vision of marriage, and her role within the public and private sphere. In doing so I hope to demonstrate something of the importance of their relationship, as well as the importance of that relationship to Dr Philip's political campaigning in South Africa.

DR PHILIP, MARRIAGE AND WOMEN

Some of Dr Philip's earliest letters are from a collection he wrote to Jane Ross, later Jane Philip, between 1809 and 1811.[12] These passages present John, not so much as the liberal, but rather as the lover concerned with husbandly and wifely roles. In April 1808 he outlined his vision of a happy marriage:

> I have widely observed that there is no happiness where the husband and wife are indifferent to the good opinion of each other … And that man and woman who values the good opinion of each other more than they do the good opinions of the world, are the happiest couple in the world, and would do more to please one another than they would do to please the world.[13]

This letter is important because it cues us in to John Philip's attitude to marriage, and his relationship to Jane. Marriage was a relationship of supreme importance. He envisaged marriage as a relationship of two people whose different abilities would complement one another in the creation of a harmonious partnership. Many statements of his give weight to this idea of emotional reciprocity in their relationship. In two letters in 1808 he wrote, 'if her own happiness is not injured by studying mine, I hope I shall always increase my own happiness by studying to make her happy' and 'it would entirely spoil my pleasure, to think that my pleasure did not promote yours'.[14]

Not only affection in equal parts was to be exchanged, but also counsel and advice. In 1825 John Philip described Mrs Philip to (presumably) the LMS as his only adviser.[15] This desire for counsel was no hollow comment, and Mrs Philip frequently gave Dr Philip her desired opinion on subjects. In 1837, when Dr Philip was in Britain, she wrote to him telling him that some of his speeches were too political and too filled with generalisations.[16]

The Philips had a close relationship. Their love and regard for one another did not diminish throughout their married life. Their correspondence between 1836 and 1838, when Dr Philip was in Britain, was full of declarations of affection. In May 1837 Dr Philip sent Mrs Philip '1000 kisses'.[17] She missed him tremendously, writing to her friend Miss Wills that 'My heart has at times nearly sunk within me during the absence of my husband'.[18]

John Philip's notion of complementarity in marriage was a commonly held view of the early-nineteenth-century European middle class.

> A good marriage rested on the man and woman bringing to it their complementary characteristics. The man would be the 'lofty pine', the woman the 'slender vine', the man would take responsibility for the stormy world of business and politics, the woman would cast her sunbeams over the

murky clouds he had to contend with and 'sweetly smile' the cares of the world away.[19]

Contemporary authors regularly emphasised the suitability of a role which cast woman as a helpmeet to man.[20] This description fitted the Philips' marriage, but in practice the distinction between their different spheres of duty tended to slip because of John's views about the need for reciprocity and support at all levels. This slippage will become apparent in the latitude allowed Jane to pursue personal and joint interests.

Accompanying Dr Philip's vision of marriage was a vision of ideal womanhood. In 1808 he wrote to Jane on the desired character of woman, quoting 1 Peter 3:3–4. 'Whose adorning let it not be that outward adorning of plaiting the hair, and of wearing of gold, or of putting on of apparel; But let it be the hidden man of the heart, in that which is not corruptible, even the ornament of a meek and quiet spirit, which is in the sight of God of great price.'[21] This meek and quiet spirit with its emphasis on internal qualities was not, however, to be socially silent, because (as I shall show) John Philip valued female conviviality. In a letter to his daughter Eliza in 1830 he wrote of 'that nameless ease, that self command, that light society, that grace in company and in conversation which give to Woman her liveliness, her Empire'.[22]

All these characteristics, felt Philip, would find their ultimate fulfilment in marriage and in the management of home affairs. This too was in conformity with the early mid-nineteenth-century middle-class perception of marriage. Middle-class respectability lay in the separation of the public and private, whereby women confined their activities to the home for which men provided. This separation of spheres was relatively new.[23] Many of the middle-class families of the mid-nineteenth century had come to prosperity through the combined efforts of husbands and wives in work, but with their greater prosperity women no longer needed to work and the house-bound wife and mother became a potent signifier of middle-class status.[24]

While John Philip's view of women as best suited to marriage and motherhood (not stated but by extension) was dictated by his evangelical and ideologically middle-class background, he was also fairly pragmatic and status-conscious in his views on the reasons for marriage. In the same letter to Eliza, quoted above, he strongly advised her against becoming a school teacher. 'His objections [were] both moral and material. Philip was concerned that, in the business of running a school, Eliza would lose sight of the all-important task of forming an appropriate female identity – of becoming the 'Lady' which her class demanded she be.'[25] This letter is discussed in Kirsten McKenzie's thesis, where she links Philip's view of women's roles to class and marriage.[26]

Marriage – and by implication the domestic arena which marriage bounded – was therefore not only the duty of a Christian woman, but the best role available to middle-class women. Clearly, though, not all women were suited to marriage according to these criteria. In his letter to Eliza, Dr Philip dwelt on the social ignominy that could accrue to middle-class women undertaking paid employment; yet in 1830 he had recruited an English woman, Elizabeth Lyndall, specifically for the task of teaching infant schools in Cape Town.[27] In his letter to Eliza, Dr Philip wrote, 'You will perceive that this is not a letter you can show to any one out of the family and there are views in it that Miss Lyndal [sic] might misunderstand. Her years, and situation, and mental character may make a thing proper.'[28] Miss Lyndall's advanced years (all of about 28) and her ill-health suited her for work, and her status was partially redeemed because that work (although paid) was of a philanthropic nature.

Dr Philip did not exclude women from working when the work was philanthropic and of an ancillary nature and such work was suited to married women, women unsuitable for marriage, or widows. These provisos would prevent that loss of social respectability which he felt attached to women who worked (Dr Philip's views on women were quite class-specific). He was full of praise for Matilda Smidt and Mrs Elizabeth Robson, Christian widows who did volunteer philanthropic work.[29] He was vehemently not in favour of Ann Hamilton, the wife of a missionary at Dithakong, because she involved herself too closely in the affairs of the LMS and performed primary mission work. Nor was this work conducted in private and she did not efface either her identity or her opinions in her dealings with the LMS.[30]

John Philip's reaction to these women reveals a dissonance between his ideal image of womanhood and that image in practice. This is best demonstrated by his relationship with his wife. After Jane Philip's death he wrote that she had never neglected her home for public duties, yet as the following section will show this was not the case.[31]

JANE PHILIP AND USEFULNESS

Although Jane Philip is mentioned in several of the works which deal with Dr Philip and the activities of the LMS, her status and work are almost always given as ancillary to his.[32] Mrs Philip, however, was as intriguing a character as Dr John, and an examination of her work and the Philips' marriage points to the relevance of gender as an analytical category in examining and understanding the Philips' missionary endeavours.

Jane Ross was born in Scotland in 1792. In 1809 she married Dr John Philip (1775–1851), her senior by seventeen years. They lived in Aberdeen, where Dr Philip was a Congregational Church preacher until 1819. Their first child, Mary was born in 1810; the second, Eliza, in 1812; the third, William, in 1814; and the fourth, John, in 1816. Dr Philip was very involved in the home activities of the LMS, and in 1819 the family moved to the Cape of Good Hope where he had been appointed as superintendent and director of the LMS affairs in the Cape Colony. Jane Philip was 27 when they arrived, and her husband 44. There the family remained – apart from a visit to Britain for three years between 1826 and 1829, and another visit of Dr Philip's between 1836 and 1838. At the Cape the Philips had three more children: (Thomas) Durant born 1819, Margaret (who died young) born 1825, and Wilberforce born 1829. Jane Philip died in 1847 after an illness that was probably cancer and Dr Philip died in 1851.

Most of what we know of Mrs Philip comes through her own writing and the writing of those around her. She wrote to her husband, children and grand-children when she or they were separated. Most of her personal letters were to her friend Miss Wills (also involved in evangelical work), who lived in England. Her official correspondence is in the archives of the London Missionary Society. In addition to Mrs Philip's own writing, the letters of her daughter Eliza to her sister Mary and her husband, John Fairbairn, and the minutes of the Ladies' Benevolent Society, of which she was a pivotal member, are available.

For the majority of their life at the Cape, the Philips lived at Mission House in Church Square, Cape Town. They were physically in the centre of the city, and socially at the hub of Cape evangelical and missionary life. Their friends and acquaintances were drawn from a wide range of society, though more gen-erally from Cape Town's evangelical professional and business classes. They were very good friends with the family of H.E. Rutherfoord, a merchant, and were also friendly with the Rev. Abraham Faure of the Dutch Reformed Church. The defining characteristic of the people with whom they associated was a commitment to liberal principles, specifically the abolition of the slave trade, the education of the poor and the upliftment of the Khoikhoi and other Africans. Jane Philip seems rarely to have gone out much in society; rather it came to her. Church Square was often full of visitors of various descriptions, and with these visitors, her family and her various duties Mrs Philip's time was occupied.

Jane Philip was very busy at the Cape. She assisted her husband with his LMS duties, while carrying out work under her own initiative. She was a founder member of the Ladies' Benevolent Society (LBS) in 1822, and in 1838 she was still worrying about who would perform the offices of the society.[33] She was sometime treasurer of the society, and wrote numerous letters on its behalf. In addition to the LBS, she also helped to initiate the distribution of tracts and Bibles in Cape Town, and in September 1831 she wrote to her friend Miss Wills, 'We have this week commenced a tract and Bible Society – it will be the object of the Society [not only] to circulate such tracts as are already printed but to select from these such as are thought most suitable and to simplify them and get them translated into Dutch.'[34] Four years later Mrs Philip was still deliv-ering tracts. 'We have lately had several arriving English tracts translated into

Dutch which it is our intention to distribute over the whole town if possible one at a time.'[35]

Mrs Philip was also heavily involved in the introduction of the Infant School System to the Cape – both the first interdenominational and later the LMS schools. According to Helen Ludlow, 'It was she, more than any other individual, who was responsible for the establishment in Cape Town of the Mission Schools during this time.'[36] Mrs Philip was very exited about the prospect of opening the first infant school and agitated strongly for the facilities to establish it. In 1830, soon after the Philips had arrived back in Cape Town, she was able to write to Miss Wills that 'we have got an Infant School opened exactly opposite to our home. We have got an excellent building for the purpose lent by Government House ... the very Store which I had always said would exactly suit for an Infant School became vacant at the time our Committee was formed.'[37] Just a few months later infant schools were also established in Port Elizabeth and Bethelsdorp, and a year later Mrs Philip wrote, 'Our Infant School flourishes – upwards of two hundred are daily instructed on that system in Cape Town and more schools will be begun as soon as the funds will admit of it, there are several up the country.'[38] Jane Philip frequently informed her friend of the progress of the infant schools and it is clear that she was very much committed to the project. These initial infant schools were soon given over to control by an interdenominational committee, but in 1836 the LMS began to open its own schools.[39] In 1836 a British school for girls was opened in premises in Barrack Street. It was run by Miss Buzzacott, and had between ninety and a hundred pupils aged 10 to 14.[40]

Not only did Mrs Philip participate in activities that were ancillary to the work of the LMS, but she was also directly involved in the operation of the Society. Her letters contain numerous references to the amount of work she did on behalf of the LMS and the cares it gave her. From 1826 onwards Mrs Philip assisted her husband with the organisation involved in supporting a growing number of mission stations throughout the country. She kept the Society's accounts, and twice a year she was required to write up these books – at least until 1835 when she wrote to the directors that she only intended sending bills once a year from then on.[41] She continued this work until shortly before her death.[42] When Dr Philip's eyesight became too poor for him to write, she kept his correspondence for him.

In 1834 she wrote to Miss Wills:

the first three months of the year are (if possible) the busiest of the twelve for me for in addition to making up and sending home the Acc[oun]ts for the half year (which is also done in July) I have to make out to each Missionary a statement of the Bills drawn by him and paid by us and also the balance of his acct on which ever side it may be – these accts as you may suppose cannot be sent off without writing to each Missionary so that before I have my work done during these very hot months I am almost exhausted & glad of a respite for a little.[43]

Over the next ten years the work involved in writing up the accounts increased greatly.

The writing connected with this place is very great there are about 48 or so Missionaries who have very often something to write about and that must be answered besides some stations which require much correspondence from the peculiar circumstances in which they may happen to be. Besides the correspondence there is the accounts which have increased very much since we first took the work in hand. There were then 12 Missionaries and about 8 stations. Now there are 28 Stations and 48 or so Missionaries.[44]

This work was tremendously important because it freed Dr Philip to become involved in Cape politics. The amount of work and the type of work she did is very interesting because it challenges so many of the gender stereotypes of middle-class and, in particular, evangelical society of the nineteenth century. Women, especially married women, were not supposed to work. As I mentioned above this differed from the period at the end of the previous century when women, married and otherwise, were prominent in and integral to family enterprises.[45] Mrs Philip not only worked but did work that challenged stereotypes of the capabilities of women.[46] While she helped her husband with his work, she also did work on her own behalf, and was known publicly to do so.

How was Mrs Philip allowed, by her contemporaries, her husband and her own conscience, to perform work that was so clearly perceived to be beyond the ambit of 'normal' female behaviour? The answer lies in several directions. At various times she managed to disguise her work as domestic labour, she managed to disguise it under the duties of marriage, and she managed to justify it because of its ultimate aim.

In the first place Mrs Philip managed to link her work to the domestic sphere. She was not seen to work. Almost all her work was home-centred, and she did not go out much. Strangely enough this strategy worked with her husband, or at least to the point that he colluded in this interpretation of her efforts. That is why he could commend her domestic diligence after her death. She was also wont to plead a female frailty in some of the work she did. While she was without qualms in giving the directors of the LMS her opinion on matters, she also pleaded her lack of expertise: 'even a much more accomplished accountant than I can pretend to be may occasionally make mistakes ... I am conscious of attending to the accts to the best of my ability'.[47] From a current perspective, and given also Mrs Philip's peremptory tone in writing to the missionaries about the accounts themselves, this appears rather disingenuous.[48] However, it was an entirely more appropriate way for a woman to behave in the early nineteenth century. It is quite apparent that Mrs Philip only wrote like this when the directors queried her accounts and it is not difficult to believe that she was pleading her gender as an excuse.

In the second place Mrs Philip conflated some of her labours with the duties of marriage. In several of her letters to Miss Wills she described the need to fulfil her duties to Dr Philip, which involved both 'that assistance which none but a wife can so well render' and performing work for which Dr Philip had not time.[49] However, some of her work was clearly not ancillary to her husband's and she accommodated this shift within her consciousness by redefining contemporary divisions of labour and blurring the line at which public met private.

> We have much cause to bless God for the mercies he is continually showering upon us. He is pleased to favour us with a considerable measure of health, and to furnish with abundance of occupation in discharging the duties of the Station we are called to fill. Much of my time is certainly occupied by secular business but then it [spares] my husbands more valuable time to be employed on the Spiritual duties of his Station so that I have never to think my labour is not altogether in vain.[50]

More important than the distinction between public and private was the distinction between secular and spiritual. Duty within marriage was also duty towards God, because proper marriage was the epitome of Christian relations between men and women. It was an enactment of faith. During Dr Philip's absence in the late 1830s she wrote, 'I miss his conversation – the elevating views which he was in the habit of holding out to me as an inducement to forget my own selfish feelings in making a sacrifice to promote the cause of God.'[51] In this instance her duty in marriage involved a separation from her husband, and this tallied with her duty to God.

Within or without marriage, the exercise of faith was central to Mrs Philip. Her Christian beliefs and her commitment to duty and 'the hope of being useful' gave her ultimate justification for her activities.[52] The following passage (written 1831) is central to an understanding of her character:

> we have much mercy to be thankful for and if it would but please God to let us see the pleasure of the Lord prospering in our hands our cup would run over but we do grieve to think of the little spiritual advantage that appears to arise from our labours when we read of what is doing in

America we feel humbled and almost discouraged and we are led to examine ourselves whether the want of eminent piety be not a bar to our usefulness – the prayer of our heart is let thy work appear unto thy Servants and thy Glory unto their children and let the beauty of the Lord our God be upon us and establish thou the work of our hands upon us yea the work of our hands establish thou it.[53]

Several words and concepts are repeated in this passage: 'hands' were mentioned three times, as was 'work'; together with 'labours' and 'usefulness' these are loaded terms, given the tone of the passage. Mrs Philip was very concerned about being a recipient of God's mercy, and believed that this could be obtained through secular labour ('the work of our hands') if it was geared towards promoting the acquisition of spirituality. Work (of a tangible nature – hence the emphasis on hands), 'duty' and 'usefulness' are key concepts in these extracts; duty to God and usefulness in God's cause. Mrs Philip was very much a practical woman – she was convinced of the worth of practical measures and concrete labours in raising God's cause among the people in Cape Town and the interior not blessed with his mercy. In this sense she was an ideal partner for her husband, who was more interested in intellectual labour.

This emphasis on 'usefulness' did not restrict itself to her perception of public activity. Duty, usefulness and hard work were equally terms which applied to Mrs Philip's private world. Jane Philip's children and grandchildren were constantly being admonished to be useful. When William ran away to sea she wrote, 'Grant me the Salvation of his soul, and if possible that he may be useful in this world in promoting the Saviour's cause'; when John wished to become a printer on a missionary station she wrote, 'but he has many opportunities of being useful in town if he is disposed to avail himself of them', and she wrote directly to Wilberforce that 'now is the time that you should employ in laying up a stock of knowledge to fit you for future usefulness'.[54] With reference to Eliza's marriage to John Fairbairn she wrote, 'I cannot but hope she will also be useful to him in many respects', and with reference to the returning daughter of a Dutch minister, 'I hope she may be useful – there is considerable opportunity if she is so disposed in connection with her father's congregation'.[55] 'Useful' and related concepts featured repeatedly in her letters and, if not by direct association, at least by implication referred to action that could be performed in the service of God.[56]

In evangelical Christianity the individual was responsible for his or her own transformation.[57] Prior to the eighteenth century the dominant European political philosophy posited society rather than the individual as the site of political and social attention. Enlightenment philosophies began to swing emphasis, however, onto the individual as the site of social and political attention. The result was a reconstructed view of selfhood, in which the social values of discipline and generosity became reconstituted as the personal qualities of self-discipline and self-denial.[58] Evangelicism, which was a reaction to the rational and established nature of Enlightenment Christianity, proposed a reconceptualisation of individual characters similar to this, but with the added component of individual energy, which was necessary to overcome the distinction between self-interest and selflessness.[59] Salvation lay in self-discipline and the individual triumph of a soul over sin. Activity, of the soul and of the body, in the right direction led to the attainment of salvation. This individual energy translated into practical action was at the core of evangelical belief.

It is very important to understand the dynamic character of early evangelicism, because this personal conception of sin and the need for salvation was what motivated so many of the early philanthropists and missionaries. 'The most radical distinction, and the root of [the evangelical's] world-view, lay in his conviction of sin and redemption, of personal sin and personal redemption, and in the readiness for complete dedication to God which was the product.'[60] Quite crucially it was this need for active intervention in one's soul that allowed evangelical women to move beyond their domestic spheres, as in the case of Mrs Philip.[61]

Usefulness provided Jane Philip with a way of assessing women that was contrary to her general understanding of the female character. She believed that women were inferior creatures to men and, unless properly occupied, a burden to society. She was quite emphatic on the subject of the sort of education future missionary wives ought to receive. Her requirements were outlined in a letter to Miss Wills:

> and while a good education is exceedingly desirable it should be united with all house [illegible] duties and a strict attention paid to the useful every day duties which females are born to attend to. I am always much grieved when I see Missionaries wives who require their husbands constant attendance and who instead of being an assistance to them in their [illegible] or duties as Missionaries hinder them by taking up their time in attending to domestic concerns. I hope usefulness may be impressed upon their minds as the great aim of their lives.[62]

She, like her husband, subscribed to the view in which women were first and foremost intended to be helpmeets to their husbands. Women, in her view, were 'born' to particular roles, and to particular spheres of occupation. This tallied with contemporary gender ideology, though her views reflected an extreme of this ideology through her belief in the benefits to spirituality accrued through usefulness. She wrote to Miss Wills, enumerating the sorts of occupation available to her were Miss Wills to come to the Cape, and emphasised the use she would be to the Ladies' Benevolent Society:

not that the Ladies are unwilling to work but most of them are so cum-
bered with families – or School or duties of one kind or another that they
really have not time to donate to the Societies. Every one of the Ladies
connected with the Barrack Street School the Benevolent and tract
Societies … have large families besides several of them on whom depends
the entire support of their families … The Treasurer and Secretary of the
tract Society have each of them large families to support by keeping
Schools … you may judge how little time they have. [63]

There was no censure here, only sympathy. While none of the women in the
Ladies' Benevolent Society undertook as much work as Mrs Philip, the work
they did was permitted by her religiously defined sense of morality. Religion
was above society for Mrs Philip and she was quite prepared to contravene the
prescriptions of one to satisfy the needs of the other should occasion require
it.

The partnership and usefulness that characterised the Philips' marriage was,
however, marred by one particular flaw, and this is important. The emotional
and professional partnership of the Philips, which was constituted by John
Philip's view of marriage and which constituted Jane Philip's role in marriage,
had its source in an emotional and sexual intensity within John Philip. In its
positive results it prompted the importance John Philip placed on marriage, but
in its negative results it laid him open to the possibility of sexual infidelity. At
the one extreme this resulted in a degree of jealousy which marred the Philips'
marriage and at the other this had implications for John Philip's faith. I wish to
end with a discussion of John Philip's sexuality because it brings us back to the
sorts of issues discussed at the beginning of this essay.

INFIDELITY, FAITH AND SEXUALITY

It is apparent from his writing that that Dr Philip was concerned about the
proper exercise of sexuality. In June 1808 he quoted to Jane a review of a book
containing letters between the

late Empress Maria Theresa to her Daughter, the late Unfortunate Queen
of France, on the very delicate and interesting subject of exciting and fix-
ing the warmth of passion in Husbands, and thereby securing their con-
jugal fidelity. If the married part of your sex and those that expect to be
married are not already possessed of a specific for this purpose, I should
think that this publication would be very popular amongst them. So far
from possessing a knowledge of the means of exciting and preserving the
affections of their husbands, I am sorry to say that a great proportion of
otherwise respectable Females are very ignorant of this matter.[64]

This was a rather explicit inclusion in the letters of an engaged evangelical couple, and it points to both the importance of such matters for Dr Philip, and his belief that the only proprieties to be observed in such a relationship were those established by the couple themselves. Dr Philip obviously saw himself as a case in point of husbands who needed the warmth of passion fixed on their wives. Elsewhere he wrote to Jane about 'the most glaring faults into which a man may have been precipitated by his passions', referring to both spiritual and physical passions, and he saw himself 'in reality to have been the very chief of sinners!!!'.[65] In the June letter he had also admonished Jane not to take what he said as applying to her, dreamt of kissing her lips gently, but also asserted that his love for her was not a 'sensual appetite'. Dr Philip, at least in 1808, was concerned with his sexuality. His was not a latent sexuality, and it was one that he felt might lead him into sin if not properly constrained.

The possibility of metaphysical marital infidelity seems to have been the result of Dr Philip's constrained sexuality. Perhaps as a response to his passionate nature, he was a man who attracted other people to him.[66] Andrew Ross makes this clear in his biography of John Philip, in writing about the circle of young people he gathered around him in Aberdeen, and the efforts his congregation made to keep him in Aberdeen.[67] However, it appears to have been women who were most drawn to Philip. Philip had various connections over the years with women to whom he was not related, or related only in friendship.

The Foulgers were friends of the Philips', and had looked after Eliza and Mary Philip in Britain until they left with their parents for South Africa in 1829. Mary Anne Foulger began a correspondence with Eliza Philip soon after the latter's departure to South Africa. The following extract concerns either a family picture of the Philips, or perhaps just John Philip and Eliza:

And the picture of you, no, not of you only, but also of my beloved dearest father – I look upon it, and kiss it till I can look no longer; but instead of the warm embrace and the affectionate words, the same cold, mute countenance seems to gaze with unmoved indifference upon me and I turn away chilled and disappointed, exclaiming with wishful ardour 'Oh that those lips had language'! Yes, my dear Eliza, he is, he will be my father and I must call him so; it will seem if possible to draw us still more closely together, we will never be more than one family.[68]

John Philip (more than 30 years her senior) had clearly made a strong impression on Mary Anne Foulger. Several more of Mary Anne's letters contain similar declarations towards her 'Dear Papa', and in the same letters she referred to her own father as 'Papa'. In addition to her correspondence with Eliza she wrote to Dr Philip personally, and he wrote to her. Only in 1838, after Dr

Philip's visit to Britain in which he had little time to see the Foulgers, and when she began to realise how old he was, did her sentiments seem to abate.[69]

Dr Philip's interest in (mostly younger) women was not restricted to Mary Anne Foulger. He personally recruited Elizabeth Lyndall to establish an infant school in Cape Town. During the 1830s he did not always communicate directly with Thomas Fowell Buxton, but wrote instead to Buxton's daughters, both before and after they were married. In Cape Town he frequented, mostly without his wife, the salons of Lady Margaret Herschel (25 to his 55), who referred to him repeatedly in her letters.[70] Close relations between fathers and daughters were a treasured ideal of middle-class families at this point, and older men often married younger women, yet this does not seem to have been the case here. Dr Philip was married already, and he did not treat his female friends as he treated his daughters.[71] His relationships fall into neither of these categories. While he obviously valued these women for self-command, light society, grace in company and intelligence, it also seems possible that the relationships included an element of sexual attraction – on their part, if not his, and he did not hesitate to take advantage.

This sexual attraction may never have been acted upon but it was apparent to at least one other person. In September 1836 Jane Philip wrote to John in Britain that she was 'really angry and hurt' at his writing so seldom, and that she feared the kindnesses and caresses of so many other good ladies.[72] Clearly this hit a nerve in John Philip, and either this or a similar letter led him to reply to Mrs Philip, giving scriptural justification for their separation.[73] Mrs Philip replied by quoting 1 Cor. 7 to him. This chapter begins, 'Now concerning the things whereof ye wrote unto me: It is good for a man not to touch a woman. Nevertheless, to avoid fornication, let every man have his own wife, and let every woman have her own husband. Let the husband render unto the wife due benevolence: and likewise also the wife unto the husband.' There is no reference to which part of this passage Mrs Philip quoted to her husband (possibly 1 Cor. 7:10–11, 'And unto the married I command, yet not I, but the Lord, Let not the wife depart from her husband: But and if she depart, let her remain unmarried, or be reconciled to her husband: and let not the husband put away his wife'), but whether she quoted part or whole the point would have been made. The chapter is on 'Duties of the Married State' and Dr Philip's behaviour at least was contrary to its precepts, and at worst emotional adultery.

Sex as sex, and not suppressed sexuality as some colonial metaphor, is not the sort of thing easy to gauge from the correspondence of early-nineteenth-century evangelical writing. Its presence in Dr Philip's writing is indicative of his personal ardour and the prominent status of sin and moral right in his life, and the struggle between them. This combination of his evangelical fervour and physical appetite revealed itself in his writing, as is shown in this continuation of an earlier quotation:

> Recollect … that the Law of god is spiritual; that there is an impurity of
> the mind, and adultery of the heart; that certain desires to please, certain
> artful emotions, certain lascivious airs, and certain attempts to wound the
> virtue of others (though we may apparently observe the most rigid rules
> of decorum) may be as heinous before God as the most glaring faults into
> which a man may have been precipitated by his passions … I see myself
> in reality to have been the very chief of sinners!!! Create in me a clean
> heart O God, and renew a right spirit within me! Hide thy face from my
> sin and blot out all mine iniquity.[74]

Dr Philip was writing this for Jane, but appears to have been more preoccu-
pied about the relevance of the passage for himself. The first line of the passage
sets up an opposition between the physical and the spiritual, Philip needing to
remind himself that the law of God was spiritual. Thereafter, according to the
rest of the passage, certain impurities of the mind are just as immoral as any
physical act, those impurities being also unfaithfulness to God. This passage
appears to be reflecting as much on Philip's relationship with other people as
his relationship to his God. Andrew Ross has described the radical nature of
Philip's evangelical beliefs, and one feature of this was the tangible, almost cor-
poreal love John felt for his Lord.[75] Dr Philip's faith was intensely personal and
the ardour with which he approached human relations was carried over into
his divine relationship. It is not entirely clear what he was referring to in the
above passage, but the language he used, of physical and sexual betrayal, certainly points to confusion within him about both the nature of his sexuality
and the nature of his faith. It is therefore important to look at his sexuality
because of what it reveals about this belief.

   This understanding of John Philip's character may not alter our perception
of his efforts in any radical way, but it does beg several questions. It alters our
perception of his faith, but it also alters our perception of his evangelical work
– his political efforts, which were motivated by his evangelical belief.

   Recent work in the field of gender, colonialism and sexuality has pointed to
the links between private lives and public worlds. Several researchers have now
described how 'representations of women have been central to the process of
constructing a male national identity in the colonial period'.[76] These kinds of
representations, according to Sara Mills, take on two forms: either the British
memsahib in need of protection from a non-European sexual threat, or the sexually available colonised woman.[77] In recent work Wendy Woodward has
described how John Philip depicted Khoisan and Tlhaping women as entirely
sexualised and as objects within a pornographic discourse.[78] It would be interesting to examine the degree to which Philip's construction of women (other
than his wife) and his unease about his own sexuality fed into this sort of con-

struction, and how his own identity fed on these sorts of constructions.

Ann Laura Stoler's work has also shown us that definitions of appropriate sexual behaviour acted as signifiers for colonial and colonised populations in French Indochina and the Dutch East Indies, so that sexuality not only metaphorically but also physically mapped out the differences between the two.[79] Nineteenth-century evangelical liberals at the Cape were particularly incensed by the sort of sexual relations and gender relations that existed between Africans. Those relations were a fundamental marker of difference between uncivilised, heathen people and civilised, Christianised people. In his description of the Tswana, amongst whom the Moffats worked, Dr Philip wrote of the degraded nature of Tswana women, forced to marry young (and by implication have sexual relations). He also included in his writing a vignette in which he described how the Tswana were always urging the Moffats to find a husband for their young daughter, in such a way as to emphasise the difference between the Tswana and the missionaries.[80] Pam Scully's research has shown how anti-slavery liberals at the Cape, Philip included, worked to reform slave sexuality in the period before emancipation.[81] While Dr Philip wrote as he did, and was involved in efforts to reform slave sexuality, such concerns did not receive as much attention in his writing as they did in the writing of other missionaries. Did such issues, given the potentially explosive nature of his own sexuality, cut rather too close to the bone? And by extension, was all his effort to create the Khoisan as 'rational beings' a reflection of a personal desire for moral elevation?

It is not my intention to answer these questions. Rather I wanted in this essay to point out the relevance of a gendered analysis of Dr Philip, for what it can say not only on a representative level, but also on a constitutive level. Whatever Dr Philip's feelings about his own sexuality they were subsumed in a marriage and constitutive of a marriage which he regarded as a partnership. His partner did likewise, drawing principally on her idea of usefulness for confirmation of this status of hers.

Mrs Philip's belief in the need to be useful in the cause of God provided her with the ultimate justification for transgressing contemporary gender norms. Ironically, part of her husband's acceptance of her behaviour came from his own gendered vision of marriage as a partnership, which at times differed from his given opinions of the true role of women within marriage. His ideal view of marriage was one of partnership, the complementary nature of two separate entities bound by love for one another and the love of Jesus Christ. Mrs Philip shared this view. It was therefore natural that they should divide the work of Dr Philip's position between them – Mrs Philip undertaking the secular nature of the task while Dr Philip undertook the spiritual, as suited their particular skills. Kirsten McKenzie has suggested elsewhere that it was Dr Philip's position that allowed Mrs Philip to do what she did.[82] While this may seem to be what I have outlined, there is in fact a difference – Mrs Philip was performing duties that were part of Dr Philip's position, a position held by the couple together through marriage. Both of them were the Superintendent of the LMS in Cape Town.

7

'WORKING AT THE HEART':
THE LONDON MISSIONARY SOCIETY
IN CAPE TOWN, 1819–1844

Helen Ludlow

The anniversary of the emancipation of slaves throughout the British empire, on 1 December 1834, was commemorated with intent in Cape Town.[1] On 6 December 1840, during a week in which he had preached on the 'privileges of liberty and the consequent duties', the LMS missionary Vogelgezang called his coloured congregation to his first missionary prayer meeting at the Dorp Street school room of the London Missionary Society. Desiring to develop a mission-mindedness in these subjects of missionary enterprise, he also 'called for any one of the Coloured brethren to speak'. Through Vogelgezang's report we obtain a glimpse into the world of this mission congregation: 'One of the deacons spoke [he has been a slave until the 1st December 1834] ... so free, earnest and impressive that I was astonished. We could hear that he had been a slave and also a slave of sin, but that from his bodily slavery he had been liberated by the Britons and from the spiritual slavery by our Lord Jesus Christ.'

The second to take the floor was a sergeant 'of Hottentot extraction', both a church member and member of the 'school for the aged'. He wanted 'to speak of a free nation of his country which equally had been treated like slaves, even in so much, that some esteemed a slave higher than one of that nation ... the Hottentots; a nation exposed to contempt.' He spoke of how, despite the hopes Ordinance 50 (1828) had raised, it had been a struggle to improve the condition of the 'Hottentots'. It had been the mission stations which had given them the opportunity to hear the gospel and to attend schools and churches.

The third speaker of the evening was 'a blind person of colour'; the fourth, a member of the church and assistant in the school who had been 'a Mohamedan'. The common theme was appreciation of the LMS for the work 'bestowed upon them' and a strong sub-theme, the appreciation of the privileges and duties of being free (and Christian) men.[2] In celebrating the gratitude of his congregants to God, Britain and the LMS, Vogelgezang was also demonstrating how the full circle of successful mission work was the ability to harness these now useful members of Cape society into mission work of their own.

The years immediately after effective emancipation provide the endpoint of the period covered in this essay, for it examines the LMS work 'bestowed upon' the people of Cape Town during the superintendency of Dr John Philip, and the relationship which developed between the LMS and the city of Cape Town from 1819 to 1844. What becomes apparent is that the LMS and Cape Town's established Christian community grappled only intermittently at first with an appropriate response to the urban poor – people such as those gathered at Vogelgezang's missionary prayer meeting. This was in the context of a growing rival religion in the form of Islam. Indeed, it was a matter of concern to shorter-term LMS missionaries in Cape Town that Philip's preoccupation with the interior missions was unmatched by any distinctly missionary thrust in the port city itself. It was only with the legal abolition of slavery in 1834 and the potential further growth of Islam, that a change in focus within Cape Town came about. By 1839 Vogelgezang had been appointed as the first LMS missionary in Cape Town dedicated to work among the coloured population.

As the LMS began to move into work among the 'lower orders' it assumed a prominent role in the provision of infant and elementary education. This was something which came increasingly to be seen as the key to winning the hearts and minds of the lower classes of all persuasions. The initial priority of Philip as far as Cape Town was concerned was, however, the building of a relationship with government and Cape Town's evangelical leadership in order to facilitate his broader task of superintending LMS missions throughout the country. Cape Town came to have a particular role in the thinking of Philip and in 1820 he stated that 'Cape Town is to the country what the heart is to the body'.[3] This was said as he sought support from his superiors in Britain for the construction of a church to house the predominantly white middle-class colonial congregation whose minister he would be at the same time as superintendent of missions. Indeed, far more than being a focus of mission, Cape Town in the 1820s and 1830s became a resource for mission – materially, educationally and in terms of personnel.

CAPE TOWN IN THE EARLY 1800s

The early nineteenth century was an important time of transition for the Cape Colony, with its incorporation into the British empire and consolidation of British rule. In 1819 Cape Town's population was in the region of 18,000[4] and the city had been the seat of colonial government for nearly 170 years. Combining this important role with that of garrison town and chief colonial port, Cape Town had through its incorporation into the British empire witnessed a new spurt of growth in a local merchant class, growth which was to gather momentum with the availability of slave compensation money from 1837.[5]

Though small, it was a cosmopolitan city. Slaves of diverse origins equalled the whites in numbers. The 'free black' population of close on 2000 constituted the heart of the city's growing Muslim community. The balance of the population comprised 'Prize negroes' and, because pass laws continued in force until Ordinance 50 of 1828 allowed their free movement, a mere 500 or so people of recognised Khoisan extraction.[6] Although Dutch-speaking colonists outnumbered their more recently established English-speaking counterparts, the more influential were increasingly coming to recognise their community of interests: though slaveowners, they were 'tied by occupation or cosmopolitan culture to the British'.[7]

Though far from the centre of debate, Dr Philip's Cape Town both pondered and had its consciousness shaped by the massive changes in the mother country. Governors, missionaries, journalists, businessmen and expatriates arrived at Table Bay from a Britain which, by the early nineteenth century, had seen 'the rise of liberalism and the emancipatory discourses of abolition, a heady ideological stew of evangelicalism, the new liberal political economy, and the domestic crises bequeathed by industrial capitalist development.'[8] In the context of an expanding commercial economy, this gradually bore fruit at the Cape in the form of diminishing patronage in government, in judicial reform, a free press and replacement of directly coercive forms of labour control.[9] It also saw the expansion of missionary activity in and beyond the colony.

ESTABLISHING A BASE IN CAPE TOWN, 1819–29

The LMS work in South Africa had nominally fallen under local supervision since Van der Kemp's appointment as superintendent in 1811. The position was only made effective, however, with Philip's arrival in South Africa in 1819. When the 44-year-old Congregational minister from Aberdeen, together with his wife Jane and children, took up residence in Cape Town at the beginning of 1819, Philip's role was supervision of the Society's thirteen stations in South Africa. He was not himself a missionary, nor was his task related specifically to the inhabitants of Cape Town.

It was Cape Town's English-speaking Nonconformists who drew the LMS representative into a local role. Soon after his arrival in Cape Town, Philip was invited to preach to the 25–30 members of the Presbyterian congregation, meeting in the hall of the Orphan Chamber.[10] Philip appears to have made an immediate and successful impact as a preacher. In April 1820 he was invited formally to become pastor of the congregation, now numbering over 150 and uncomfortably packed into the Orphan Chamber. Amongst these were a number of 'the most respectable English residents in the place'.[11] He accepted the position on the understanding that his missionary duties took precedence over those of pastor and that the church government take the Congregational form.

Philip then set out to persuade the LMS directors that it was in the interests of the Society to depart from usual policy and finance the building of a chapel.[12] The core of his argument was the need to establish a strong base in Cape Town because of the city's uniquely important position in relation to the work of the missions in South Africa in general. He wrote, 'if good is to be done on an extensive scale in Africa, it must be done in Cape Town'.[13] In December 1820 he said:

> I am satisfied the society must have a chapel in Cape Town for the sake of the missions. Cape Town is to the country what the heart is to the body, it is from here that the streams of life or death all lead to the furthest extremities. Building is very expensive in Cape Town but if the Society means to lay its mark upon South Africa and do good upon a certain and extensive scale nothing should prevent the erection of a place of worship in the Town.[14]

Impressed by his immediate success as a pastor, the directors accepted Philip's argument. They recognised Cape Town's significance as the seat of government. It was here that permission would have to be obtained for work in the colonial interior and government cooperation in the cause of missions would be solicited. Not only did the 'prevalent sentiments and habits' of Cape Town's population exert a great influence on those of the rest of the Colony, but successful work among the more influential Capetonians would win local support for the wider missionary effort. Indeed the directors were keen to harness the financial and human resources of Cape Town's evangelical middle class in the cause of converting and civilising Africa.

The directors thus both raised donations and contributed directly to the financing of what became known as the Union Chapel on Church Square, as well as of Mission House to accommodate the superintendent and other missionaries in transit.[15] Opened on 1 December 1822 and seating three hundred congregants, Union Chapel was described as 'an elegant building, and ... generally admired'. A Sunday School was opened at the same time.[16]

It was a reciprocal relationship which subsequently developed between the LMS and the Cape Town community. The LMS provided a pastor, chapel, some financial assistance, and much later a full-time missionary. While genuine piety is not possible to measure, members of the congregation of Union Chapel displayed the concerns and behaviour of those 'serious Christians' whom Davidoff and Hall identify as the core of British evangelical and philanthropic activities.[17] They attended prayer meetings, Bible studies and Sunday services. They became increasingly involved in work beyond their own immediate private concerns. Sunday schools were started up in other parts of the town, adult classes taught, tracts were distributed far and wide.

With the establishment of the Cape Town Auxiliary Missionary Society in

1823,[18] members of the chapel, as well as of the wider Christian community, became committed to ongoing, formal support of the LMS in its work of spreading Christianity and the 'blessings of civilisation' among the 'Heathen'. This was done particularly by raising financial assistance for LMS projects throughout the country. In Cape Town the Auxiliary Society would play a vital part in financing the construction, equipping and teaching of LMS schools there. The committee of the Auxiliary Society was solidly dominated by Union Chapel members in later years.[19] It was chapel members such as H. Rutherfoord, John Tredgold, Ralph Arderne and John Fairbairn who also played leading roles in shaping Cape Town society through the commercial and philanthropic institutions they founded and led, as well as in local politics.[20]

As in Britain from which so many of them had come, men and women of the Union Chapel congregation participated in the religious and social life of Cape Town in gender-specific ways.[21] The men headed committees, selected pastoral staff, controlled finances, spoke on behalf of the community. The women's roles were more supportive and informal – extensions of appropriately nurturing and formative activities of the home. They participated most notably in teaching Bible classes for adult women; running, through the auspices of the Ladies' Benevolent Society, a school of industry for lower-class girls; and in Sunday school teaching.

The woman who played a decisive role without violating her position as supportive wife was Jane Philip. In the documents which form the basis of this essay, hers is the one woman's voice expressing clear opinions on matters of education and deployment of personnel among the dominant male voices in the correspondence between the Cape Town station and the London directors of the LMS.

Despite different roles, the activities of the Chapel members show them to have been united in their sense of responsibility towards their society, and in this they can also be equated with their British counterparts. M.J. Jones writes of the continuities between the old puritanism of eighteenth-century mercantile Britain and the new puritanism of evangelical, industrial Britain (and the springboard of both missionary work and educational reform). The coincidence of individual wealth and personal piety was crucial:

the consecration of self and work to the glory of God ... taught [the puritan] that wealth ... was a trust, whose expenditure was governed by the same rule as its acquisition – the glory of God – and since God could best be glorified by making man fit to glorify Him, the puritan was irresistibly drawn towards the service of man, who through misery, or ignorance, or debauchery, deprived God of the glory which was His due. To men of such a mould charity was obligatory.[22]

While accepting that the poor would always be with them, they identified true charity as capable of promoting the usefulness of people. It was an investment – in people's salvation; in training pupils in habits of order and decency; in 'forming little garrisons' against false beliefs.[23]

Dr Philip remained pastor at Union Chapel for 24 years, actively assisted by his wife Jane. There is little direct information about the nature of the relationship between Philip and his congregation but, as far as policy towards Cape Town was concerned, Philip's role was certainly decisive. The actual functioning of the work would depend largely on these 'ordinary' people of Cape Town and a variety of short-term missionaries. For Philip's duties as superintendent took him away into the interior for periods of between four and six months at a time and his two visits to England (1826–9 and 1836–8) meant that for almost six years he was totally removed from the situation in Cape Town.

His responsibilities as superintendent were immense and Cape Town was a very small part of the total missionary enterprise. Issues of Khoisan restrictions, Lord Charles Somerset's vendetta against him, vagrancy laws, frontier relations and many other matters affecting the colony at large were preoccupations which rivalled and probably eclipsed Cape Town in Philip's thoughts.

In January 1826 Dr Philip left for England at the request of the directors in order to present to the Colonial Secretary, Lord Bathurst, his evidence concerning the condition of the 'Hottentots' in South Africa. He would also use this time to write his *Researches in South Africa*. The superintendency and pastorate of Union Chapel were filled in Philip's absence by the Rev. Richard Miles, a controversial appointment.[24] The congregation at the chapel decreased considerably during this period.[25] At the same time, Miles expressed his dissatisfaction with the spirituality of Capetonians in general, and the failure of Union Chapel to fulfil a missionary role in particular.[26] The few coloured people who attended the chapel were the domestic servants of white members. Otherwise 'none of their class of inhabitants are even present at the services held in the Mission Chapel. Neither is there any suitable provision made for their accommodation even if they were disposed to attend. No direct efforts have yet been made by the Society for the moral and spiritual improvement of the heathen population of Cape Town.' Miles wrote in October 1830 that Cape Town offered a wide field of activity for a missionary 'who would condescend to men of low estate', particularly as the Muslims were actively and effectively proselytising the black community.[27]

While the plaintiveness of Miles's correspondence and his own condescension are not attractive, he had identified a very real divide in Cape society. As Worden says, 'Cape Town was … a harsh place for the old, sick and the poor in the first decades of British rule'.[28] It was in fact really two towns. 'Behind and between the neat grid of streets of the colonial town was a maze of "steegs" – lanes, alleys, squares and culs de sac. [Here] every square foot of spare ground contained shacks and sheds and ... livestock. [The poor] were crammed also into the basements and cellars of the old houses.'[29] A deficiency in sanitation and drainage, inadequate water supply and easy access to the consolation of canteens and drinking houses resulted in a singularly unhealthy labouring class. The over-crowding and poverty subsequently worsened with the freeing of slaves. While poor people of Irish and English extraction were part of this population, it was largely defined by race and the Dutch language. With practically no social sup-port other than that beginning to be provided by the religious communities (Muslim and Christian) and the Somerset Hospital, a 'catch-all for Cape Town's indigent sick', the average life expectancy in the city in the 1830s was 23–40 years.[30]

Miles clearly represented those in Cape Town for whom the spreading of the gospel had a vital, even essential, social function; that is, those who were of the opinion that 'the moral and religious improvement of this numerous class of inhabitants whereby they may become sober, honest and industrious members of Society, and partakers of the invaluable benefits of the Christian religion is intimately connected with the general prosperity and happiness of the com-munity'. For this reason he urged the LMS or the government to provide a mis-sionary for the low-ranking 'heathen' of Cape Town.[31]

The LMS did in fact have a missionary working among these people in Cape Town. In July 1828 Miles had agreed to take into service the South African Missionary Society (SAMS) missionary William Elliott, the financial support for whose work in the Muslim community had come to an end.[32] Despite achiev-ing little success in converting Muslims to Christianity, Elliott continued the work begun under the SAMS, operating mainly among 'persons of colour' but also among English boatmen and fishermen in the poor waterfront area of Roggebaai. At a school room in Roggebaai, Elliott orchestrated a pattern of day and night instruction and Sunday activities which became familiar at various sites of LMS work as the years progressed. In addition, Elliott held Sunday morning services for the 'vagrants' at the House of Correction and the 80 con-victs at the Amsterdam Battery.[33]

This, then, was the state of the Cape Town station of the LMS at the end of the first ten years of Philip's superintendency. A fairly firm base for LMS work had been established in the white community; opportunities for work beyond this community had been perceived and grasped by some, Miles and Elliott for example, but the directors were as yet uncommitted to extending operations in this arena.

THE WORK AND ISSUES OF THE PERIOD 1830–5

When the Philip family returned to Cape Town in October 1829 after their four-year absence, they found a newly installed governor, Sir Galbraith Lowry

Cole, in office, and much agitation amongst the colonists at the effects, real and imaginary, of Khoi emancipation. Philip's role in achieving this made him very unpopular amongst many colonists and, together with a libel suit arising out of the publication of *Researches in South Africa*, made the years 1830–2 among the most discouraging of his career.[34] It is evident that Philip considered leaving the Cape permanently at this time but felt that this would be surrendering too easily to those who would be glad to see him go.[35] Jane Philip did not want to leave Cape Town. She felt that there was no one capable of adequately replacing her husband as superintendent and that she herself was of use in Cape Town. A motherly desire not to leave her daughters also restrained her.[36]

Preoccupation with these troubles, with sorting out the financial problems of the mission in South Africa,[37] and a lengthy visit to the interior missions from August 1832 to March 1833, followed by his involvement in the problems of the eastern frontier, may account for the limited attention paid by Philip to the expansion of the work in Cape Town during this period. Certainly numbers at services, prayer meetings and a new fortnightly Bible study grew once he was back at the helm.[38] Other than in annual reports, however, Philip's correspondence with the directors contains few direct references to the 'Cape Town station'.

The 1830s did see the establishment of a number of interdenominational bodies in Cape Town on whose committees Philip and members of the Union Chapel were to serve and whose work supplemented that of the LMS. Among these were the South African Infant School Institution (1830), the South African Christian Instruction Society (June 1831) which employed a missionary to work amongst the coloured population, and the South African Tract and Book Society (September 1831).[39]

The work at Roggebaai was continued with the addition of classes for 60–100 children on three evenings a week, while the Ladies' Benevolent Society, founded by Jane Philip, used the Roggebaai school room during the day for a School of Industry for girls.[40] The Rev. Christie, arriving from Calcutta in 1832, helped at Roggebaai and began to learn Dutch in order to be more effective in this community. Ill health forced his departure in early 1834, however, and he took with him his new wife, Mary Philip.[41]

Meanwhile the provision of other shorter-term missionaries in Cape Town was shaped by events in Madagascar where the spread of Christianity was seen by the new ruler as an unacceptable threat to traditional culture. That the provision of schooling for this island population had proved to be the most effective way to do missionary work may have been a lesson brought to the Cape Town station.[42] At any rate, fearing expulsion, the Rev. J.J. Freeman, later LMS foreign secretary, left for Cape Town and stayed from 1830 to 1831. The Rev. and Mrs Theophilus Atkinson followed (1832–3), as did the artisan missionary John Canham (1835–7).[43]

Soon after his arrival, Canham became involved with Malagash residents of Cape Town, probably largely 'Prize negroes' confiscated from illegal slave traders and distributed as 'apprentices' by the British authorities after 1807. Canham was unable to ascertain the numbers of Malagash in Cape Town but they formed an identifiable minority amongst whom he was able to put to use his knowledge of the Malagasy language. Vernacular services for between fifty and eighty Malagash were held at Church Square twice a week, as were evening classes for adults. In summer, however, long working hours interfered with attendance, which seldom exceeded fifteen. Instruction in reading was given to 'adult females' on Sunday afternoons and two evenings a week by Mrs Canham and the two older daughters of Mr Powrie, a Union Chapel deacon. Canham, like Miles, felt that the LMS should employ 'at least one missionary for the Coloured population in Cape Town'.[44]

While the Society's missionary work in Cape Town was progressing in this rather *ad hoc* fashion, two matters did occupy a fair amount of the superintendent's attention; the first was related to education, the second to slavery and Islam. The establishment at the Cape of a seminary which would provide education for missionary children and prospective 'native' schoolmasters had long been a matter of concern to Philip and the directors. Philip saw the need to provide not simply sound education, but the kind of training which would supply the LMS with the teaching missionaries it would require in the future. As a missionary who felt that all people were capable of attaining an equal level of civilisation,[45] he regarded education as a vital ingredient of missionary work and the mission schools as 'the most important institutions we have in South Africa at the moment'. Without 'native' teachers the work would never progress adequately.[46]

The directors went as far as sending William Foster to establish a seminary for missionary children at Hankey in the eastern Cape, in 1825. But disagreements over leadership and the suitability of this location saw the project stall. It is likely that Philip was determined that the seminary should be in Cape Town.[47] In 1831 the question of the seminary was temporarily set aside when Philip concluded that there was no suitable person to run it. Agreeing that no inherent difference existed in 'the mental capacity of the Coloured races and whites at the Cape for acquiring knowledge', Philip and Foster argued that missionary children should be educated at LMS mission schools, 'suitably adapted'. The opening of the South African College in Cape Town in October 1829 helped Philip make this decision, for it provided the opportunity for the 'more promising boys' to attend College for two or three years preparatory to becoming schoolmasters ('let the dunces go from the institutions to the trades').[48]

As far as education of the poor was concerned, Cape Town was directly influenced by developments in Britain at the time. The people of import with whom the Philips corresponded when in Cape Town and interacted when in

Britain moved within intersecting circles of mission supporters, abolitionists and educational reformers.[49] The Philips, while not the sole innovators, drew on their friends for information and support as the Sunday school movement, monitorial schools and infant school system were all translated to the Cape context.

Just as Philip saw the South African College as helping to solve the problem of providing teachers for mission schools, so he recognised in the infant school system, introduced to Cape Town in 1830, a means of improving the quality of mission education. Philip was from the beginning involved in the establishment of the system in Cape Town and Miss Lyndall travelled from England to South Africa with the Philip family 'for the express purpose of introducing the Infant School System to the Colony'. The system did not remain the preserve of the LMS, for an interdenominational Infant School Society was soon established[50] and thereafter supervised and supported the functioning of the first infant schools.

In the introduction of the infant schools, Cape Town had a direct link with the more creative pre-schooling of contemporary Britain. It was William, the eldest son of Scottish weaver James Buchanan, founder of the infant school system, who arrived to set up an infant school for the poor at the same time as Miss Lyndall did so for more affluent children.[51] James Buchanan had run the New Lanark infant school at the time that Robert Owen, his famous employer, was experimenting with creating optimal conditions for healthy and happy social development. By all reports a gentle man, a lover of children who had used dance, music, stories, free play as well as 'object lessons' to occupy his charges, Buchanan was moved to London in 1818 by educational reformers keen to use his methods. It was Samuel Wilderspin who learnt from him and then became self-appointed populariser of the 'infant school system'.[52]

The initial freedom within the infant school system seems to have given way, under Wilderspin, to increasing regimentation and stress on the performance of memorised tasks by the 2–7-year-olds targeted.[53] It is nevertheless tantalising to speculate what Buchanan had learnt from his father and indeed from Mrs Buchanan, who had assisted in the London school; both of them eventually came to live with him and his half-brother David in Cape Town.[54] Certainly the infant schools shocked some Capetonians with their bold display of racial and cultural inclusiveness as their pupils paraded hand in hand on festival days, singing songs and proclaiming their unity.[55]

Initially two schools were established; the Lower School in Church Square which had William Buchanan as its 'Master', and the Upper School in St George's Street under Miss Lyndall.[56] Children from all economic classes were to be catered for, separately, with the more expensive Upper School aimed at those 'in better circumstances'. Miss Lyndall's school soon closed for lack of support, however, and it was for its role in the provision of education for the poor that the system was significant.

Neither 'nation' nor 'colour' was to play a role in deciding who should attend infant schools like that run by Buchanan for the 'Poor and Slave Population'. Here, it was hoped, was the means of moral and intellectual improvement for the poor of all groups. It was believed that the whole community would benefit if the poor were rescued from the vices associated with their poverty and trained in the habits of industry and responsibility. In 1831 the Lower School was attended by '24 free blacks, 37 English pupils, 17 Dutch pupils and 75 slaves sent by owners'.[57]

The success of Buchanan's school so impressed Philip that in 1832 he secured the permission of the Committee to send Buchanan to introduce the system to the mission institutions.[58] It was Buchanan's success in general, and particularly his success in drawing Muslim children into his school after 1834, that Philip later cited as a reason for his wife's efforts to establish mission schools in Cape Town on behalf of the LMS.[59]

The rapid growth of Islam amongst free blacks and especially amongst slaves in Cape Town had first been remarked upon by observers in the early 1820s. By 1825 there were 2167 Muslims in Cape Town, 1268 of whom were slaves.[60] The strength of Islam in Cape Town was first seriously brought to the attention of the LMS when Elliott joined the Society in 1828 after his four years of mission work aimed at converting Muslims to Christianity.[61]

Miles appears to have advocated an LMS mission directed specifically towards the Muslims but Philip, on his return to Cape Town, felt compelled to dispel any such ideas. It was not that he did not think that Islam was the religion of the 'false prophet', but rather that the strategy was ill founded. He could see no scriptural authority for isolating a section of a mixed community and concentrating efforts exclusively upon it. The call was to preach to every person.[62] His opposition to the LMS undertaking a separate mission to Muslims was further based on Elliott's own experience. Besides the fact that few Muslims could understand the archaic Malay in which his materials were printed, the imams had used their considerable influence to prevent Muslims from accepting Christian literature, nor would they allow Muslim children to attend the school which Elliott had proposed to establish for them.[63]

Philip felt that the 'aggressive operations' of Elliott's Muslim mission had done the very opposite of what was desired – it had closed the doors to Christianity. By 1831 Elliott was agreeing with Philip that any future work should take the form of 'a general mission to the Coloured people, heathen and Muhammedan'; he had in fact found that several Muslims allowed their children to attend Roggebaai school when they perceived that there was no intention of imposing the Christian religion upon them.

The matter was not simply one of converting Muslims to Christianity. It was gradually realised by the LMS missionaries that the Muslims were in fact more successful at mission work among the slaves in Cape Town than any Christians. They continued to be assisted by the slaveowners' opposition to Christian work among their slaves, believing as they did that a Christian slave could not be sold and might in fact be freed.

Both Philip and Elliott saw the institution of slavery as in itself corrupting society and hindering the cause of Christianity.[64] 'The consequences of slavery are complicated, extensive and awful and are not confined to any one class of the community,' wrote Philip. In his lengthy discussion of Islam and slavery in 1831 Philip stated: 'The treatment the Malays have received from what is called the Christian population, and the evils of slavery, have placed barriers in the way of our attempts to bring them to the knowledge of the truth as it is in Jesus, that nothing but some extraordinary exertion of Divine power, or some revolution that will break up and sweep away the existing forms of society, can remove.' The fact that the masters in their society were called Christian, as well as the kind of treatment received from these men, disposed slaves to turn to another religion.

Regardless of the kindness with which a slave might be treated by his master, a 'heathen' slave was not 'recognized as a member of Society; but [was] regarded as a base fragment, detached from the family of man, for the purpose of rendering unrequited services to them.' Should such a slave adopt the Christian faith, he might be admitted to a Christian church and 'be addressed from the pulpit as a Christian Brother' but that was the extent of his changed status. 'There is a wide difference in colonial estimation between a Christian slave and a Christian man; the former may be a member of a church, but the latter only is recognized as a member of Society.' Elliott contrasted this with the way a Muslim slave became fully included in that community. Another appeal of Islam was the appreciation that Muslims manumitted their slaves far more readily than did Christian owners. Doctrinal differences had their appeal too, for Islam promised the slave 'eternal separation from his Christian lord, and a separation much to the advantage of the oppressed party'.

Philip had never trespassed on the terrain of the SAMS by attempting to undertake work on behalf of the LMS among slaves, and he still did not. But a change of great significance – the 'revolution' which would 'sweep away the existing forms of society' – was thrust upon the Cape Colony in August 1833. In that month the Emancipation Act was passed by the British parliament, abolishing slavery throughout the empire as from 1 December 1834. A period of four years would follow in which ex-slaves were to remain as apprentices with their masters, making emancipation effective only from 1 December 1838. Nevertheless, from 1833 a new dimension was added to Philip's thinking about the work in South Africa and in Cape Town.

He hoped, in the first place, that the removal of the structures of slavery would result in 'a change for the better as regards vital religion in Cape Town'.[65]

He also realised that the release of thousands of slaves hitherto largely inaccessible to missionaries would provide new challenges for the LMS.[66] Some 5555 slaves lived in Cape Town, where the population now totalled 19,226.[67] With the strong appeal that Islam already had for Cape Town's slaves, the question was whether the LMS would stand aside and allow them to be drawn into the Muslim community; or would it prepare itself to do battle for the spiritual allegiance of these people?

It was the latter course that Philip later chose.[68] The introduction of a new system of education to Cape Town had already been perceived as a weapon in the battle. In addition, the revival taking place at the LMS Chapel was well on its way to producing the motivated corps of workers and supporters to help carry out the campaign. By January 1836, James Read jun. could write of Union Chapel:

> There is quite a stir among the dry bones in the place. Never was the Doctor's church in so flourishing a condition. At one time you would see the people all sit like statues, and one could almost read their wandering thoughts in their very countenances, but now you would [see] panting and longing for the good things of the Lord's house. There are no less than 10 prayer and other religious meetings kept by the members of the church during the week.[69]

EDUCATION BECOMES A PRIORITY, 1836–40

The period 1836–40 saw a burgeoning of LMS work in Cape Town, both that undertaken directly by the Society and that carried out indirectly through or in conjunction with members of Union Chapel. It was marked by great activity in the field of education, both religious and day school; the development of branch congregations in the poorer sections of Cape Town; and finally the appointment in December 1839 of the first permanent working missionary in Cape Town.

Between February 1836 and February 1838, Philip was once again absent from the city. This time he was in England, primarily to present evidence to the Select Committee on Aborigines about conditions on the Cape eastern frontier. Again there was a succession of missionaries arriving at and departing from Church Square. The Freemans, Williamses and Lockes held fort at different stages before Philip returned in August 1837, while Canham left the city during this time.[70] Shortly after his return, Philip set off on another tour of the interior stations and during his four-month absence, from October 1838 to February 1839, Henry Calderwood deputised in Cape Town.[71]

There was one person in particular who provided continuous leadership during this time, and the directors did not fail to recognise the value of her efforts. 'During the absence of Dr Philip from his post, the South African mission has been largely indebted to the unwearied attention and active zeal of Mrs Philip,' they wrote in their 1838 report.[72] The letters to the directors which accompanied her biannual accounts assumed virtually the nature of superintendent's reports during her husband's absence. It was she, more than any other individual, who was responsible for the establishment in Cape Town of the mission schools during this time.

Both Freeman and Williams were impressed by the diversity and vigour of the work carried on in Cape Town by the Union Chapel members. Besides services, prayer meetings and Bible classes at the Chapel,[73] they displayed a missionary zeal most evident in their efforts to distribute tracts throughout the city and to provide religious instruction for young people.[74] Ten Sunday schools containing 674 pupils had been established and were conducted by Union Chapel members at venues throughout the city by 1837, although the number of schools had declined to six by 1839. It appears that by the end of 1841 the Dorp Street Sunday schools operated independently, with Union Chapel members helping in the Barrack Street and Roggebaai Sunday schools.[75] In addition new evening classes for coloured men were started at the end of 1838, specifically for Malagash, which had apparently ended with Canham's departure.[76]

In England, from the last decades of the eighteenth century, the Sunday School Society had played an important role in teaching religious knowledge and reading to working-class children.[77] It seems that likewise in Cape Town in the 1830s Sunday schools were fulfilling some kind of educational as well as religious function. At the same time they removed from the streets children who might be drawn into the inappropriate Sabbath activities which at times disturbed respectable Capetonians.[78]

In 1836 the LMS embarked upon a new venture in Cape Town – the provision of day school education for the poor and predominantly coloured people of Cape Town. The advance of the LMS into this sphere was to be a feature of the years 1836–9. The social function of education for the poor had been acknowledged in the establishment of the infant school system in Cape Town. Its appeal became much stronger when it was realised that the day of final slave emancipation was drawing nearer and the challenge of Islam had not abated. Every apprentice child, heathen or Muslim, who could be brought into a Christian school could be 'nurtured and saved' and, through him, possibly his parents too. As Philip said in October 1837, 'Education [is] one of the most efficient remedies we can apply in the present circumstances.'[79]

There were two types of school established by the LMS during this period: the infant school already discussed and the 'British' school. The latter followed Joseph Lancaster's monitorial system and was promoted widely by the largely Nonconformist supporters of the British and Foreign School Society, established in 1813.[80] British schools generally catered for elementary school pupils from the age of 8. According to this system a single teacher could run a school for large numbers of pupils using monitors to teach the other children. The LMS schools in Cape Town operated with one teacher for often as many as 70 pupils.

During his brief return to Cape Town in 1836, Freeman oversaw the opening of an infant school in a Roeland Street store, principally for the children of the Malagash. This school was placed under the supervision of the committee of the South African Infant School Society and so, although its origin lay with the LMS, it did not remain under LMS control.[81] Thereafter Mrs Philip became the person to plan and organise the Society's schools. She also coordinated the financial arrangements, receiving sums collected in Cape Town by branches of the Auxiliary Missionary Society, allocating money for teachers' salaries and running costs, and reporting to the directors. She also received from the LMS in England money which seems to have been used primarily for the purchase of the school buildings.[82]

Philip described the LMS day schools as being 'taught by members of the Congregation and supported by them in connection with the London Missionary Society'.[83] On his return to South Africa, he tried to make up for the lack of a seminary in the country by tutoring certain young men, a practice he continued until 1843 at least. Among these were the young Jewish convert Edward Solomon, W.Y. Thomson and Mackay, all of whom helped at various stages with the schools and work based at the schools.[84]

Some of the teachers were brought to Cape Town from England in order to fill positions in the mission schools. In 1837 Philip maintained that they generally 'got more service out of educated young women in our schools than from men from England' and for this reason he would take three young women with him when he returned to Cape Town at the beginning of 1838.[85] This was at a time when the proportion of females to males was rising steadily in the British population, creating the 'largely ... middle-class problem of finding careers for unmarried middle-class ladies'.[86]

By this time, the new methods of education were making teaching a more acceptable activity, and one relatively easy for women to move into. Teaching was seen as 'an extension of childrearing' and requiring not more than a few weeks training.[87] Davidoff and Hall's research on the Birmingham area shows that 'many schoolmistresses were on the fringes of the middle class, particularly in the British and Foreign schools', which 'contributed to the low social standing of a woman in teaching'.[88] This could make a colonial position with a respected body like the London Missionary Society desirable, and provide the modest upward mobility and respectability which accrued to foreign missionaries of humble origin.[89]

The first day school established and operated by the LMS in Cape Town appears to have been a British school for girls in the old Wesleyan chapel in Barrack Street.[90] Through friends in London, Mrs Philip acquired the services as schoolmistress of Miss Buzzacot, who must have stood as proof of Philip's assertion that women teachers gave good service; in addition to teaching her 70 girls during the day she was, by December 1838, running an evening class for 'Adult Coloured females … several evenings a week besides the Sabbath'.[91] An infant department in a newly built school room was added at Barrack Street in 1839.

The acquisition of a school room provided the Society with the facilities and contacts for further work in an area. Day school pupils became Sunday school pupils, and vice versa, and services were held at the school room for the whole family. In March 1837 Williams wrote that, with the aid of a Dutch interpreter, he was preaching 'to the natives' in the Barrack Street school room on Thursday evenings.[92] Both prior to Williams's arrival and after his departure, Mr Vogelgezang of the Christian Instruction Society preached there and also supervised the Sunday school.[93]

The location of the third LMS school was a short way out of town at Papendorp, later known as Woodstock, where a new school room was erected on ground donated by a Union Chapel member. The poverty of the community and availability of cheap housing for former slaves convinced the Philips that it would be a good location for a school, but it did not prosper and was closed by 1841.[94]

In a letter dated 5 October 1837, Mrs Philip reported the purchase of a double-storeyed warehouse to be used for both a British and an infant school. She felt that it was in a good location as it was some distance from any school and 'in the midst of a large native population'. These must have been the Dorp Street school rooms, opened during the course of 1838. Meanwhile the old Roggebaai school room was abandoned – 'the schoolroom was so close and unhealthy' – and its pupils transferred to Dorp Street with their teacher, Edward Solomon.[95]

By August 1839 Mr Vogelgezang had replaced Solomon as teacher of the upstairs British school, and his eldest daughter Ann had replaced Miss Mathews at the infant school.[96] Vogelgezang subsequently became the LMS missionary based at Dorp Street, and the reports on his work for 1841 and 1842[97] describe pupils at the two schools as 'children of heathen, Mohamedans and of Christians'. In 1842 they totalled 300, of whom 288 were the children of former slaves. This indicates that these LMS schools were reaching the people whom they were intended to reach.

The infant school pupils, 110 in 1841 and 156 in 1842, were all under the age of 6. The infants were initially taught in Dutch, although later English was taught too. Miss Vogelgezang appears to have spent a good deal of time preparing materials in Dutch as only English 'reading books, hymns and other nessesery [*sic*] means for the guidance of the teacher' were available.

The upper school, also referred to by Vogelgezang as the juvenile school, catered for children over the age of 6. From 1840 he had as assistant teacher Abraham Johnson, the Muslim convert referred to in the opening paragraphs of this essay. The children were taught in English one day and Dutch the next. They learnt reading, writing, arithmetic and history. In the afternoons the girls were instructed in needlework by 'Mrs Molts, widow Wylen and G.M. Geyer', in order 'to make them useful for themselves and for their parents'. In his 1842 report Vogelgezang asked the LMS to distribute books to reward the most deserving children for their perseverance.

In May 1839 an infant school was reported to have been opened a few weeks previously for poor Dutch-speaking pupils in Rose Street but does not appear to have continued.

These, then, were the seven infant and juvenile schools started by the LMS between 1836 and 1839. Mrs Philip appears to have planned at least one more; this 'should be in a central situation and have a good house to accommodate the Head teacher and such as are acquiring the system.'[98] If such a school materialised, it fell under the control of the infant school committee and was not regarded as a LMS school. The question of obtaining someone to supervise the existing schools and to train teachers persisted, and led to the issue of a seminary in Cape Town being raised again for the first time since 1831.[99]

The LMS had relied almost completely on British or European recruits going to South Africa as missionaries and teachers. At the same time the Cape Colony was beginning to produce its own candidates for these positions; Union Chapel in particular was a source of teachers and potential missionaries. Edward Solomon and David Buchanan, younger half-brother to William and also an infant school teacher, were both reported in 1837 to be interested in acquiring training as missionaries.[100] As the situation then existed, they would have had to go to Gosport in Britain to obtain this. There seemed to be a strong case for the LMS allowing Philip to establish a seminary in Cape Town to train local white and 'native' missionaries and teachers. As Philip argued, not only would it save the expense of sending such men to Britain or of bringing already trained men from Britain, but locally trained men would possess special advantages. They would already have a knowledge of Dutch and 'of the habits and feelings of the natives'.[101]

Nevertheless, much to Philip's disappointment, the LMS failed to establish the seminary – possibly because by the 1840s finances were becoming a problem with the waning of evangelical enthusiasm in Britain.[102] Before the 1840s were very far under way, the LMS was beginning to think of ways of reducing costs and involvement, not of increasing its commitments.

In 1839, a government education department was established in the Cape and James Rose Innes appointed first Superintendent-General of Education.[103]

In January 1840 Philip wrote favourably of plans being formulated for colonial education, these including the subsidisation of mission schools. On condition that finances were provided for the education of 'the aborigines of the country and the children of Freedmen', he saw no reason to refuse the offer of aid. If the Society did refuse, it would itself have to pay out increasing amounts in teachers' salaries 'or have the mortification of seeing the education of the colony pass into less competent hands, and of losing our hold on the young generation, and with it the hope of our missionary labours'.[104] In December 1841, after having been involved in a struggle to have the newly established public schools opened to pupils of all classes and races, Philip was less optimistic. No relief had by that stage been given to the mission schools and he was convinced that government money would be absorbed by those able to pay for the education of their children, to the detriment of 'the colored children'.[105]

However, by 1844 there were, in and around Cape Town, 25 mission schools subsidised by the Cape government.[106] Almost certainly the LMS schools were included in this number, and they continued to play a very important part in the provision of education for the coloured community.

THE LMS IN CAPE TOWN GAINS A MISSIONARY AND LOSES A PASTOR, 1840-1

It is significant that, after 1840, the reports to the directors of the LMS contain very little information about the work at Union Chapel and an increasing amount about that based at Dorp Street. There appears to have been discussion and a great deal of uncertainty about the position of pastor at Union Chapel at this time. By contrast, the appointment of Mr M. Vogelgezang, a Dutch-speaking colonist, as LMS missionary 'to the coloured population, who speak the Dutch language',[107] saw the enlisting of a most energetic missionary.

Vogelgezang's appointment in December 1839 was directly connected with the recognition of the strength of Islam and the reality of slave emancipation. For years, and to no effect, the need for a LMS working missionary in Cape Town had been put forward. For the first time, in October 1837, Philip gave his support to the idea. His word appears to have been the directors' command in this instance, and by July 1838 he was able to write, 'I am truly thankful that we are to be allowed a missionary for Cape Town'.[108]

1 December 1838 arrived and went with a lack of disruption, which seems to have surprised and pleased the LMS missionaries.[109] Statistics indicate that the slave population moved almost wholesale into the Muslim community. From 2167 in 1825, the Muslim population had grown to 6492 in 1841.[110] Yet immediate impressions were that there was a notable move of former slaves into the churches. Nine months after emancipation, the *Commercial Advertiser* reported and lauded an increase in attendance at the churches, chapels and Sunday

schools of Cape Town, Wynberg and vicinity. This increase was 'not confined to any one class or color, and we hail it as a symptom of general improvement, and as sure indication of growing intelligence and refinement'.[111] And, in the words of the historian Shell, 'in the long run, emancipation aided Christianity more than Islam. The massive machinery of Victorian missionary endeavour, freed of the immoral association with slavery, began to gain more and more converts.'[112]

It was in this first year after emancipation that Vogelgezang's appointment was decided upon. He must have been well known to Philip because he had, as Christian Society missionary, been working closely with the LMS in Cape Town from March 1837 at least. It was an easy transition for Vogelgezang to make to LMS missionary based at Dorp Street, as his work there was already fairly well established.

Vogelgezang now formed a church which would become the heart of a new religious community in Cape Town. The church had an initial membership of 42,[113] and the church members appointed their own deacons, 'which [was] a strange thing in this place, considering that they [were] coloured men'.[114] His congregation comprised mainly former slaves, now mainly poor servants. In 1842 he explained the poverty of his church by stating that 'the income of the labourers and servants is very low through scarcity of work and the arrival of so many emancipated Africans. Some of these people work for a very low price, and some without receiving wages from their masters hence such a decrease in their wages.'[115]

The range of activities based at the Dorp Street school house in 1841 was extensive. Besides the two day schools operating there every day, an adult school was conducted by Vogelgezang's family and friends on Tuesday and Thursday evenings. Candidates for baptism met on Monday evenings before the 'very popular' public prayer meeting. Vogelgezang maintained that he had at times 400 persons under instruction. On Sundays services were held at Dorp Street, morning and evening, while two Sunday schools operated. That for children was conducted in English and that for adults, upstairs, in Dutch. The church acquired its own burial ground and formed, among its members, a United Assistance Burial Society to help members pay for medical care and funerals.

Vogelgezang's weekday afternoons were spent visiting the prison, 'the improving house', the hospital for aged and disabled slaves, and members of the congregation. He also tried to engender a missionary spirit in his church, so that his congregation was not simply the subject of missionary enterprise but the agent of this too. To this end he formed a branch of the Auxiliary Missionary Society, held monthly missionary prayer meetings and got his scholars to help him distribute tracts 'in public places, as on the parading plain, public road, jettee and the government garden'.

Subsequent reports are very much in this vein. An impassioned and graphically contrived plea for assistance in building a chapel for his ever-increasing

congregation was repeated on several occasions, ending, in one report: 'generous, philanthropical british christian hearts, do give us a place'.[116] It took some
time before it was granted but by the beginning of 1843 when church membership stood at 90,[117] money was being raised by the Cape Town Auxiliary
Missionary Society, amongst other benefactors, to build the chapel.[118]

Meanwhile an ageing Philip faced disputes with members of the Union
Chapel congregation[119] and with fellow missionaries over the appropriateness
of the old pattern of superintendency.[120] Feeling that he could not be effective
in this role while still pastoring the Capetonians, he resigned from the post in
1841.[121]

It was, despite his resignation, another three years before Philip's connection
with Union Chapel was finally severed. He agreed to continue as pastor until
the directors sent a suitable replacement to Cape Town. This person proved to
be difficult to find, for the shrinking but respectable congregation at Union
Chapel insisted that he had to be an experienced preacher and an 'able' man.
In arguing the case for such a person being appointed to Cape Town, representatives of the congregation followed some of the same lines of reasoning
presented when the establishment of an LMS chapel in Cape Town had first
been mooted. With an outstanding pastor and a growing church, the further
work of the LMS in South Africa would be promoted. Missionaries could be
raised on the spot.[122] 'Able ministers once established in the chief towns with
efficient churches, by them and their efforts the cause will extend to the rural
districts.'[123]

Eventually, on 27 August 1844, the man whom the directors had decided
upon, the Rev. J.C. Brown, arrived in Cape Town to take over from Philip as
pastor at Union Chapel. By this time Philip had also resigned as superintendent,[124] a position seriously under question in some circles by this time.
Although he was anxious to surrender the position, he still saw it as crucial:
'The interest in Cape Town cannot be lost without a prodigious loss to the
Society. I might say much upon the religious and moral influence of the
Agency in Cape Town not only on the Town itself, but also on the whole
colony.'[125] His measured, if emphatic, words were echoed by a typically impas-
sioned plea from the Dorp Street missionary:

> Dearly Beloved, where do you find a man which shall have a heart for the
> poor Aboriginees, for the neglected sons of Ham in Africa. O! let Dr
> Philip not have your permission to come to his native Country, and leave
> the sons of Africa; this worthy man has nearly shed his blood for the poor
> of my country ... There is one loud call, we must, if he leave us, have a
> person in this Town, to speak in time of need, (and this time is always) by
> the Government of this Place for your missions.[126]

We close with the directors vacillating about the role of superintendent. It had been over 25 years since Philip had assumed pastoral responsibility for the Union Chapel congregation and his departure signified the end of an era in Cape Town's ecclesiastical history.

CONCLUSION

There were two distinct features of the work developed by the LMS in Cape Town over the years under discussion. One was the relationship formed between Cape Town's white community and the LMS. By 1844 Union Chapel was still important enough to the LMS for it to supply the pastor, although the Chapel had passed the peak of its evangelistic activity. It had always been an almost exclusively white congregation and was by then very much a regular white urban church.

The other feature was the movement of the Society into more clearly recognisable mission work in what became known as the coloured community. At the beginning of the 1840s it was here that the focus of LMS work in Cape Town lay. It is impossible to assess the legacy of this work. Overall, little has been done to investigate the social history of the descendants of Cape Town's slaves in the decades after emancipation.[127] What is evident is that, as Vogelgezang pointed out regularly with regard to ex-slaves in his congregation, they were poor and generally stayed poor. They lacked access to capital, possessed few skills, and typically pursued occupations like fishing and laundering, and so freedom rarely meant social mobility.[128] It is not possible to judge whether missionary intervention elevated a particular segment of the Cape Town community. Greater access to education and church support structures may have helped; Abraham Johnson, the Dorp Street assistant teacher, for example, earned £35 per annum in 1842, which enabled him to support his family.[129]

There is no doubt that former slaves valued their freedom, as is demonstrated in the way emancipation was commemorated each year.[130] For many, this was done in a consciously Christian and communal way. We began the essay with one such occasion. We conclude with another. Commenting in October 1842 that on the third anniversary of 'our congregation', the Union Chapel was 'full of the coloured sons of Africa, under my care', Vogelgezang reported that his deacons had called for another meeting at 6 p.m. on 1 December. 'They felt they should have a meeting of the whole community for most were slaves before, but now emancipated through the goodness of God ... though mainly poor servants now.'[131]

CONGREGATIONS, MISSIONARIES AND THE GRAHAMSTOWN SCHISM OF 1842–3

Robert Ross

The London Missionary Society was founded as an interdenominational, evangelical body. Its early missionaries came from a variety of ecclesiastical backgrounds. It was broad enough in its appeal to include Dutch Calvinists, German Lutherans, Scottish Presbyterians and even a few low Anglicans among its employees. As the nineteenth century progressed, however, it became increasingly associated with the Congregational, or Independent, churches, both Scottish and English. In part, this was because the other churches came to found their own societies, which naturally enough attracted the vast majority of those in their ranks who were potential missionaries.

As its name implies, Congregationalism has stressed the importance of the local Christian community in deciding, under God, upon matters affecting individual churches. For as far back as the reign of Elizabeth I, Independent congregations have had their *raison d'être* in the rejection of any ecclesiastical hierarchy. It is the community of believers which calls, which pays and which can dismiss its minister, and which is in general responsible for the good running of the church.

This is a form of church government which necessarily sits ill at ease with mission work, though it does not in any way preclude the impulse to preach the gospel as widely as possible. The essence of a mission entails a degree of authority. A missionary is, almost by definition, an individual who proclaims the Word to unbelievers. Thus, given the assumption, which missionaries (and their converts) shared, that Christians are superior to non-Christians, he – very rarely she – is above, and has authority over, those who are new in the faith. Certainly, the heathen should have nothing to say about the specific qualities of the missionary from whom they were to be privileged to receive the good news.

This sort of description is, of course, a caricature of missionary views. Equally, it is factually untrue, at least in South Africa. Very shortly after the arrival of the first missionaries, Africans came to understand that there were all sorts of distinctions to be made between the various missionaries. In consequence, certain individuals and certain societies might answer their secular (and

indeed spiritual) requirements better than others. But this was altogether different from the tensions which could arise between a missionary and a church
which was establishing itself. At what point did the newly founded church have
the same rights as any in the country from which the missionary derived? This
was not such a problem for Wesleyan Methodists, Anglicans or Catholics, who
had institutions, such as conference or the bishopric, which could make and
impose decisions from above. For the Congregationalists, in contrast, this could
create major difficulties.

The way it should have gone is clear. In 1856, James Read jun. described
how the church in the Kat River was run.

> Our church is half Presbyterian and half Independent, that is there are lay
> elders & their office [is] to watch doctrine, to exhort at the out-stations,
> catechise the young & the inquirers. The work of the deacons is to attend
> to the wants of the poor & other secular matters of the church such [as]
> keeping the church and ministers' house in repair while they also take part
> in the general running [?] of the church. The choice of Pastor & other
> church officers & the reception and exclusion of members is with the
> entire body of the church.

This constitution, 'well-defined and written down', allowed James Read to be
certain that the church was functioning well even when he was 700 miles away
in the western Cape, recovering his mental health and lobbying in the aftermath of the Kat River Rebellion.[1]

This form of church government could only work when there was a degree
of confidence between the minister and the congregation, that is to say when
the missionary was prepared to view the members of his congregation as his
equals, even though they might be called to a different station in life. This was
certainly the basic orientation held by Johannes van der Kemp and James Read
sen., who had created the church order which the latter's son was describing.
Read indeed was proud of the fact that 'half a word of dissatisfaction would
remove me, old as I am, into the wilderness'.[2] It was not an attitude which was
shared by all the missionaries, even of the LMS. As the nineteenth century progressed, the effort which was required to assume equality was replaced by a far
greater emphasis on tutelage, by a stress on the subordination of the flock to the
pastor and by what can only be described as latent racism. It is difficult to be
certain whence this came. Certainly, the social distance between missionaries
and their flocks increased. The sexual scandals of the 1810s had led to the ending of marriages between missionaries and their converts, and thus the absence
of kin links between them.[3] Further contributions to this trend included the
institutionalisation of missions in Great Britain, and the waning of the influence
of Van der Kemp, probably the only LMS missionary for whom his calling to

the field entailed a sharp decline in social status; most rose socially as a result.

This change of attitude had initially most effect within the ranks of the missionaries themselves. Conflicts developed on two fronts. The first was with regard to the establishment of a district system within the Society. At first sight, these might seem to have been innocuous bodies, as they provided for regular communication between the missionaries in the various parts of South Africa, and allowed them to discuss matters of common interest. In fact, of course, they were anything but innocuous. Their proponents, notably Robert Moffat in Bechuanaland and Henry Calderwood on the eastern Cape frontier, sought a radical reorganisation of the way in which the missions of the LMS were governed. Power was to be concentrated in the hands of the ministers, as the laity, even including 'native teachers', were not accorded access to them.[4] Their proponents believed that the committees would do away with the monarchical powers exercised by the superintendent, Dr John Philip, who was despised and hated, particularly by Moffat. Their opponents, notably Philip himself, argued that such committees would take the running of the churches away from the congregations themselves, and place them under 'a Presbytery of Ministers', without even the representation of the churches themselves, 'which is the Presbyterian principle'. This was a problem particularly for the Griqua and Kat River churches, which, not being mission institutions, were differently constituted from those at, for example, Bethelsdorp.[5] Philip might have added that the same problem would occur in the town missions. In private, opponents might comment that the committee system was a ploy orchestrated by Robert Moffat to allow him to control the Griquatown church, with which he had a long conflict and whose accusations of adultery against him almost cost him his career.[6]

These committees worked to restrict the access of the converts and their descendants to power within churches. Such a matter revolved around the question of African 'agency', as it was described, that is to say the extent to which Africans would be allowed to act as paid agents of the mission, to preach and teach, and broadly to take over the tasks of the missionaries. In the early years of the LMS mission in South Africa, and elsewhere, African agents were widely employed. The Rev. John Campbell, defending this, even commented that the early church would not have got very far if the apostles had not allowed converts to preach the gospel.[7]

After about 1820, though, there was increasing distrust among many missionaries of such agents. There were Europeans jealous of Africans whose access to potential converts was so much greater; they wished to maintain their own hierarchical control over the churches and judged the African agents by an impossibly high standard, and found them wanting. On the other hand, there were those, notably James Read sen. (again), who did all they could to foster African agency. Indeed his church in the Kat River valley, with its many outstations, would not have prospered as it did without the active involvement of the elders, deacons and paid school masters in its work. Read compared those who were trained by his son with his own accomplishments when he had first come to South Africa almost half a century earlier, a comparison greatly to the advantage – in his eyes – of his converts.[8] He also considered his colleagues as being particularly lax in this matter. In a bitter letter to his friend, the Rev. James Kitchingman, he wrote as follows:

> Few of the Brethren think as we do respecting Native Agency in any way, and I fear the feeling respecting colour is retrograding. With us [in the Kat River] we are pushing on to raise the people in the scale of society: others are for leaving them behind or pushing them back … It was assuring to James [jun.] and I at our last meeting to hear the Brethren speak of Native Agency, how to raise it, etc. I thought of Rowland Hill, who said that when a Socinian spoke of Christ it was like an ass eating raw thistles.[9]

In general, these matters remained between the missionaries, although it is reasonable to assume that their congregations knew rather more of the discussions and dissensions among them than many of the missionaries would have cared to know or admit. In the 1840s, however, these attitudes came out into the open within the LMS church at Grahamstown, in a conflict which spilled over beyond the bounds of that town.

Grahamstown, which had been founded in 1812, was by the 1840s a rising commercial centre. It was, of course, the spiritual home of the British 1820 Settlers, and had a population of around 6000, three-quarters of whom were white.[10] Also, a considerable number of men and women of predominantly Khoikhoi descent came to live in the town during the 1820s, if not earlier. By 1829, there were said to be as many as 400 living in mat huts or 'temporary sheds' around the town. A year later, a location was laid out for the Khoi, but was described as containing 'a parcel of wretched straw or rush hovels'.[11] As elsewhere, many of these came to be associated with the LMS. It was for the LMS that the Graham's Town Auxiliary Missionary Society built the Union Chapel, which was consecrated in 1827. In that year, there were said to be 'upwards of 200' Khoikhoi in the Sunday school and, by 1834, 305, 'of whom only 48 are children of European parents'.[12] Nevertheless the congregation was of a variegated background. The Rev. Colin Fraser, a Scottish clergyman who was the Dutch Reformed minister in Beaufort West, preached on one occasion there to 'a crowded congregation of Boors, English, Hottentots, Caffres and Mantaties promiscuously seated and united in solemn worship.'[13]

This easy non-racialism did not last. The foundation of a Dutch Reformed Church in the town drew away the white Dutch-speakers. In the Chapel, services were soon held alternately in English and Dutch. The former attracted

British settlers of Congregationalist (and no doubt other Nonconformist) per-
suasion; the latter primarily Khoikhoi living near the Grahamstown burial
ground in the 'Hottentot village', which had been founded around 1830. While
English prosperity in Grahamstown waxed, that of the Khoi declined, particularly it would seem during and after the war of 1834–5.[14] The degree of social
distance within the town was clearly increasing, as was political tension, exacerbated by the attacks made by the *Graham's Town Journal* against the Kat River
Settlement, in particular.[15]

In 1838 the Rev. John Monro, who had served the LMS in Grahamstown
since the foundation of the mission fifteen years earlier, was replaced by the
Rev. John Locke, a man of a very different stamp. Monro had been a schoolmaster in Bethelsdorp before moving to Grahamstown, and had imbibed much
of the ethos of that place. For him the spiritual life, and the social advancement,
of his Khoi congregation were paramount. Locke, who was by this time in his
mid-thirties, was nevertheless new to the Colony. He had been a minister for
five years in England, and was described by James Read, after he had met him
in London, as 'one of our sort'.[16]

This was not a prediction which was to be borne out. Locke did not speak
Dutch, at least initially, and on his arrival in Grahamstown was drawn into the
English society of Grahamstown. His 'ideas of the people were begotten and
matured in Graham's Town Society and must bear resemblance to it'. It was
rumoured that he did not invite the coloured church members into his house,
'seldom spoke with them in any other place than his kitchen', and did not
encourage any intercourse between them and his wife. 'He used to say that the
people were still in their pupillage, and should be treated like children. Would
not such an opinion lead to his treating them with contempt?'[17] Much of his
work in his early years was concerned with the building of a new chapel, in
Bathurst Street, in a much more salubrious neighbourhood than the old
church. On 13 April 1840 the Civil Commissioner of Albany, Martin West, laid
the foundation stone after a procession through the town, including the 91st
Regiment of the British army, led by Colonel Somerset. Eight months later it
was opened. Its exterior was not yet finished, but it was clear that the propor-
tions were good. Its front, so the *Graham's Town Journal* claimed, had a 'chaste
simplicity'. In total it cost £2369, including £800 raised on a loan, which was
to be paid off over the next four years. Furthermore, 'the Chapel hitherto used
by the Independent congregation will be in future appropriated for the
Coloured Classes connected with that denomination.'[18]

During the early years of Locke's ministry, the pastoral care for the Dutch-
speaking members of the church – who in the nature of things were the principal objects of mission work – devolved on Nicolas Smit. A native of South
Africa, he had been converted to evangelical Christianity, apparently by Monro,
and had given up a lucrative position as a clerk in a commercial establishment

to become a teacher for the mission. His motives were at once religious and philanthropic, and he later commented that 'the Hottentots were the first people towards whom my sympathies were awakened', possibly by seeing the degradation in the town.[19] 'He came down to [the coloured people] and having been used to the coloured people from his youth there was a natural sympathy between him and the people.'[20] He was very energetic for the cause of the mission. As James Read later described his actions, in addition to running the school for coloured children, 'He continued … to itinerate round the town, and to visit the homes, or rather huts of the Hottentots and other coloured people for whose souls no one cared, especially in the time of the measles and small pox. He likewise exerted himself for the poor deluded people attending the canteen and was the means of reclaiming many of them.'[21]

He was by this time regularly preaching twice every Sunday, and more frequently when he went to visit the outstations of the Grahamstown mission, and in addition two or three times during the week, as well as visiting the sick and attending 'the several meetings of the Hottentots for prayers'. The deacons of the Grahamstown church, all Englishmen (to judge from their names), recommended that Smit be ordained, as not only did he deserve the attention but it would also make matters far more convenient if he could 'administer the ordinances of the gospel'.[22] On 26 August 1842 this ceremony was duly performed. Smit was henceforth to labour alongside Locke. He worked hard, describing his work as follows:

> I have school five days in the week, commencing at half past nine in the morning and closing at three in the afternoon, letting the children go out for a short time at twelve. I preach twice on Sundays. On Monday evenings I preside at the Native Prayer meeting. On Tuesday evenings I preach at the Chapel, and after the service I preside at the inquirers meeting. On Thursday afternoons I preach at the Native hospital. I have commenced a Dutch service at a private house (my mother's) on Friday evenings, to which many of the colored people (I believe as many as know of it) come. I visit the sick whenever there are any. To make the practice of visiting the people at their houses here is not as convenient as at the institutions, most of them being in service. The members, however, often visit me at my home. The inquirers also are in the habit of constantly visiting me at my house, where besides talking to them about their state at the inquirers meeting, I endeavour to instruct them in the things of God. Saturdays I spend in the study of the Word.[23]

It quickly became evident that cooperation between the two ministers would not run smoothly. Even aside from the political differences between the two men in an increasingly polarising LMS, there were tensions inherent in the circumstances of their relationship. Locke had to accept as his equal a younger man who had once been his protégé, whom he denied ever having recommended for ordination, and who was much better accepted by part of the congregation. Nevertheless, he himself was determined to maintain his hierarchical superiority. As he said, 'Have I not been the recognized pastor? I have sole charge, both in the white and native church.'[24] The relative responsibilities and competencies of two men within a single cure were not spelled out, and were interpreted differently. The potential for conflict was great.

It erupted within six months of Smit's ordination. About 17 October 1842 Smit received a request from the congregation at Long Bush, a farm forty to fifty miles from Grahamstown which was apparently one of the few places in the Colony where people of Khoisan descent owned land in freehold.[25] They sent horses for his transportation and requested that he bring the marriage register with him, so that he could marry a couple whose banns had been called some time previously. Smit therefore went to Locke to collect the register, but was refused it. Locke claimed that it was only lawful for the pastors of churches to marry, and that as Smit 'was neither pastor nor co-pastor', he could not perform the ceremony or indeed any other religious ordinance without Locke's leave. Smit therefore went off to Long Bush merely to preach, and left the couple in question unmarried.[26]

Locke later admitted that he had made a mistake in ecclesiastical procedure, and perhaps the matter should be left at that. However, there are hints that there were deeper questions involved. The people in question – we do not know their names – had been 'living together in sin for several years', and as a result of Locke's refusal Smit could not 'draw them out of the sin' in which 'they continued some months longer'.[27] It had been regular practice in Grahamstown under Monro for couples who declared that they had 'intermarried with each other' some years earlier, and had had children, to have their marriages solemnised in church.[28] All churches which impose discipline on their members have in such cases to decide whether it is preferable to end the sin as quickly as possible, by marrying the parties, or whether some show of remorse and period of separation is necessary before the marriage can take place. It is difficult to say how far Locke, who came from the disciplinarian background of British Nonconformity, held views on the matter which differed from those of Smit, and indeed the Khoikhoi congregation, but the possibility is certainly there.

The consequence of this difference of opinion was a full-scale breakdown of relations between Locke and Smit. The situation became unworkable, and within a few months Smit had decided that for the good of the church he should remove from the town. He went to live in the Kat River Settlement, under the aegis of the Reads, and here his skills as a printer were much appreciated.[29]

The quarrel did not remain simply a quarrel between the two men. Had it done so, it would have been merely one of many, as missionaries were notoriously combative, and would scarcely be worthy of extended treatment. It was, however, taken up by the congregations in question, particularly the coloured one. Locke found this painful, particularly as he prided himself on the success of his work among them. When he arrived, he wrote, 'there was no temperance society, no native miss[ionary] society, no church meeting, no deacons in connexion with the native church, only me preaching on the sabbath; no visiting any out station. These arrangements have all been made by myself. I have been accustomed to preach to them twice every week.'[30] There were certainly those among the congregation who supported Locke. Three deacons, Philip Arian, Plaatje Nieuveld and Adam Johannes, wrote to claim that a majority had remained within the church.[31] It seems unlikely that their analysis of the relative strengths of the parties was correct. Another letter, signed by three other deacons, Piet Vandervoort, Dirk Cole and Christian Slinger, and by nine subscribers, was sent to the directors of the LMS in the following terms:

We the people lately under the charge of Mr. Smith[32] who is now removed to Cat River for what reason we know not, all that we can now say it was against our feeling, as we considered him our Minister and he was ordained expressly in the presences of the Church of the Union Chapel of Graham's Town as our lawful minister. We never did understand that Mr. Lock was our Minister no more than other Servants of God who might occasionally preach to us.

But as Mr Lock still continued to claim the exclusive right to administer the Sacraments of the New Testament to us, we as a church began to call his claim in question as we did not nor are we inclined to acknowledge him for our Minister. We therefore wish to know from you why Mr. Smith might not be allowed to administer to us the Ordinance of the Gospel instead of Mr Lock.

They were aware that Smit had left of his own accord, but disputed the suggestion that he was the cause of the disaffection. Rather, 'since Mr. Monro left us the said Mr. Smit was our Schoolmaster and our preacher except the Sacrament and Baptism, and since Mr. Lock began to build his church for the English people we began to talk together that we will have Mr. Smit for our minister for then we will have a church for ourselves.' Of the 130 members of the church, they believed, a hundred had seceded and only thirty remained with Locke.[33] They were busy arranging a subscription so as to be able to pay Smit, and indeed in 1842 they had raised £75 for his salary.[34] Later they were able to promise to raise £60 per annum for him on a regular basis, no small sum for a poor congregation which was vulnerable to the wild fluctuations of the commercial economy of the eastern Cape.[35]

In an attempt to achieve a settlement in this dispute, three ministers, including John Monro the previous pastor, were sent to Grahamstown to mediate between the parties. Their efforts failed, however,[36] and the matter was brought before the newly instituted Eastern District Committee of the LMS, which was attended by Robert Moffat, who happened to be in the area, as well as by those who were present by virtue of their eastern Cape charges.[37] The majority, led by Moffat and Henry Calderwood, saw the actions of the seceding portion of the Grahamstown church as a threat to the authority of the ordained missionaries, and thus by extension of white pre-eminence.[38] Locke expressed the matter most cogently. He argued that Smit's conduct had

> rendered the opposition to his having the sole charge of the people absolutely necessary, not merely for their sake, but for the promotion of a proper spirit among the native churches generally. If these people, through unreasonable and wicked opposition, had succeeded in their object, would it not have furnished a precedent for others to follow when any dispute may occur between them and their missionaries. The unhallowed spirit of the persons whom Mr. Smit has encouraged and cherished has been displayed not to me only, but to others. The Miss[ionary] brethren appointed Messrs. Moffat & Brownlee to talk with them, but, the attempt quite failed, for while the former was affectionately pointing out to them their duty and showing them whence dissensions in churches originated many of them following in the rear of their leader rose up and left the chapel.[39]

An alternative description of this episode, the one that reached the Reads, is that the exodus followed Moffat's remarks that there is a 'devilish feeling among you'. A deacon then told him that the people had taken great umbrage 'because you call God's church devils'.[40]

Nearly three years later an attempt was made by John Philip to resolve the schism in the Grahamstown church by offering the pastorate of the coloured congregation to Gottlob Schreiner, but he declined. He refused because he did not want to become involved with a church which believed that it had the right to appoint its own minister, particularly as it had not called him. He believed that the Reads had been responsible for developing this spirit among the people, not apparently believing that the congregation could articulate independently the ideas which were inherent in the LMS's denominational background. Schreiner had considerable animus against James Read, who had been very critical of his actions during his first ministry, in Philippolis. Schreiner had moreover suffered there from his inability to work together with a powerful church council.[41] It is, however, interesting to speculate how different South African literary history would have been if Schreiner's daughter

Olive had grown up in Grahamstown, not in the Herschel district.

In the nature of the divided politics of the LMS, there were those who thoroughly supported Smit and, more importantly, the congregation. By far the most prominent of these were the James Reads, father and son. There is certainly a degree of personal animosity in the comments which they make towards some fellow missionaries, above all on Robert Moffat, an old enemy who had nearly ruined the elder man's missionary career a quarter of a century earlier. There is an excusable glee in their description of his humiliation in Grahamstown. On the other hand, they saw the whole episode both as an opportunity to develop their own ideas of proper ecclesiastical government and as yet another battleground on which the rights of the converts had to be defended.

Initially, James Read sen. saw the actions as presaging 'the commencement of voluntaryism among the Hottentots or natives in this country and of independency or congregationalism'.[42] Soon, and certainly at the meeting of the Eastern District Committee, he found himself having to defend the right of congregations to call their own ministers. He found numerous precedents in South Africa, notably in his own call to Philipton in the Kat River and, most damningly, in the fact that the whites of Grahamstown had given Locke 'a regular call' without their committing themselves to paying his salary.[43] The Reads' stance was supported by the elders and deacons of their own church in the Kat River, who had met Smit – he had come to live among them – and had many contacts and probably bonds of kinship with the Grahamstown people. Their basic argument, impeccably Congregational in its tenets, was that 'as long as a church and a people can agree and the moral character of the Missionary is good, no Missionary should be removed from a regularly formed church without the church being consulted.' Conversely they claimed their right, as they saw it, to give a regular call to its ministers.[44]

In time, the conflict at Grahamstown lost its urgency. Smit and Locke were reconciled, although exactly how and on what terms is not known. Smit returned to Grahamstown in 1846,[45] where he laboured until he died in 1881. Locke got cancer, and died in 1848. The two churches remained separated, as they have to this day, the white church as Trinity Church within the Congregationalist denomination[46] and the coloured, eventually, transferring to the Dutch Reformed Sendingkerk.

What, then, was the significance of all this? It would seem to lie in two directions. First, within the mission church itself, it formed the overture to a major restructuring, the discussions about which dominated the LMS in the 1850s – at least once the problems surrounding the so-called Kat River Rebellion had died down. In the discussions about the form of independence to be enjoyed by the Grahamstown coloured church, matters of money continually came up. The assumption, surely not very scriptural, was that a congregation could only have the rights it could buy, or, to put it another way, the right to choose a pastor entailed the duty to support him.

This was most attractive for the LMS, whose financial circumstances were becoming increasingly straitened. The mission communities of the eastern Cape were seen as draining the resources of the Society to a degree which was no longer justifiable, given their prosperity. They should be required to find for themselves, as in the long term charity would be 'a real evil rather than a benefit'. The money so saved should be used for the true purposes of the Society, namely the evangelisation of the heathen, preferably to the north of the Cape, among the Tswana. (This last is the subtext which explains why Robert Moffat in particular, who had attempted to bring the people of Grahamstown back to allegiance to their pastor, was now so keen to impose independence on them.) Indeed it was also suggested that the missionary institutions themselves, including Bethelsdorp, should be divided up between their inhabitants. In this way, they could acquire the property and thus progress in civilisation, at least within the property-driven ideology which was now taking hold.[47]

The second area of significance was less tangible but no less important. It has to do with the development of political consciousness. After all, the whole matter would not have been a serious problem if the majority of the coloured congregation had not held firm to its decision in favour of Smit, and against Locke. This entailed an affirmation of rights by a group whose position within colony society had hitherto been subordinate and silent. It was thus one of the several expressions of Khoikhoi nationalism which were to be heard from around 1830 up to the early 1850s. Most of the others were more specifically political, such as the agitation against the vagrancy laws in 1834.[48] That this sort of political awareness should be manifested within the confines of a church is, however, neither strange nor unusual. There were a number of other similar events at more or less the same time, involving people attached to other missions, mainly involving congregations of primarily slave descent.[49] The churches provided arenas for self-expression and self-definition that were otherwise still largely absent in Cape colonial society.

The congregation, or at least the coloured community of Grahamstown, remained politically involved. In about 1847 they sent their own memorial to the government in respect of the Masters and Servants Ordinance.[50] Smit himself had this community, among others, in mind when in 1851 he wrote that 'many of the Hottentots attend the public meetings of the English at which they have examples to satisfy their minds about the real state of feeling towards the coloured races. Many of them also read the frontier papers which with scarcely an exception exhibit the very state [?] of feelings towards them.'[51]

Admittedly, by the middle of 1851, it was not difficult to be political in Grahamstown. There were rumours flying around that people in Grahamstown were in contact with the Kat River rebels. In the month before Smit wrote, a hundred men of the Albany Rangers, under the leadership of Thomas Stubbs, had gone rampaging through the 'Hottentot location', burning it to the ground, after the magistrate had ordered that the huts be searched.[52] In the year or so following, a number of rebel Khoi, quite possibly with kin among Smit's congregation, were hanged publicly in the town.[53] In the subsequent years, the descendants of the eastern Cape Khoi tended to be politically reticent, except for their participation in elections. The experience of the rebellion makes this thoroughly understandable.[54] Nevertheless, the coloured community of Grahamstown maintained control of its church. Congregationalist principles of ecclesiastical organisation had given them and their fellows elsewhere in the Colony the space in which and the confidence with which they could assert themselves.

WHOSE GOSPEL?
CONFLICT IN THE LMS IN THE EARLY 1840S

Elizabeth Elbourne

By the 1840s, the character of the British missionary movement as a whole was shifting in significant ways with the rapid growth of settler colonialism, the institutionalisation of missionary activity, the growing respectability of evangelicalism and the entwining of missions with the imperial project more broadly. In this essay I wish to examine the lesser known transformations, which were of political importance to a number of African communities, as they found the LMS an increasingly unreliable partner in the struggle to maintain political rights and to forge direct links with the British crown over the heads of antagonistic whites. At the same time Africans both within and beyond colonial boundaries were either making an independent use of Christianity increasingly divorced from missionary input, or moving away from earlier expressions of interest.

Several key interrelated processes were at work. The LMS was being compelled by social and economic circumstances, including financial problems, to make the transition from a missionary society in southern Africa to an institutionalised church. Like other missionary societies, it often handled this transition badly. A growing corps of African school teachers and 'native agents' were developing career paths within the church, even if they themselves might not have thought of their evangelical activity in such instrumentalist terms. Their professionalisation, and the rapid development of an African clergy, were being blocked at the mid-century by the racial anxieties of many of their white colleagues.

Many white missionaries, furthermore, were unwilling to accept the more self-confident claims of black congregations whose fledgeling attempts to exercise the privileges of Congregationalism, including the choice of ministers, were threatening to an insecure group suffering from status anxiety in both 'black' and 'white' communities. The increased respectability of the missionary movement, combined with the growth of settler society, led to an influx of missionaries who did not want to sacrifice membership in the white community and who emulated the higher status of domestic ministers. Missionaries therefore were arriving, expecting to be ministers with powerful control over their congregations; African churches wanted white missionaries to missionise other Africans and in some cases to act as intermediaries for them with the state, not to control existing churches. Partly in consequence, there were significant power struggles among white missionaries themselves, in which different models of church government and current conflicts in Scotland were mobilised in order to bolster competing claims to authority. Theological debates with European roots were, however, reinterpreted at the Cape through the prism of racial politics and struggles over the ownership of the gospel.

I want to address these issues through the microcosm of an intense conflict in the early 1840s between two white missionaries, the elderly James Read sen., missionary maverick bound by kinship ties to the Khoikhoi community of the Cape, and the younger Henry Calderwood, a Scotsman who had arrived in 1839, eventually to become a government agent in 1846 and a prime mover in efforts at the forcible 'civilisation' and christianisation of the Xhosa in the wake of the War of the Axe. The two men thus represented very different interpretations of the relationship between missionaries, Africans, empire, and white settler society. Calderwood's attempt to destroy Read and his son James in 1843 is a useful way to begin to unravel the complicated tensions of the early 1840s – and in some ways a microcosm of the ambiguous role of missions in imperialism. The ambiguity of lines of authority in evangelical Christianity, and the slipperiness of Christianity as a political tool, may even help explain why creative Xhosa chiefs such as Maqoma ultimately turned away from experimenting with missionaries as potentially useful political agents and became willing instead to experiment with innovative millenarian prophecy with Christian elements.

POWER STRUGGLES WITHIN THE LMS

Tensions were already high in the LMS in the early 1840s, as also in the broader Christian community. The most immediate cause of conflict in the LMS was over the issue of whether African congregations could call their own ministers, and veto the choice of missionaries to their communities made by the parent missionary society. The question exploded in debate over the so-called Grahamstown schism, in which part of the congregation of the missionary John Locke left in order to follow another missionary, Nicolas Smit, after Locke attempted to oust Smit. Robert Ross discusses this case in detail elsewhere in this volume, in an essay which is very apposite to this one.[1] As Ross points out, the affair brought to the surface tensions over the rights of African congregations, theoretically permitted in the Congregationalist tradition, to choose their own ministers. In the Scottish Presbyterian kirk in which a few Scottish missionaries of the (dominantly Congregationalist) LMS and probably all of the (Presbyterian) Glasgow Missionary Society had been brought up, the issue of a congregational veto over the choice of ministers was a topic of virulent debate by the 1830s and 1840s between 'moderates' and 'evangelicals' – in fact, as good evangelicals most Scottish missionaries ought in fact to have been more firmly on the side of the Grahamstown seceders than they were.[2] James Read and his family, most importantly his eldest son James, were firmly behind the Smit faction and upheld the rights of congregations to independent choice. The quarrels I examine here are in a sense the next stage of the story told by Ross, as the underlying disputes over authority which had ignited the conflict continued to fester.

A second, related cause of deep-seated tension among LMS missionaries was, as Robert Ross also underscores, debate over whether the existing system of having an LMS superintendent for Africa, who oversaw relatively autonomous stations, ought to be replaced by one of district committees on which only ordained missionaries would be represented, and through which missionaries would come to majority decisions and discipline one another. No final decision had been reached on this issue by the LMS directors in the early 1840s, but a large number of LMS missionaries in southern Africa were pushing for it. In June 1843, on his return from Britain, Robert Moffat helped organise a committee for the eastern frontier in conjunction with his colleague Henry Calderwood, before proceeding north to organise another committee to run his home region of Transorangia, encompassing the Griqua and Tswana missions.[3]

Deeply committed to the principle of congregational autonomy, the Reads saw a committee system as a covert form of oppression. Read sen. was convinced that men such as Robert Moffat (missionary to Tswana groups at Kuruman beyond the colonial frontier) and Henry Calderwood (initially stationed among Xhosa groups at Blinkwater near the Reads' own territory, the independent Khoikhoi community of Kat River) wanted a committee system in order to centralise power in the hands of white missionaries and to bypass African influence. In particular, Read felt that missionary committees would bypass the local church government of deacons and elders staffed for the most part by Africans. This was of particular importance in view of the centrality of church officials to the running of churches within both the Congregationalist and Presbyterian traditions. Deacons and elders were selected by congregations themselves. Not only was this an important instance of local democracy, particularly given the considerable power wielded by churches in Khoikhoi communities, it was also a vehicle for proclaiming the respectability of those chosen for the office and thus more broadly of the community itself.

In contrast, Robert Moffat had been involved for years in power struggles with neighbouring Griqua communities on whom, ironically, he had depended for military protection throughout the turbulent 1820s, if not beyond.[4] Griqua chiefs, who had an instrumentalist attitude to the many LMS missionaries whom they compelled over the years to leave their own communities, saw Moffat as a threat to their local political hegemony, including their own attempts to missionise the Tswana; some had even attempted to get Moffat dismissed on the time-honoured grounds of adultery.[5] Read thought that Moffat fought for a district committee system beyond the northern frontier of the Colony in order finally to get the Griqua church, its outstations and officials firmly under his control.[6] For its defenders, however, the committee system was more democratic than the potentially despotic rule of one man.[7]

Behind these debates, not surprisingly, loomed intense conflict over the role of the actual superintendent, John Philip, and his political actions such as agitation in Britain for the return of Xhosa land in the wake of the 1834–5 frontier war and support for the post-war treaty system along the eastern frontier. Quarrels were lent further piquancy by even longer-standing divisions: Moffat's hatred of Read, for example, dated back many years to Read's adultery and the related fact that Moffat had taken over a mission founded by Read and evangelists from Read's early station of Bethelsdorp whom Moffat had then proceeded to oust.[8] Throughout his long life in southern Africa, Read, already tainted by scandal and politically a more vulnerable figure than Philip, had borne the brunt of attacks from his colleagues and other fellow whites in part for what were perceived to be his naive and dangerous pro-African political stances, particularly his testimony before the House of Commons Select Committee on Aborigines.[9] Read, Philip and the LMS more broadly had been bitterly attacked by settlers over the past half-century, and at least some LMS missionaries found the widespread criticism difficult to bear.

In 1843 Calderwood, Richard Birt and others of their party had censured Philip for the role he played in the Grahamstown affair. They would continue to do so late into 1844, and would send a letter reiterating their case against Philip in the same package as their documents against the Reads.[10] In the face of conflict the elderly Philip would first tender and then withdraw his resignation in 1844. Read was Philip's closest ally in South Africa, as well as a key player in the disputes of the 1830s; as such, he became a symbol of unwarranted metropolitan interference in both disputes, and one of the most hated men in the Colony. The attack by several missionaries against Read was therefore political in ways which went well beyond the immediate questions.

THE QUARREL

The actual affair that triggered a two-year split between factions of missionaries in both the LMS and the former Glasgow Missionary Society, as well as an attempt to oust James Read sen. was, all the same, as James Read jun. put it in May 1844, 'in itself a very silly one, and scarcely worth noticing'.[11] In early 1844 the Reads, father and son, were summoned to a meeting at Block Drift on the

Tyhume River, within the boundaries of what was then Xhosaland. The ostensible goal of the meeting was to adjudicate the smouldering quarrels between missionaries of the two factions of what had been the Glasgow Missionary Society (GMS), both working among the Xhosa. Political and theological conflicts in Scotland over the relationship of church and state had divided the GMS – although tellingly the split had been concealed from Xhosa congregations in order to avoid 'imprudent excitement'.[12]

The 'voluntarists' who formed the new Glasgow African Missionary Society (GAMS) argued for the complete disestablishment of the state-supported Church of Scotland, and felt that religious allegiance should be voluntary and churches financially independent of the state. Their rivals in the Glasgow Missionary Society, adhering to the Principles of the Church of Scotland, continued to believe in and belong to a tax-supported Scottish national church, even if Scottish evangelicals in general did not feel that the state should have any control over doctrine and ecclesiastical discipline.[13] Although the two societies had initially continued to hold common presbytery meetings, the presbyteries split during the conflicts of 1842. The passion involved reflected the disputatious, even envenomed, nature of Scottish religious culture in the 1830s and 1840s, in the run-up to the final split of the Church of Scotland itself in 1843. What this suggests more broadly is that disputes over spiritual authority and its relationship to temporal authority were occurring in parallel in Scotland and the Cape Colony, both industrialising countries with an expanding potential electorate in which debates about political citizenship interacted with debates about the relationship of church and state.

The immediate dispute was more mundane. Shortly after his arrival in Africa, Robert Niven of the GAMS had established an outstation at John Pringle's farm of Glen Thorn in the Mancazana valley at the instigation of the Pringle family, who were without 'religious Instruction for themselves, their families and dependants'.[14] John Pringle – brother of the better known poet, newspaper man and evangelical ally Thomas Pringle – built a new church and supported a 'female Native Teacher' named Notishe. Two white missionaries preached there alternately once a month, with Notishe presumably left in charge the rest of the time, until the arrival in Africa of GAMS missionary John Cumming, who settled temporarily at Glen Thorn while awaiting a permanent minister, the Rev. Mr Hepburn and a school teacher, a Mr Withers, from the home society. Once Hepburn finally arrived several months later, however, he found fault with the arrangements: he claimed that his accommodation was 'not fit for a Minister', and moved to a new house at Baviaans River twenty miles away from the new church, where he ministered to a white congregation. He demanded that Notishe be sent away, and threatened that if she did not leave then, he would not baptise her. By this point Notishe was running a 'school for the native children', while Withers was running an 'academy', presumably for the white children.[15]

In all this, there were power struggles over the degree of respect to be accorded to a white missionary. Hepburn was able to call on the white man's exclusive access to the sacred power of baptism in order to rein in Notishe – underscoring recurrent conflict in Christianity over whether sacred power is individual or channelled through institutions and community rituals. Hepburn also mobilised existing disputes between white power-brokers in the neighbourhood, as he exploited divisions between John Pringle and his brother to get up a 'party'.[16] After extended quarrels, accusations of falsehood and furious exchanges of documents, the GAMS finally decided to dismiss Hepburn. Henry Calderwood of the LMS and a number of other missionaries to the Xhosa from the other Glasgow Missionary Society branch opposed the GAMS board decision and called a missionary conclave to urge the directors to reconsider.

The Reads later attested that they assumed this meeting would include representatives from both the quarrelling parties. They were shocked to discover on their arrival that only the supporters of Hepburn were present, all from the opposing wing of the former GMS, and that his opponents had absented themselves, considering the meeting 'a piece of unjustifiable interference with the private affairs of a kindred society, and as setting a bad precedent in future cases'.[17] Read sen. in particular felt that the meeting was illegitimate and that it was wrong to read the documents of another society and to meddle in its affairs.[18] His objections were, however, overturned. Ultimately the meeting voted unanimously to urge the GAMS board to review the case of Hepburn. After the meeting, Read wrote privately to his friend Dr Gavin Struthers, GAMS secretary, to explain his participation in the meeting and to express his discomfort at interfering in the affairs of another society.[19]

Henry Calderwood heard that someone in the meeting had written to the GAMS through a convoluted chain of rumour, which in itself points to the strained relations among the frontier missionaries and the fervour with which some were looking for any excuse to bring down the Reads. Read sen. mentioned his letter to Cumming of the GAMS; Cumming then told his fellow GAMS missionary Thomas Campbell, who in turn, while at dinner at Frederick Gottlieb Kayser's house, informed the aged LMS missionary to the Xhosa that someone at the Block Drift meeting, whom Campbell refused to name, was opposed to their proceedings and had written to Glasgow. The 'old German Gentleman', in the words of the Xhosa diplomatic agent and Calderwood foe, Charles Lennox Stretch, 'asserted there was "Treason" and putting his own construction on the case wrote to *his* friends from whom have emanated documents which for their own sake I wish had never existed'.[20] Calderwood required each person who had been present at the original meeting to sign a document attesting that he had not written to the GAMS to 'controvert' the resolution passed by the meeting; he took Read's initial refusal to sign as an admission of guilt. On 30 April 1844 Calderwood located, supposedly through a fortuitous accident, a letter awaiting delivery at the Fort Beaufort post office, addressed to Dr Struthers in James Read's handwriting. This at last was the proof for which he had been hunting to condemn Read.

The following day, eleven missionaries spearheaded by Calderwood circulated a statement of censure of Read sen., accusing him of acting 'dishonestly' and 'insiduously' and of 'dishonorable' conduct. They attested that unless Read could explain himself they would be 'obviously under the necessity of withholding their confidence from him in future'[21] – a 'wretched exhibition of animosity and uncharitableness', according to the Read supporter and GAMS missionary Niven.[22] 'Eleven,' lamented Read, 'just the number that sold Joseph for an Egyptian slave … The Doctor [Philip] pities *them* and other Brethren consider that I have not acted wrong, but a broken, shivered *reed* against eleven *cedars* is, as the Caffres say, *no joke.*'[23] With the exception of the German Kayser, all the signatories were Scots; four worked for the LMS and six for the old GMS, while W.R. Thomson was a Scottish Presbyterian minister and government agent at Kat River who opposed Read's frontier policy.

Although Read transmitted the gist of his letter to Struthers, Calderwood and his allies accused Read of lying. In the meantime, Cumming and Campbell denied that their evidence was as conclusive as Calderwood claimed, while Campbell in particular furiously attacked Kayser for having abused the privacy of the family dinner table.[24] With increasing anger over the next few months, the missionary committee tried to compel Cumming and Campbell to rescind their testimonies. 'Unless you adopt measures to clear yourself we will be compelled to regard you as deliberately abetting falsehood and calumny,' wrote William Govan in fury to Cumming in December 1844.[25] This, responded Cumming, echoing Scotland's past history of political violence around church–state relations, was

> the language of one holding the Bible in one hand and a sword in the other saying – if you do not acknowledge the truth of this Book you shall feel the power of the destructive weapon. Is it possible think you that any Christian man should succumb so far to the sword *in terrorem* as to comply unconditionally with your request?[26]

By the end of January 1845, the missionary committee was meeting on the issue of Cumming and Campbell, hinting at censure should they not change their stories. Despite these background quarrels and mitigating circumstances, the anti-Read group persisted.[27]

A further piece in the case against the Reads fell into place seven months after the original Block Drift meeting, in September 1844, when the indefatigable Calderwood intercepted another envelope, addressed, as he put it, in a woman's handwriting to two Khoikhoi church officials, Arie van Rooyen and Valentyn Jacobs, of Calderwood's own parish at Blinkwater. Through the thin paper he saw nonetheless that the handwriting of the letter itself was that of James Read jun., and assumed immediately that an attempt at deception was under way. Calderwood therefore violated his policy of not discussing missionary politics with non-whites, and called together 'the Hottentot portion of his Deacons and Elders'. In Calderwood's words (note the status distinctions of naming):

> Mr C asked Arie & Valentyn if Mr Read had informed them of what had happened between him & the Missionaries – Arie said, *Mr. Read* had said nothing – Valentyn said he had heard something. – Mr C did not like to press them further on this point – He then related to them what had occurred & knowing Messr Read had acted secretly in the Grahamstown affair, he related also what the three Brothers appointed by the Directors had done in Grahamstown. – And this statement respecting the conduct of the Reads should never have been made to any of the Natives had not, in connection with other circumstances, J Read's letter been put into Mr C's hands, which excited suspicions that have proved too well founded. Mr C then produced the letter addressed to Arie van Rooyen and as Arie was proceeding to open it Mr C said 'I feel strongly impressed with the conviction that there is something improper in that letter. I see through the paper that it is James Read's hand and the address is disguised & after what has happened I have a right to suspect that there is something more in that letter. I therefore as your Friend & Pastor beg a sight of that letter.' After much hesitation Arie allowed Mr C to read it, & after Mr C read it he stated that 'such a letter could not be *fairly* considered as private property'. Mr C therefore begged the letter in order if possible to check the dishonourable & serious conduct of Mr Read towards the people & his Brethren …[28]

The letter included an informal discussion of Read's joint plans with Van Rooyen and Jacobs, and referred to 'the suspicious C.', for whose opinion Read affirmed he did not care tuppence: 'ik geef geen dubbeltjie'. Read threatened that the missionary committee should 'feel it' if their upcoming meeting mentioned his name or that of his father. He discussed the injustice of the Grahamstown case, disagreeing with the principle that the LMS ultimately enunciated of only allowing congregations freedom of choice regarding ministers if members were able to support the minister from their own pockets. He concluded the letter by instructing Van Rooyen and Jacobs to burn it after reading.[29]

This second letter, and a very angry subsequent exchange of letters between

Read jun. and Calderwood on one another's sins, furnished sufficient ground for Calderwood and his associates to forward all the relevant documents concerning the events of that year to London on 26 September 1844, and to call for the dismissal of the Reads from the service of the LMS. The attempt failed, however; neither the LMS superintendent and Read ally, John Philip, nor John Fairbairn, when asked by the LMS directors to adjudicate the affair, could find anything reprehensible in the conduct of either of the Reads. The 1846 War of the Axe between the Xhosa and the Cape Colony eventually overrode these more parochial concerns. By the end of 1846, Calderwood had left the service of the LMS and had accepted a post as government agent in newly conquered Xhosa territory.

IMPLICATIONS: AUTHORITY AND THE GOSPEL

The issue of authority was at the heart of this convoluted and unappealing debate: who had it and how was it to be enforced? This occurred at a number of levels. The first was dispute over church government. The meetings which condemned the Reads were presented as acts of collective will, representing the district committee system in action. As minutes and letters frequently attested, meetings opened with prayer, as God was invoked as speaking through the acts of the community. The meeting initially condemned Read for seeming to concur with and then supposedly seeking to undermine a majority decision: 'we learned that a member of our meeting had violated the confidence which we are bound to repose in one another and had done a previous injury in the cause of truth and to his Brethren by attempting to controvert a decision in which he himself had fully concurred', as Govan put it in a bitter letter to Cumming.[30] Calderwood wrote in the first person plural, representing himself as the simple conduit of the meeting's opinion, even discussing himself as 'Mr. C.'. An underlying trope in this approach was that of God moving a group to action: the rhetoric of group solidarity permitted an intrinsic appeal to divine authority.

Calderwood and his allies were obviously using this dispute to attack Philip and to entrench the committee system of which Read was such a passionate opponent. Read was essentially accused of being a maverick who worked in secret to undermine the decisions of the majority of his brethren; this paralleled his position against the district committee system. It was no coincidence that two days before the Calderwood faction sent its documents back to London to obtain Read's dismissal, the Reads were the first signatories of an appeal against committee government. Not only, this document claimed, was such a system absurd in a country in which missionaries were too remote to function effectively as a collectivity, but a committee permitted the suspension of individual moral conscience: 'it may commit the most egregious blunders, or the most flagrant injustice, and there is no one to bear the blame and individual character is often merged in the movements of associated bodies, so that the wisdom and uprightness of the persons forming such associations are no guarantee for the wisdom and equity of their corporate acts.'[31]

Three weeks later, Calderwood and others wrote a lengthy document attacking Read's arguments: only those guilty of ungentlemanly and dishonourable conduct truly had to fear the so-called tyranny of the majority. To prefer a superintendency was worthy only of an episcopalian: 'for Dissenters and *congregational Dissenters too*, to argue that they must have Bishops or mock-bishops placed over them *because* an association of Brethren is an irresponsible and dangerous thing, is surely like a new thing under the Sun'. A superintendent was potentially tyrannical; he might, for example, gain information from 'improper quarters', while a 'missionary who may be so dishonourably inclined, has *peculiar facilities* for acting in an underhanded manner against his Brethren'.[32]

Debates over church government had inescapable echoes in European history and contemporary politics for their European participants. On the most basic level they reflected splits between episcopalians, Presbyterians, who had fought civil war in the seventeenth century to establish church self-government through presbyteries of ministers rather than bishops, and Independents or Congregationalists, who favoured self-government by each congregation alone. Read sen. commented to a friend that the district committee system 'strikes at the very root of the fundamental principle of our Society. It is establishing Presbyterianism ... The thing is worse than Presbyterianism, because in their synods and presbyteries there are always laymen to represent the churches. In the system proposed the churches are entirely at the mercy of the reverends.'[33]

In the Scottish Disruption of 1843 the national church split into two as evangelicals left the established church to form the Free Church of Scotland, in a dispute with wide-ranging political implications.[34] Although there were many underlying tensions, the issue on which the church split was precisely that of state control over the appointment of ministers over the objections of a majority of male heads of family in a given congregation.[35] Read considered that the 'fatal' struggle in the Scottish church had arisen precisely because 'to force a pastor upon a church without in any way to consider its judgement or feelings would be to hand over God's heritage', and used the example to illustrate the need for South African churches to choose their own ministers.[36] The GMS as a whole, like most missionaries, voted in 1843 to join the Free Church, as did other Scottish ministers at the Cape.[37] To support the free choice of congregations in 1843 was thus a very political act, which proclaimed the independence of the church from secular authority.

What Read was doing that riled fellow evangelicals was implicitly comparing the missionary society to the intrusionist state, and equating the rights of black (or mostly black) congregations to choose ministers with the right of the church to be free from secular interference. Scottish missionaries, even fervent voluntarists such as Richard Birt (who eagerly requested the LMS to dispatch his deceased wife's sister to the Cape Colony so he could marry her despite such a marriage's technical illegality), failed to see the parallel. The LMS as a corporate whole argued that only congregations which paid for their own minister had veto rights – and indeed in Scottish Presbyterianism the right of veto was vested only in the male 'heads of families'. As was the case in debates over democracy, the notion of political rights founded in property could be used to limit that of universality, with particular application in a racially diverse community.

In societies – African mission stations and industrialising Scotland alike – in which ministers and elders had great power over the members of their congregations, including wide-ranging powers of discipline for moral offences, these disputes over church government were important for community life. Note too that ministers in the established Church of Scotland by the early nineteenth century tended to be at an educational, financial and social remove from their poorer parishioners.[38] Debates over church government mattered particularly for a Scottish tradition in which synods acted as powerful church courts. Like the Scottish-dominated synod of 1817, the Block Drift meeting and its successors were essentially trying to act like Scottish church courts, exerting legal as well as moral control over the community of the faithful.

At the same time, vigorous Scottish reformers in the 1840s, like their reforming counterparts in England, tended to want the tightening up of church control, in parallel with extending actual church presence in poor areas (often seen as dechristianised and 'savage'). Thomas Chalmers, leader of the Free Church forces, called for a more tightly disciplined parish system which would give churches and church officers much extended social control over their parishioners in poor areas; he saw this as a solution to the immiseration and moral decay occasioned by industrialisation, and opposed demoralising state 'charity'. The implications were for the most part conservative, as Chalmers recommended tighter social control over the poor, rather than the alleviation of their material misery.[39] The confrontation between the older Read and the younger Calderwood was also, then, a confrontation between different evangelical cultures. In South Africa race complemented class, but similar issues were at stake in the drive to christianise, or rechristianise, the masses: after conversion, was the church an institution for moral police directed by accredited agents, or was its primary aim the continued spread of Christianity by the newly converted themselves, whatever the loss of institutional control this involved?

Secondly, the debate over church government echoed debate over the role of the imperial government in white settler colonies. By the 1840s, white British settlers across the political spectrum were pushing for a legislative assembly in South Africa and a correspondingly greater degree of local autonomy from imperial rule. The aftermath of the 1834–5 frontier war, in which LMS superintendent, John Philip, had been instrumental in gaining the return of Queen Adelaide's land to the Xhosa in large part through a relationship with parliamentary abolitionist leader Sir Thomas Fowell Buxton that permitted Philip to intervene at the imperial centre over the heads of settlers and local officials, was taken by many as a prime example of problems both with imperial government and with the LMS system of superintendency. Both committee government and settler self-government were presented as inherently more democratic, although in both cases opponents might argue that democracy permitted the hegemony of white men. During the frontier war of 1850–3, for example, many Khoikhoi joined the side of the Xhosa in part because they disliked the advent of settler government and the loss of the potential for the imperial government to act as a referee in local power disputes; Griqua leaders in the 1840s, manoeuvring to avoid Voortrekker dominance and keen to mobilise missionaries as diplomatic agents, opposed the district committee system on similar grounds.[40]

Authority relations were also at stake in less tangible ways. Underlying the complaints of fellow missionaries against Read, as indeed against Smit and Philip in the Grahamstown case, was the sense that they had crossed over the line between missionaries and 'the people', and owed their allegiance to converts rather than to fellow missionaries. This came out with particular acuity in Calderwood's attack on James Read jun. in the wake of the incident of Read's letter to Van Rooyen and Jacobs. Read jun. had a foot in two camps: he was the child of a white missionary and an African mother, and had been raised in an African community while being active all his life in missionary activity, in common with a number of his friends and associates in the important Khoikhoi missionary drive which I discuss in more detail below. Read jun. clearly troubled Calderwood. He was indubitably a missionary, but could he be trusted? In a lengthy attack on Read jun., Calderwood complained, for example:

> Considering the circumstances and natural disposition of the Natives generally, all who know this country will admit that a more serious offence against the souls of the people and the comfort and confidence of Miss[ionary] Brethren could scarcely be committed than that which Mr Read has many a time committed in speaking and writing to the Natives in the manner of which this letter is a sample. It should also be here considered that there is an important difference between Missionaries conversing however freely amongst themselves, about their fellow missionaries, and this *kind* of intercourse which the Mssrs Read have with the Native people. To speak or write of his Brethren secretly, in this manner to any one even the most intelligent Europeans would be highly dishonourable & [wicked to do?], but to do so to the Natives is *cruel* to them &

unfairness towards his Brethren in no common degree. It is also worthy of remark on this point that while Mr. J. R. speaks with the greatest disrespect & *affected* scorn & that [too?] in the *lowest terms* of the Missionaries, he speaks to & of the people in terms of marked respect and affection.[41]

To this Read jun. responded tartly:

That I wrote a letter to Arie and Valentyn is true: but that I wrote to the one *as an elder* and the other as a deacon is not correct but *friends* with whom I was on terms of intimacy long before you thought of coming to this country: and with whom I was in the habit of corresponding before you knew anything of them, or they of you …[42]

Read conveyed a keen sense of the missionary as an outsider, without the roots in a given community to claim the kind of respect men such as Calderwood expected to command as ministers. Calderwood, on the other hand, clearly wanted to build up a brotherhood of missionaries bound together to one another above all and separated from their congregations by complex etiquettes of racial and professional exclusion. Indeed, he and others inadvertently conveyed a sense of their own loneliness and isolation as they stressed, as part of their plea for a committee system, that 'missionaries are necessarily removed from many of those social, moral and religious advantages which are continually operating for good on Brethren at home. It is therefore a most serious evil to keep up any system the natural tendency of which is to diminish our dependence upon and responsibility to one another.'[43]

Locke cast his complaint against Nicolas Smit in similar terms of the violation of boundaries in a letter to the LMS board of 25 September 1844, written a day before the district committee called for Read's dismissal. Smit had illicitly shared private information with the Grahamstown congregation, Locke contended. In a striking denial of Khoikhoi agency, Locke continued to claim that Smit and 'some other parties' had 'acted upon' the Grahamstown seceders, and that Smit had 'countenanced and encouraged them in the manifestation of a most improper spirit towards me and their fellow members'. In injured tones, Locke described his relationship to his congregation in terms of a violated relationship, undercut by a skilful competitor: 'until the period of the unpleasant occurrence I had always been on the best of terms with the people & had every reason to believe that I had a place in their affections'.[44] Similarly, even the accusation of 26 September brought against Philip by the district committee was, as Birt and Calderwood put it, precisely

not that he had removed Mr. Smit but that he had written to Mr. Smit to inform him (Dr. P.) as to the feelings of Mr. Locke's people on certain points, and that too without first communicating with Mr. Locke. Dr. Philip may blame Mr. Smit, as he does, for having communicated with the people *as he did*, but how could Mr. Smit possibly answer *with truth*, the questions of Dr. Philip without communicating with the people, and which communication we must still think could produce *only* evil in the Church.[45]

In all these cases, it was the crossing of boundaries between the missionary brotherhood and the missionaries' congregations which was at the heart of the problem. This reflected a preoccupation with drawing lines between the private and the public: communications between missionaries were private, while the missionary's relationship with his congregation was in the public sphere. James Read straddled the division between private and public, as did his entire 'mixed-race' family. He thus became a spy within the ranks. Cumming's attack on Kayser for his betrayal of a 'private' conversation reflected a similar anxiety about the need to keep private and public separate.

The distinction between minister and 'people', the private world of white equals and the public world of work with unequal blacks, which Calderwood was so anxious to mobilise was surely reflected in the social stratification of Cape society by race: worlds coexisted and overlapped, but the majority of whites did not for the most part accord non-whites the social status of equals. An anecdote in passing told by James Read sen. about Tys Jurie, who had recently died at the Kat River Settlement, is revealing:

altho a man of colour he was in his dress and address the Gentleman. He had once to call at a house in Grahams Town, the servant opening the door and not taking notice of the face, ran and said there was a gentleman at the door – he was ordered to the Parlour, but when the Lady came she was surprised to find that it was a gentleman with a brown face.[46]

In a similar play on notions of gentility and of race, James McKay, even though he criticised racial prejudice and struggled to persuade rural Dutch-speaking whites to attend school with blacks in the 1860s, told the following anecdote about the Khoikhoi rebellion of 1850–3, during which he was a sergeant in the British army. A man and his wife escaped from Wilhelm Uithaalder's rebel encampment, which was in a state of starvation.

The vrouw said that it was pitiful to see so many fine *young ladies* going about perfectly naked and half starved. On enquiring what ladies she meant, she replied bastard and Hottentot 'ladies'. Of course I and others laughed heartily at the expression, and wondered what the ladies of

Britain would think when they heard of the miserable plight their sisters were in.[47]

It is telling that Calderwood's complaints against James Read and his son dwelt so extensively both on gentility and on false appearances. The Reads posed as gentlemen, but in reality they were 'dishonourable', acting in secret an 'ungentlemanly' role. The missionaries would therefore be compelled to 'withdraw the right hand of fellowship'. Hand-shaking had an important role in dissenting churches, as it was a sign of community inclusion; there was also, as Robert Ross has written, a complicated 'etiquette of race' around the shaking of hands at the Cape. As Nicholas Pos put it bluntly in 1868, 'no white inhabitant of the Cape gives a coloured his hand'.[48] While it would be deeply unfair to suggest without further evidence that the signatories of the letters against the Reads upheld these colonial prejudices, it is nonetheless noteworthy that to withdraw the right hand of fellowship was still a racially and socially charged gesture.

English speakers had strong prejudices about race, respectability and 'civilisation' which permitted even those who deplored Afrikaner and (more problematically) English settler behaviour towards Africans nonetheless to distance themselves socially from non-whites and to elaborate a code of honour which still categorised non-whites as intrinsically less honourable than whites. In this one can see the emergence of a newly dominant form of white missionary liberalism which defended black rights from a careful social distance, while assuming white superiority.

Despite these racial expectations about a white community of the honourable and respectable, worthy of black esteem, it does not seem farfetched to suggest that many missionaries actually felt very insecure about their personal relationships to their congregations (and thus all the more likely to rely on their colleagues emotionally). Furthermore, this insecurity was justified. Calderwood was much disliked by most in Kat River, as James Read jun. stressed when he rehashed old incidents and reminded Calderwood that he and his father had in fact fought to 'reconcile' the people to Calderwood.[49] According to the Reads, they had given Calderwood 'a portion of their Missionary sphere (Blinkwater) with a good Kaffre and Hottentot congregation many members and inquirers with two schools and Schoolmasters', and had then struggled to 'heal breaches caused by his (Mr. C's) temper abrupt manners and ignorance of native character'.[50] The work of Donovan Williams and others on Xhosa reactions to missionaries before the cataclysmic events of the 1850s has long suggested that the bulk of white missionaries in Xhosaland were relatively ineffectual.[51] Even a laudatory and quasi-official 1873 history of Free Church missions comments gloomily that in the early days 'the [Xhosa] men, as a rule, treated their preaching with indifference, and the women with bitter hostility', while in the late

1840s a cash-strapped Free Church contemplated abandoning its South African missions altogether.[52]

By the mid-1840s, many missionaries to the Xhosa, with the exception of Ross and Niven of the GAMS, were perceived by Xhosa chiefs as working against their political interests in supporting changes to the treaty system.[53] In March 1845 Philip stated baldly to the LMS, 'you must know that the Caffreland missionaries have lost the confidence of the chiefs … The Reads form the only party among our missionaries in whom the chiefs have confidence and this is one cause of the hostile feelings manifested against the Reads and the reason why they find it necessary to give up holding intercourse with the chiefs'.[54] To take just one example, despite Calderwood's stated admiration for Maqoma's intelligence and ready wit, the relationship between the two men was very strained by the early 1840s: a substantial part of Calderwood's 1858 memoir *Caffres and Caffre Missions* was devoted to a vindication of his side of quarrels with Maqoma.[55]

A further underlying issue related to these questions of racial distinction and of social insecurity was that of whether the missionary should work with 'white' congregations. There was a growing tendency among churches, including the Grahamstown church, to segment into white and black congregations which worshipped separately, even in different buildings. Kat River congregations were mixed. Read felt strongly that missionaries should not work at all with white congregations, as they inevitably absorbed most of the missionary's time and effort. On the other hand, Calderwood's *Caffres and Caffre Missions* called for missionaries to minister to both whites and blacks.

One particular anecdote in support ironically underscored the status anxieties that afflicted Calderwood: the minister, by then employed as government agent, recounted that he had helped spiritually a white colonel's wife on her sickbed, despite the fact that the colonel himself had earlier treated Calderwood with a 'marked disrespect', due to his 'enmity to my religious views and character', such that Calderwood requested the Governor to 'cause him to understand the respect that was due at least to my official position'. The colonel's wife recovered but the colonel unexpectedly died in a most satisfactory manner after being seized with a cold following Calderwood's spiritual ministrations. 'All this rose out of the circumstance, under the Divine blessing, of Mr. Laing and myself being led to keep up an English service every Sabbath.'[56] It does not seem far-fetched to read between the lines of Calderwood's account considerable anxiety to be included himself in the community of the respected and the respectable.

Similarly, one of the underlying criticisms of Locke in the Grahamstown affair was that he focused too much on his white congregation. This was also one of the issues at stake in the Hepburn case, which started the entire attempt to oust Read: Hepburn had been concerned to live in a salubrious situation with a white congregation. Commenting on the Hepburn affair, Read criticised the whole policy of having missionaries work with whites in his infamous letter to Struthers.

White missionaries arguably felt all the more insecure because people of African backgrounds, particularly Khoikhoi, were carrying out evangelisation in a way which threatened white control. In theory (and in practice for some agents), the London Missionary Society was committed to creating an African ordained ministry and phasing itself out. This was typical of the preaching patterns put into practice in Britain during the early years of the late-eighteenth-century evangelical revival: itinerant preachers in the 'dark areas' of Britain, often themselves unlicensed as ministers, tried to evoke religious conversions, rather than establishing themselves as the permanent ministers of new congregations. The late-eighteenth-century tradition, in which James Read had cut his teeth as a young itinerant preacher among the 'dark villages' of Essex in John Eyre's revivalist Hackney church, was in fact self-consciously opposed to the sclerosis of excessive institutionalisation and stressed the action of the Holy Spirit through the most humble and unlikely of vessels.[57] In practice, by the mid-nineteenth century in South Africa the concept of missionary tutelage for an indefinite period seemed firmly entrenched.

Several parallel developments were taking place. In Britain itself, evangelicalism had become far more institutionally dominant and less oriented to revival, as well as politically more conservative. The missionary enterprise was far more seen as an expression of British cultural superiority to the non-Western world and less as an offshoot of a shared revivalist culture with little initial distinction made between darkest Africa and darkest Essex. A romantic discourse about missions was already well entrenched in British popular culture by the mid-nineteenth century, as the character of St John Rivers in *Jane Eyre* would suggest: the white missionary met African people with little or no experience of civilisation or of Christianity, preferably dwelling in wildernesses, who were brought to Christ under his paternal guidance. In the meantime in southern Africa itself, on the one hand, African networks were actually becoming more professionalised and more extensive – a reality which it was often hard for the newly arrived missionary operating with a romantic self-image to grasp. On the other hand, the white LMS itself was in retreat from the concept of an African ministry, as many missionaries claimed that Africans were not sufficiently civilised, while more advanced training for native agency and eventual ordination in itself was becoming a topic for acrimonious debate.

It had not escaped missionary notice, furthermore, that Christianity was often used as part of a subversive spiritual bricolage: had not Nxele, war prophet in 1819 and Xhosa national hero, initially preached a version of Christianity, to be transformed into the idea of separate Gods for whites and for blacks? What was Christianity if its boundaries could not be policed by its accredited agents?

In this context, native agency, which both exemplified the successes of Christianity and yet threatened to take it in worryingly uncontrolled directions, evoked ambiguous reactions for many. Henry Calderwood unwittingly expressed some of that ambiguity well in *Caffres and Caffre Missions.* Calderwood extolled several Xhosa 'native agents' and stressed the importance of native agency by Xhosa and Mfengu (not, one notes, Khoikhoi) in Xhosaland. Nonetheless, 'they require, however, constant superintendence and assistance ... There is a certain inertia in the native mind that requires continual pressure from without, with judicious instruction and superintendence. But with such instruction and supervision, native agency is of the very highest importance.'[58]

By the 1840s there were well-organised networks of 'native agents', based at the Kat River Settlement, who were running a network of outstations and *de facto* mission stations under the leadership of James Read sen. and his sons but certainly without 'constant superintendence and assistance'. Kat River native agents were partially financed by Kat River inhabitants; the Auxiliary Missionary Society, for example, held annual meetings and publicised the names of donors and the size of their contributions, like its sister organisations elsewhere, in a way which doubtless also publicised the respectability of contributors. In 1844 Read was able to report that 'we had a good meeting. Our income was then [three weeks ago] about £220; 'tis now upwards of £250, and daily more coming in; 'twill reach at least £260, if not £270.'[59] Agents were also funded by private donors in Britain. Like the school teachers who were important intermediaries in the Kat River Settlement (some of whom resigned in the 1840s because they weren't being paid enough), a number of these 'native agents' were essentially employees – although contractually of whom is not entirely clear – in the sense that they were working full-time in exchange for a small salary. Read was able to mobilise monetary support for these agents and school teachers, particularly after the visit of himself, James Read jun., Andries Stoffels, Dyani Tshatshu and John Philip to Britain from 1836 to 1837 in order to give evidence before the Select Committee of the House of the Commons on the status of aborigines in the British empire. Extensive speaking tours by the South Africans publicised the Kat River Settlement. In 1839 Read had over £100 in private donations from Britain to support eight 'native teachers',[60] while in 1844 he had over £100 from England for the Kat River mission to the Thembu.[61] In 1843 Read sent reports on five native agents to financial backers in Britain; he seems to have been paying these agents between £15 and £28 per annum, depending on the size of their families.[62]

These agents included men such as Matroos Jaris, who been brought up at Bethelsdorp, where he was a playfellow of the christianised minor Xhosa chief Dyani Tshatshu. In 1815 Matroos Jaris had helped found the short-lived mission to the Xhosa of Joseph Williams and Tshatshu. Many years later, he accompanied the new LMS agent Brownlee and Dyani Tshatshu to found a new mission station for the Xhosa at the Buffalo River. After that he was sent to the Thembu chief known to Read as 'Kagalla', where he replaced the Khoikhoi agent Boosman Stuurman at a station which continued after Kagalla's removal and death. In 1843 Matroos was struggling unsuccessfully to irrigate the station and contending with the results of the previous year's crop failure, which had created serious problems for his large family.

Another agent, Andries Jager, supported by a Miss Hewitt, had likewise been an early inhabitant of Bethelsdorp. He had then moved to Theopolis after the creation of that station, where he had so distinguished himself at school that Dr Philip had sent him to the LMS English school at Salem. About 1822, according to Read, ' it pleased God to change his heart', and he 'became a decided follower of Christ', so esteemed by missionary and church alike that he was chosen deacon and held the office seemingly continuously until he left Theopolis around 1838 to come to Blinkwater in the Kat River. Throughout this period, Jager 'had likewise been employed to exhort at different times and different places'. After his arrival at Blinkwater (where Calderwood's station would be established in 1839) Jager went as a native teacher to the new settlements on the Fish River, established by the government for new Khoikhoi settlement although shortly thereafter abandoned. There Jager had a school, taught people to read, held services on Sundays and twice during the week, and was responsible for several conversions.

Once the Fish River settlements were disbanded, Jager went to work as a native teacher at the Philipton church's outstation of Bruceton, originally set up in order to serve local San inhabitants, or former clients of San. There Jager maintained in 1843 a Sunday school and a 'good day school', in addition to running religious worship. Jager also acted as an agent of the LMS civilising project, trying to teach agricultural techniques and encouraging the acquisition of material goods: when the station was first founded, the inhabitants of Bruceton 'were in fact living upon wild geese, Qwagga's meat and wild Roots they were almost in a state of nudity, and living in miserable habitations ... [and] seen ploughing with ploughs without an ounce of Iron'. Now they were 'living in comfortable dwellings are well dressed and have good ploughs and are in most comfortable circumstances and above all very many are members of [the] christian church – and enjoying the benefits of christian ministry'.[63] Men such as Matroos Jaris and Andries Jager were indubitably motivated by profound Christian belief; they also had career paths. There was not much difference between what the unordained Jager was doing at Bruceton, including holding divine services, and what the ordained Calderwood, for example, was doing at Blinkwater – and it was Calderwood who was perceived as the unwelcome interloper into a functioning system.

The relative autonomy of Khoikhoi native agents is suggested by the fact that there had even been a theological schism at Bruceton some eight years previously, well before the trouble at Grahamstown – not, of course, that Read saw parallels between the cases. As he recorded,

> the first native Teacher they had – was afflicted about 8 years ago with the brain fever. He has never been right since and has taken up with strange notions – as not to believe in original sin – not to believe in the Deluge not to credit the Epistles as part of the word of God &c and tis to be regretted that several of those to whom we had reason to hope he had been usefull to adhere to him, and they have their separate worship. But some of them are getting tired of the poor man's nonsense and we hope will soon leave him.[64]

The Kat River community ran an important mission to the San of Chief Madoor (which ended in disaster and military conflict between Mfengu, Mpondomise, San and Thembu groups). Despite some tension between Khoikhoi and Mfengu, native agents also worked among the Mfengu who were rushing into the colony and in particular into the Kat River region. Khoikhoi agents also worked among Thembu groups to the north, as well as in Kat River outstations.[65] Such activity, which continued in a more formal manner the evangelisation work of earlier Khoikhoi converts to Christianity, reflected broader regional patterns – as Khoikhoi-descended groups elsewhere tried to take over the missionary mantle of spiritual authority with important political implications. In areas of considerable ethnic diversity, such as Kat River was becoming in the 1830s and 1840s, Christianity also furnished a means (however fragile) of integration and the possibility of an imagined common community.[66] Khoikhoi evangelisation posed a threat, however, to a number of white missionaries, insecure as they were in both black and white communities. It is telling that one of the main bones of contention between the Read and Moffat–Calderwood factions in the district committee debate was that the committee system deliberately excluded the unordained; Read thought this was clearly designed to exclude native agents.

Beyond the Cape Colony, native agency was already being used by some African societies to shore up the power of particular interest groups. Missionary attempts to exert their own control over the selection and maintenance of preachers and other agents and officials interfered with the political uses being made of Christianity by groups involved in local power relations. Paul Landau has shown this process in operation with particular force in the kingdom of Khama, among the Ngwato Sotho–Tswana of modern-day Botswana, where younger royals mobilised Christianity to establish a new form of regional hegemony. As Landau argues, in GammaNgwato 'African preachers and teachers, *baruti*, were far more important in restructuring 'missionary' Christian life than a handful of missionaries'.[67] Throughout the late nineteenth century and early twentieth century, Tswana converts ousted unpopular missionaries as they ceased to serve their purposes, and Africans and white missionaries tended to compete for the management of missions. The senior Read's evidence would suggest that similar processes may have been at work even earlier, and that Tswana groups in the vicinity of Griquatown may have been more receptive to Christianity than Moffat's personal experience implies.

The example of conflicts between the entourage of the chief Mothibi (with whom LMS missionaries had first settled in 1816) and the LMS missionary Holloway Helmore is telling – and provides a broader context for the Grahamstown schism. On an extended visit with Philip to the interior, Read acted for three days in 1842 as an interpreter between Dr Philip and Tswana men, all, as the proletarian Read respectfully noted, 'young Princes, most intelligent pious Men', who were attempting to get rid of an unpopular missionary, Helmore. The dispute came at a time when African groups were manoeuvring to avoid Voortrekker hegemony. Philip tried to persuade both African leaders and the British to accept British imperial overlordship as a counter to Boer incursions. The LMS missionary at Griquatown at the time, Peter Wright, was an ally of Philip's who worked closely with Griqua leaders and was far more popular with Tswana leaders than Helmore.

The initial complainants included Tabe, son of the 'well known chief Tyso', Mothibi's two sons, 'Jantze (or John) and James', as well as Mothibi's son-in-law and his nephew Koka, 'all office Bear[er]s, or managers or had been so at Sekatlong, they had been my school children from 1816 to 1820'. They wanted to be rid of Helmore among other things because he had deposed Tabe as school master and native teacher, and had fired Jantze, Mothibi's son, as deacon of the church, 'both for a frivolous act, and both without consulting or the Sanction of the Church'. He had barred a woman from communion against the wishes of the congregation. Furthermore, Helmore had broken his agreement, sanctioned by the LMS directors, with Griquatown missionaries that Sekatlong was to be considered an outpost of Griquatown and indeed that the two communities should think of themselves as one church: 'he had broken off all friendship with those Missionaries, and all the regulations established by them had been dispensed with, and without consulting those missionaries, or the office Bearers of the Church'. Running through all these complaints, then, was the critical issue of the relative authority of the local church, particularly its officials, and of the missionary.[68] At this time and place, as missionaries and Christian chiefs negotiated with the British government, that relationship had much political importance.

Dr Philip insisted that a meeting be called with Helmore in attendance to answer the charges; at this meeting, other members of the male elite attended including Mothibi, Tyso and 'several others of the most respectable, and influential members of the church and community'. Philip indeed dismissed Helmore from his post at Sekatlong, although the LMS directors in London would overturn this decision. Wright and Read were later attacked for their role in this affair (Wright posthumously; his widow was much distressed by the letter of censure from the LMS directors, according to Read). Read, however, defended the right of native agents as employees of the LMS to appeal directly to Dr Philip, as the superintendent of the LMS in southern Africa, over the head of local missionaries – in a debate which arguably again echoed that occurring over settler democracy.

It is significant for my overall argument that in his discussion of this earlier rift with the LMS, Read underscored that native agents and churches would increasingly demand autonomy in the future in southern Africa, and that directors and missionaries alike essentially needed to work out how to deal with a fact that they were powerless to change. The churches in 'heathen lands' were beginning to understand the nature of church membership and the constitution of a Christian church, not only regarding the 'duties' of members (above all, to spread the gospel – a very evangelical conception) but also regarding their 'privileges':

1st the admission and exclusion of members 2 in the election of [...] deacons to serve the church 3 The third privilege the right of assisting in the choice of a Pastor this last has hitherto lain dormant from the fact of the people not paying their own ministers, but from many concurring circumstances, and from communications received from the Directors of the time having now come that the churches in this country should support their own ministers or subscribe more liberally towards the funds of the parent society: the other part of the question namely the right of the people in the choice of their Pastor has been facilitated the one was dependent upon the other. – The people have asked, and have been told that if they support their own Pastor, or Missionaries they have a right in their choice – this is a new state of things for which the Directors & the Churches of England must be prepared. Tho I have been 42 years in the missionary work in Africa, I never spoke to the people upon this subject or preached upon it till the thing has been forced upon us by the natural course of events; our people know well now not only what is their duty but what is their privilege.[69]

This wider framework brings us back to the question of whether the Calderwood–Read dispute actually mattered in some sense beyond that of the injured careers and egos of the missionaries involved. I would argue that it did. First of all, it made some difference to Cape politics that the Philip–Read party ultimately lost influence so extensively both in South Africa and in Britain, among both the LMS directors and the staff of the Colonial Office. This is evident, for example, in the ultimate failure of Philip's efforts in the 1840s to act as broker between the Griqua, Moshoeshoe and the imperial government in opposing Voortrekker expansion to the north. Calderwood lost in the short term, leaving the LMS to work directly for the government, but internecine strife within the LMS was a symptom of much broader problems with LMS radicalism by the 1840s. The brief promise of direct relationships between the imperial government and African groups which seemed enticing in the 1830s was essentially broken by the 1840s, although the hope of a return would remain powerful. The attacks on Read in 1843 and 1844, followed by more serious attacks on the Kat River Settlement and on the vestiges of LMS radicalism as a whole in the wake of the 1850–3 rebellion of many Christians of Khoikhoi background, helped put paid to the notion of the LMS in particular as a useful conduit of African opinion. As rebel leader Willem Uithaalder at the Kat River Settlement commented to the DRC minister W.R. Thomson in 1850:

'Sir, you and Mr. Read were both young when you came among us, and you are now both old, and klein Mynheer (young Mr. Read) had no beard when he came to Kat River, and he is now getting advanced in years, and yet these oppressions won't cease. The Missionaries have for years written, and their writings won't help. We are now going to stand up for our own affairs. We shall show the settlers that we too are men.'[70]

Conversely, Calderwood was an important figure in the government's later programme to 'civilise' and christianise conquered Xhosa groups, and functioned as an 'expert' on the Xhosa. It is scarcely surprising that his authoritarian brand of Christianity under such circumstances was profoundly resented as tensions built towards renewed warfare and the cataclysm of the Cattle Killing.

Secondly, the example of Mothibi's counsellors manoeuvring to get Helmore dismissed hints at the political issues at stake behind the theological and organisational disputes of the early 1840s. Who controlled the church, and how much control ministers and elders actually had over community life, could have implications for broader African uses of Christianity for the consolidation of control by particular social groups (as the example of Mothibi's people suggests); it also affected the degree of self-control over their communities of more embattled groups such as the Kat River settlers. Not surprisingly, African leaders tried to choose missionaries in pursuit of their own interests and rejected those both wedded to strong ministerial control and unwilling to cede the ministry to Africans.

There were real theological and intellectual issues at stake for all concerned in the quarrels of the 1840s (and there seems no reason not to believe that at least some in the Kat River Settlement kept abreast of theological debates in Scotland, given that the Reads were well informed). Theological debates were, however, mediated through political conflict, and in particular through the larger question of authority and spirituality. Most importantly, perhaps, racial conflict at the Cape transformed European theological debates and disputes over church government. The interaction of political and theological questions is scarcely surprising. Christianity provided (and provides) a powerful language of authority. How was that authority to be harnessed, however? What restrictions should be placed on the unrestricted spread of ecstatic news, for example? How were the authority relations implicit in Christianity (and arguably necessary to communal organisation) to be balanced against its liberationist potential, and how did both interact with ideas of race in a politically charged environment? Who, more bluntly, owned the gospel? Who spoke for God?

In 1844, it was James Read who looked like the old-fashioned minister, opposed by younger men such as Calderwood, Brownlee and Birt. These latter men were part of the reformulation of missionary liberalism which would reshape the nineteenth-century missionary drive. The attacks on Read also symbolised, to my mind, a rethinking of the initial promise of an interracial church, with a colour-blind career path for white and black ministers and church officials, as well as racially mixed congregations. The disputes of 1844 and 1845 seemed far less significant in the wake of the War of the Axe, which erupted in 1846. The issues they raised, however, were weighty with implication for the future.

10

THE STANDARD OF LIVING QUESTION IN NINETEENTH-CENTURY MISSIONS IN KWAZULU-NATAL

Norman Etherington

By choosing to live as humbly as the impoverished Khoi, the LMS pioneer, J. T. van der Kemp, launched one of the most remarkable experiments ever attempted in the evangelisation of southern Africa.[1] Unfortunately, it was not appreciated by either government officials or white settlers. Far from applauding a saintly imitation of Christ, Cape society reviled him for lowering the white man's prestige. When Van der Kemp and fellow missionary James Read married Khoi women and fathered children, they created scandals that would last as long as South African laws against miscegenation. For all who opposed Khoi liberation, these examples proved the LMS to be a dangerous, impractical, 'visionary' movement. The general view of white settlers and officials was that missionaries would succeed best by playing their part in maintaining white prestige. Unless they were respected by Africans, their message would be ignored. Andrew Smith put the case succinctly in 1836:

> From what I have seen and heard, I should, without hesitation, declare that it is injurious to the success of missions that those employed to instruct the savage should ever have occasion to descend to the performance of any labour which is understood and practised by them; more especially to house-building and the cultivation of the soil which they consider as inferior employments and only fitted for the occupation of the women. The consideration of these points I would submit as worthy of attention, more especially as I am confident that the little extra expense which would be required in order to avoid the necessity of religious instructors appearing in the capacity of builders, and standing for weeks together before the gazing populace, with perhaps the sleeves of their shirts rolled up to their shoulders, would be more than compensated by the increased influence they would ensure from avoiding it.
>
> It is generally supposed that savages pay little regard to the condition of others, but that is a mistake; they are acute observers and distinguish quickly the different grades and show their consideration accordingly.

Thus if they see a white man doing inferior work for another white man, they will not listen to the inferior. [2]

On becoming superintendent of LMS operations in South Africa, John Philip took up Van der Kemp's courageous campaign against state-sanctioned injustice, but he set his face firmly against any further experiments in living like Africans.[3]

The examples of Van der Kemp and Read cast long shadows over missionary endeavour in South Africa. They did not, however, settle the standard of living question. In nineteenth-century Natal, missionaries from many different denominations and nations carried on long, revealing and sometimes acrimonious debates on the issue – debates which illuminate fundamental contradictions of evangelical enterprise in a colonised society.

There were occasional attempts to revive the theory of simple living on both practical and theoretical grounds. The most notorious example was set by the pioneering Norwegian apostle Hans Schreuder, a highly educated man and a gifted scholar of linguistics. A disapproving American missionary described in 1852 how Schreuder

> can make a dinner of pumpkin, roast his meat on the coals, without salt, cut it and eat it without a plate, fork or knife except his pocket knife. He can get along without soap, or water either, except to drink, and that he can drink without a dish. Indeed he would suit that class of Christians who say that missionaries ought to live as the natives do: that is, become a heathen with them, instead of remaining a Christian, and laboring to make the same of the heathen.[4]

Such accomplishments earned him a huge reputation among his Norwegian supporters and future biographers but made little impression on contemporaries in Natal and Zululand. Anglican Bishop Colenso and his daughters were typical in regarding Schreuder as an unwashed boor unfit for polite society.[5] And it is not clear that the big Scandinavian's adaptation to local customs was anything more than a pragmatic response to his circumstances. His candid opinion was that Zulu huts were intensely uncomfortable, crowded, smoky, leaky, bug-infested hovels.[6] His insistence that his clergy share his willingness to suffer hardships in the sacred work aroused resentment, particularly among the unordained artisan 'assistants'. So did his arguments that a missionary ought ideally, like Paul, to be unmarried; and that those who did marry should never allow their family life to be a hindrance to the mission as a whole. Some of his clergy rebuked him for a heretically unprotestant preference for priestly celibacy.[7]

Others who practised or preached the ideal of evangelical simplicity were certainly more sympathetic to the Catholic faith. The Church of England's Tractarian Dean, James Green, wrote enthusiastically in 1849, 'Methinks fellows of colleges might well spend their incomes by coming out as missionaries. Those who come out could live a year or so in Caffre huts without much discomfort and uniting together their expenses need not be great.'[8] The like-minded Bishop of Cape Town argued that a few dedicated men willing to live near, if not at the Zulu standard would be the best way of speeding the work of evangelisation.[9] The first Roman Catholics priests had prepared for their work in precisely this way, living in a Zulu hut at an ordinary rural homestead.[10] When Charles Mackenzie was plucked from Natal to begin the ill-fated Anglican mission to central Africa, he advocated a communal venture based on his understanding of medieval Catholic simplicity.[11]

It may be no accident that the most fervent advocates of self-sacrifice came from the most privileged backgrounds. Van der Kemp was born into a well-off and distinguished family; before his conversion he had lived a privileged and licentious life as an army officer. Hans Schreuder likewise left a wealthy family and a comfortable urban life when he went into the mission field. Although he could be satisfied with a dinner of roasted pumpkin, he held an exalted opinion of the episcopal office, leaving the Norwegian Missionary Society when they refused to grant him the same powers enjoyed by bishops at home.[12] Dean Green, Bishop Gray and Charles Mackenzie were university men from Britain's upper middle class. Perversely, missionaries who had known unusual comfort in their youth could more easily contemplate hardship than those for whom an evangelical vocation represented a step upward on the ladder of class distinction. Aldin Grout, the American who reproved Schreuder for living like a heathen, had been a stone mason before hearing his call to the clergy. The artisans Arntz Tönnesen and Siver Samuelson were brought by Schreuder to Natal as mere 'economic assistants'. Resenting their lowly status (and pay), they jumped at the chance to be ordained as Anglican priests by Colenso.[13]

The pervasive class distinctions of Victorian society in all of Europe and North America created endless problems for missionary organisations. The Presbyterian and Congregationalist missionaries sent by the American Board of Commissioners for Foreign Missions jealously insisted on what they called the 'republican principle' that all ordained ministers should be treated alike.[14] All received the same salary, equal allowances for 'infit' and a fixed family support based on the number of children. Even on this basis, jealousies could arise. When George Champion drew on his private means to make his home more comfortable, another American pointed out that as a consequence others without such means were likely to make unreasonable demands on the missionary society in order to keep up appearances.[15] The Lutheran communities founded by Louis Harms's Hermannsburg Missionary Society turned their back on the nineteenth century, hoping through Harms's ideal of medieval communalism to create an antidote to the atheism of the French Revolution and the capitalism of industrialising Germany.[16] The inception of this experiment inspired one Anglican missionary to pray that God would raise up a Harms in Britain.[17] 'Mission stations', he wrote, 'ought to be collegiate in their character, embracing crafts of various kinds, working upon the heathen around and preparing others for more extended work.' By the end of the 1860s, however, the Hermannsburg experiment in Christian communism had ended, wrecked by the irresistible temptation for skilled German farmers and artisans to join the larger white settler society of Natal.

Bishop Colenso, in contrast, built class distinctions into his church edifice from the foundation to the spire. Schreuder may have looked down on the Anglican bishop's 'low birth',[18] but in all the affairs of Natal Christianity, Colenso assumed that his bishop's 'letters patent' from the Queen entitled him to a leading role. (When a Bible society meeting in 1855 refused his right to take the chair, Colenso walked out.)[19] On his arrival in Natal, the bishop asked the Society for the Propagation of the Gospel to send him ten reinforcements:

> 4 Clergymen, Priests or Deacons, if possible with university Degrees, or, at least, with good education, and gentlemanly manners, which as Sir George Grey justly says, are essential for having proper influence with such natives as ours – and 6 Catechists, who would be received as Candidates for Holy Orders, after they have laboured as catechists for 3 years ...[20]

His policy on salaries was likewise shaped by considerations of class and education. A respectable Englishman with a university degree

> might receive £72 per ann. £60 if of a lower class & £84, if university men with degrees. If married men, without children, 1/3 as much again might be allowed – and for each child £6 per ann. additional ... Of course for first class men, M.A.'s or M.D.'s of good ability and experience, the payment should be higher from the first perhaps, £150 for a single man, £200 for married, with £12 for each child ... and after 3 years, £180 for a single man, £240 for married, and children as before.

Quibbles about salaries and conditions pervade missionaries' correspondence with their home societies. Probably the most poorly paid Europeans were the Norwegians, whose annual wages in the 1850s ranged from £35 to £60:[21]

Ministers married	60
Ministers unmarried	50

Mission helpers married	45
Mission helpers unmarried	35
Economic assts. married	40
Economic assts. unmarried	35

American mission salaries were initially set at a base rate of £150 for married men. By the 1870s, the level had risen to £200.[22] Even then, some complained that their clothing would not be 'considered respectable in any part of New England, except for poor folks'.[23] Whether that constituted a respectable wardrobe in Natal was naturally a matter of opinion. As a point of comparison, the Secretary for Native Affairs, Theophilus Shepstone, who was one of the better-paid colonial officials in the 1860s, earned £300 per annum. Bishop Colenso, at the time of his appointment, was probably at or the near the bottom of the salary scale for the Church of England's bishops in overseas colonies, which ranged from £500 to £3000.[24] His archdeacon, Henry Callaway, who gave up a lucrative London medical practice when he took holy orders, argued that 'a missionary ought to be allowed at least £300 a year for his own bona fide income; and incidental expenses, if he is to work with efficiency.'[25] Lesser Anglican clergy complained of being paid less than the Wesleyan Methodists, whose married agents – none of whom had university or theological degrees – were being paid £150 a year in 1859.[26]

Missionary standards of living cannot be strictly equated on the basis of salary, because the sending societies applied different policies in relation to leave, housing, farming and trade. Americans and Anglicans were forbidden to engage in any sort of commercial enterprise, but the Norwegians and Hermannsburgers were allowed to supplement their meagre wages through trade. This must have been a valuable privilege in Zululand because it provoked complaints from white traders.[27] The Church of England's Society for the Propagation of the Gospel forbade any use of funds for the erection of buildings, except at the inception of a new mission field.[28] The American Board of Commissioners, on the other hand, made generous provisions for housing. Some missionaries invested heavily in livestock to run on their stations, while others had no opportunity to farm.[29] Such disparities led to personnel problems like those which plague any modern corporate enterprise. Behind all the petty jealousies, however, lurked a really important question: what manner of living would best forward Christ's cause among the heathen?

Much of the missiological argument against living as Africans did rested on the alleged necessity of setting 'an example of civilisation'. Missionaries of all denominations in colonial Natal were fond of quoting the biblical injunction that Christian communities should be as 'cities set upon a hill'. They were, argued American William Ireland, so many 'centres of light whose rays shall pierce the deep darkness which surrounds them'.[30] When the Berlin Missionary

Society agreed to buy Emmaus station, Carl Posselt rejoiced that his new farm might be 'eine Stadt auf dem Berge, deren helles Licht weit hinausscheine'.[31] Anglican Henry Callaway likewise looked on his new station of Springvale as 'a city set on a high place'.[32] For that very reason,

> The missionary must have a house. I would on no account allow it to be regarded as a matter of indifference, how or in what kind of dwelling a Missionary should live; nor let it be imagined for a moment, that there is any merit in making oneself miserable in one's external position; or that untidiness or slovenliness in the dwelling, diet, or person, is any thing proper to be seen at a Mission-Station. The Missionary comes among a savage people; and whilst not shrinking from any amount of self-denial, which his work may require, he must not sink to them; nor think he is exercising any great Christian virtue, when he can boast that he has learnt to live as they. He must be their example in everything that is of good report. In his dwelling, his person, his diet, they must be taught to look to him as their superior.[33]

Using the same argument about setting an example, American Hyman Wilder explained that it was an important point of evangelical policy that their mission dwellings should bear no resemblance to Zulu structures.[34] Such arguments put an extra spin on the celebrated nineteenth-century debate on whether 'civilisation' was a precondition or a consequence of Christianisation. What appears to later readers as unthinking Eurocentrism was presented by many missionaries as a divinely ordained prescription for spreading Christianity through exemplary cities set on the African hills.

This argument meshed neatly with the widely held opinion that Africans would not respect missionaries unless they upheld the white man's 'prestige'. Andrew Smith recommended that all missionaries should be married; if they were not, Africans would think they were too poor to pay bride wealth.[35] The implication was that no one would listen to the Word of God if it were preached by what would later be termed 'failed Europeans'.[36] To 'maintain prestige' in a gathering of Africans seated on the ground, Anglican missionary S.M. Samuelson always sat on a chair.[37] The American Zulu Mission (AZM) worried that their prestige might be irreparably damaged if a person of colour from their own country joined them in Natal. It would be impossible for such a person to conform

> readily (so much as will be required) to the mode of living among the African blacks. The whites are regarded by the natives as a Superior race.
>
> Query. Will the Zulus look up to the Colored American, with that respect which is due to his superior intelligence?[38]

It was so easy to slip from the posture of 'maintaining respect' into unthinking adherence to the racial practices imposed by white settlers. Another member of the AZM suggested that if a black American must be sent to join them, 'he should come well taught from history that the white settlers of S. Africa are not, generally, the enemies of his race, but the only really intelligent friends they have on earth.'[39]

Though all the Protestant missions were theoretically committed to raising up self-supporting, self-propagating African churches, it was difficult to see how the ideal could be achieved so long as they clung to the idea of the white man's peculiar prestige. When pressed by the governing body to select an African pastor for one of their stations, American missionaries objected that their black congregations would probably feel slighted if their white missionary were taken away. Besides, wrote Andrew Abraham, a supposedly staunch Congregationalist, 'We have no native who has the requisite qualifications to become the Bishop of this important station.'[40] If a big house, comfortable furniture, a wife dedicated to indoor domestic duties, respectable clothing and a decent salary were prerequisites for the conversion of the heathen, it is difficult see how the job could ever have been passed on to African hands.

In fact, mission societies and their white agents applied totally different standards when it came to employing indigenous assistants. Anglican James Green complained that the two African itinerant preachers, to whom he had offered the reasonable sum of £2 per month in 1874, refused to go for less than £4 each. It would be a good idea, he suggested, to demand that they 'take vows of poverty'.[41] Henry Callaway paid £24 per annum to one of the men he was training for holy orders, and £16 to another with lower qualifications.[42] The American missionaries held that only in exceptional circumstances should any African agent be paid more than £36 per annum. The trouble was that other societies were paying more. According to Henry Martyn Bridgman, 'The Wesleyans pay some of their Native preachers as high as £60 per annum' in 1871 (neglecting to mention that the Methodists had already begun to ordain African clergy). He thought that if the American schools could 'glut the market with good Teachers, then it will be easier to convince other Societies, that they pay too high for Native labor'.[43] A few years later, one of his colleagues suggested that it was time they 'quit giving Kafirs money for preaching the Gospel'.[44]

Not only did this smack of hypocrisy in a mission where white agents were paid £200 per annum in order to uphold their prestige, it was out of line with economic realities. Able Africans could earn far more in secular occupations such as farming, trade and transport riding. Market forces decreed that if any black teachers were to be found for mission schools, they would have to be paid more than a pittance.[45] A most embarrassing question arose in the American Zulu Mission when Charlie Abraham, the son of one of the missionaries, refused to carry on teaching school unless his salary were raised above £75 per annum. Justice would seem to demand that his black colleague Jeremiah, who did exactly the same work with no less efficiency, be given equal pay. However, such a rise might have a bad effect on the 'other native helpers'.[46] So would the appointment of black American missionaries. The committee appointed to report mission feeling on the question pointed out that if the new recruits were given an equal voice, then 'our native helpers' might 'think they ought to have the same rights and privileges, and we should not think it wise to grant them'.[47]

Once missionary society authorities accepted the argument that Van der Kemp and Read had been wrong to lower their standards of living to the level of their African congregations, it became difficult to maintain a consistent line on relative salaries for white and black assistants. The influential writings of Henry Venn in Britain and Rufus Anderson in America advocated self-supporting, self-propagating churches on practical as well as idealistic grounds.[48] Converts who supported their own ministers and evangelists relieved foreign missionary societies of a financial burden and enabled resources to be diverted to other fields. Every penny saved on the South African mission field helped open the way for the gospel in other lands. The logic of the argument from prestige and example entailed that as African agents were recruited, they too should live in cities set upon hills, spreading the light of civilisation through their outward and visible lifestyles. This implication was ignored by cost-cutting missionary society officers. Thus Nathaniel Clark, who succeeded Rufus Anderson as Secretary of the American Board of Commissioners, wrote to tell the American Zulu Mission in 1867:

> The Committee [had] voted the allowance asked for the helpers, viz £3 a month each for the four, and the £5 each, asked for building materials … We … notice the amount allowed them, as being to our view quite large. We would be very careful of making it a secular object to be in the employ of the mission. Of course what is strictly necessary must be allowed, but not to foster tastes and habits, unfitting the helpers for the fullest sympathy and activity with and among their own people.[49]

Although it was the long-established policy of the American Board that its missionaries should hold university degrees, it took a different line in relation to African agents. The Natal mission was warned not to educate 'too highly … Men raised in intellectual culture much above their countrymen, acquire habits unfitting them to labor among them. Give them the Bible, let it be the instrument of educating and developing their minds, and there is no trouble.'[50] If more support were needed, said Secretary Nathaniel Clark, African pastors should roll up their shirtsleeves and grow their own food: 'I would not have the native pastor above doing something for himself – working his own garden, and giving some time to manual labor. I think the result would be bad if the impression is given that because a man has become a preacher and a pastor, he is removed from all manual labor.'[51]

It is not uncommon for twentieth-century mission historians to imagine that missionary authorities pushing the idea of a self-supporting indigenous church were in fundamental conflict with their own local white agents, who resisted African ordinations. As these examples show, there was not such a sharp dichotomy. White missionaries in Natal tended to insist that any Africans received into the pastorate should have qualifications and manners similar to their own. Missionary secretaries such as Nathaniel Clark of the American Board and John Kilner of the Wesleyan Methodist Missionary Society, on the other hand, recommended ordaining a second-class African pastorate who would live at a lower, cheaper level.

Thus, over a period of years, policies on standards of living all tended in the direction of isolating white missionaries from their own converts as well as the 'heathen' about them. Sometimes the argument for making mission stations cities set on hills was turned upside-down to justify isolation, as though missionary families were more likely to be corrupted by their African neighbours than those neighbours were to be exalted by their example. In 1861 Aldin Grout pleaded for financial help to get his son away from temptation.

> We ... desire to send our son away to our native land. He will be sixteen years old next Dec. and in this country early marriages are common, both among the whites and blacks, and we can see that he is possessed of the common instincts of his race already and temptations lie in the way ... If Mr. Lindley shall be at home when you get this, he can tell you some of the temptations to which boys are liable here... Daughters can better be kept out of the way, still they suffer badly by the situation.[52]

Anglican Thomas Jenkinson in 1878 took drastic action when he found his infant children prattling in the Zulu tongue. To forestall 'corruption' he dismissed their black nurse and forbade them to wander among the houses of his African congregation. The dangers that might arise from undue familiarity were, he said, vividly presented by the case of a Wesleyan missionary's son who had lately run away with an African girl.[53]

Van der Kemp and Read had scandalised white society at the Cape by marrying Khoi women and raising families intimately associated with the people they hoped to convert. The LMS, under John Philip's superintendence, turned its back on that wonderful, audacious experiment. Later entrants into the southern African mission field followed suit. By avoiding domestic entanglements with African society, missionaries lessened friction with white settler communities and colonial governments. It is not clear, however, that they advanced their central objective of spreading the Christian faith. The work of evangelisation in Natal and Zululand was unavoidably and inextricably entangled with the basic institutions of both black and white society. No mission could isolate itself from those realities and hope to grow very large. Many of the earliest mission station residents had been acquired through compromising and entangling alliances – for example, by applying to the Natal government for 'apprentices' or by presenting cows and material goods to the guardians of young women.[54] Those who were thus attached, or who chose to attach themselves to communities of believers, retained familial and cultural bonds to the larger world around them. In the long run it would be their ability to translate – in Lamin Sanneh's sense – their understanding of the Christian faith into the ordinary language of human interactions used by their fellows that would decide the fate of the evangelical enterprise.

This is not to say that by putting on the ragged clothes and worn-out shoes of Van der Kemp and Read, subsequent missionaries could have reaped the longed-for 'abundant harvest of souls'. The modern consensus of mission historians is that in every land the core work of Christianisation was done by unsung legions of indigenous believers, not by European missionaries. On the other hand, the historian's verdict must be that absolutely nothing was gained by 'upholding standards', 'maintaining prestige' or attempting to 'set examples'. And, if regret is an appropriate emotion for our profession, there are many reasons to regret there were not more shabby, humble men like the LMS pioneers.

AMERICAN MISSIONARIES AND THE MAKING OF AN AFRICAN CHURCH IN COLONIAL NATAL

Les Switzer

The Congregational tradition in colonial Natal was represented primarily by a missionary society that was known throughout South Africa as the American Zulu Mission (AZM).[1] The Americans arrived in December 1835, only eleven years after the first white hunters and traders had established a small, loose-knit community around the future port of Durban, but a permanent mission was not ensured until the British annexed the region between the Thukela and Mzimkhulu rivers in 1843 and proclaimed it the Crown Colony of Natal two years later.

After years of struggle, the AZM had established a string of twelve mission stations by 1850. Five stations – named Amanzimtoti, Imfume, Amahlongwa, Ifafa and Umtwalumi – were near the coast between 22 and 78 miles south-west of Durban. Six stations – named Inanda, Itafamasi, Umsunduzi, Esidumbini, Umvoti and Mapumulo – were also near the coast between 15 and 70 miles north-east of Durban. One inland station roughly 40 miles from the coast near the town of Pietermaritzburg was named Table Mountain.[2] In 1850 it was estimated that each station was 'surrounded by from two to five thousand natives residing near enough to attend worship'.[3] The mission was granted free-hold rights to station land as a 'glebe' (as land given to a church is called in religious law) in 1856, and the first titles were issued in 1860. Each station was also allocated a 'mission reserve' – a unique land grant in colonial South Africa – where the AZM (as with other missions allocated reserves) would have direct access to the resident African population. Although Umzumbe, the southern-most coastal station founded in 1861, was not granted a reserve, the Americans had now established the centres where the AZM would take root in the next generation.

The struggle to establish a new religious discourse among the Africans of Natal was conducted at numerous levels – within white missionary circles and with white settlers, between white missionaries and African Christians, within the African Christian community, between African Christians and African non-

Christians. Three issues informed these conversations. The first issue involved access to land and relations of production on the land. The second issue involved access to schools and the making of an educated African Christian elite. The third issue, which will be the focus of this chapter, involved access to the church and the mission's struggle to control religious discourse in an expanding African Christian community.

Critical scholars in South African studies tend to view relations between missionary and African as a subtext in the conversation between coloniser and colonised in Africa, and these relations are inevitably understood in bipolar terms. The Comaroffs, for example, suggest that conversations between the missionaries and the Southern Tswana were sharply distinguished in 'two cultural repertoires' that found expression in the opposition between *sekgoa* (European ways) and *setswana* (African ways). They do seek to deconstruct these 'profoundly historical' dichotomies, but in the process Christianity is often reduced to narratives involving the missionaries and Christian converts.[4] A similar distinction has been made between believers and non-believers among the Xhosa in the eastern Cape, where the site of struggle pitted the School people (the Christians) against the Red Blanket people (the non-Christians). A generation of social anthropologists sought to demonstrate that in both cultures these cleavages were embedded in the linguistic and social practices of everyday life.[5]

More and more contemporary scholars, however, are seeking to break down the boundaries of religious discourse, which they suggest are shaped by struggles within, as well as between, competing ideologies. Christianity on the mission frontier was contested terrain, and relations between African Christians and their missionaries were not limited to strictly religious matters. African religion, moreover, was not the monolithic, undifferentiated force that mission apologists have imagined, and those who spoke for African religion often offered shrewd, convincing accounts of their religious practices in debates with missionaries.[6] Like companion narratives in pain and healing,[7] religious narratives were open rather than closed. The voices of missionaries, African Christians and non-Christians in colonial Natal, to paraphrase the Russian literary critic Mikhail Bakhtin, were both monologic and dialogic, and religious discourse should be read in terms of these encounters.[8]

GENDERED NARRATIVES IN MISSION AND CHURCH

Gender roles on the American mission, for example, reflected dominant white,[9] patriarchal perspectives. Male missionaries were the decision-makers: they sat on mission committees that set policy, presided over the mission's pastoral, preaching and teaching activities, and administered the mission's glebes and reserves. And when the AZM was eventually forced to recognise African church leaders and formalise church structures, the conversation was almost exclusively between white and black males. Indeed, patriarchal narratives constructed within the American mission provide a kind of subtext to the patriarchal narratives constructed between coloniser and colonised elsewhere in Natal.[10] They were narratives argued in the public sphere by spokesmen from competing patriarchal systems, and they are best represented in narratives by male American missionaries and African churchmen that survive in the record.

They were also narratives constructed within a racist discourse that precluded much social contact between the patriarchal leaders of mission and church. As one missionary admitted in 1874: 'We do sometimes invite to our tables the native preachers, but we do not wish them to expect such favors.' AZM researcher Myra Dinnerstein, for example, has emphasised the importance of interaction between Natal's settler community and American missionaries in the middle and later decades of the nineteenth century. The pervasive racism in colonial society was 'overpowering' and most newly arrived missionaries 'quickly succumbed to the prevailing attitudes'.[11]

All male missionaries had to have wives – preferably before they arrived in South Africa – and these women (and their children) were supposed to provide a moral compass for the African community. But Etherington's sketch of 25 American missionary wives who served the AZM in Natal before the mid-1880s indicates they suffered from numerous physical and emotional problems ('the association of so many of the illnesses with psychological tension suggests the strains of isolated life') and spent the duration of their missionary careers confined to responsibilities in the home. Any teaching or evangelical work they might assume would be conducted within the domestic sphere, and they were expected to emulate their male counterparts in refraining from unnecessary contact with Africans.[12]

The dominance of the male speaker within mission circles did not preclude other options, and they would not be confined mainly to single women ('widows and spinsters') recruited as teachers, as Etherington suggests. But they do not really appear as autonomous voices in the mission record before the 1860s, and they do not constitute a significant discourse until the last two decades or so of the nineteenth century.

The most outspoken female missionary in the 1860s was apparently Katherine Lloyd, a woman of privileged background who had been a 'fervent abolitionist' as a volunteer social worker among poor blacks in New York City before she arrived in Natal in 1862. Mrs Lloyd's husband, Charles, died three years later, but she stayed on as a teacher in the station school at Umvoti. Mrs Lloyd did not have a high opinion of the mission's male leadership, and she was not afraid to voice her opinions to the home board. Her sometimes passionate defence of traditional African life (they 'have many better laws and customs

than ours') and her willingness to treat African parishioners as social and intellectual equals ('what they say has force and weight') clashed with mission
orthodoxy. This independent voice was apparently lost when Mrs Lloyd remarried in 1870 and left the mission field soon thereafter. While few missionaries
agreed with her views, Mrs Lloyd did represent a new generation of women
who were to play a much more active role in the life and work of the mission
than they had in the past.[13]

The Americans were unusal in Natal because they worked exclusively among
Africans and did not attempt to establish a separate, settler church. But the
Africans who came within the sphere of American missionary activity in the
Colony were not the pillars of Zulu society whom the missionaries had hoped
to influence in their ill-fated attempts to establish a mission north of the
Thukela River in the heartland of the Zulu kingdom during the late 1830s and
early 1840s. Their converts were displaced people from fragmented chiefdoms
or people who had separated themselves from chiefly authority, and they sought
asylum with the missionary for reasons that rarely included the search for a new
religious experience.[14]

Some Americans in their zeal went to the extreme of contracting with
African parents to rent out their children to live in missionary homes. The parents would be given small amounts of money, and the children would work at
household tasks and be fed, clothed, given religious instruction and taught the
rudiments of literacy. The pattern established by pioneers like Dr Newton
Adams, the missionary doctor resident at Amanzimtoti, was followed by missionaries at other American stations, who would employ from 10 to 20 children
in these 'family schools' at any one time. Dinnerstein even suggests that virtually all the mission's early converts were 'employees living with the family'.[15] If
individual salvation came only after years of domestic training in missionary
households, however, so did the growth of the church. And it was almost
painfully slow.

The number of admissions recorded each year rarely corresponds with the
total church membership, which indicates that many converts either became
disillusioned and left the church or were excommunicated. Three congregations
(at Umvoti, Inanda and Amanzimtoti) had been organised by 1849 with 43
members and there were twelve congregations with 186 members in 1858, but
the numbers fluctuated up and down from year to year. There was a record
increase of 262 members between 1858 and 1868 (when total membership
stood at 448), but between 1868 and 1882 the increase in membership was less
than 200, the number of new admissions each year generally declined and there
were only thirteen congregations-cum-churches. Membership did not exceed
1000 until the late 1880s – after more than fifty years of focused missionary
activity.[16]

REFORMATION AND RENEWAL IN THE MISSION CHURCH

Religious discourse between black Christians and white missionaries was characterised by tensions that at times appeared to threaten the very existence of
the American mission. The missionaries in the early and middle decades of the
nineteenth century lived on stations that were isolated from each other and
from much of the world outside the mission. Secure on their stations – their
authority virtually unchallenged even in the reserves – they were free to adapt
the Congregational idiom to the needs of their congregations as they saw fit.
As a form of local church government, however, Congregationalism as practised in Britain and North America was not in vogue anywhere on the AZM
in Natal. 'Congregationalism needs a good deal of modifying to fit it to this
people … Even if we ourselves could prosecute Christian work along these
lines we cannot reasonably expect Zulus, of all people, to successfully follow in
our steps.'[17]

Most mission groups in colonial Natal were critical of 'heathen' African customs,[18] but the Americans – especially from the 1860s – were zealots in attacking these customs. They condemned traditional African medical practitioners
and their medicines to ward off evil. They tried to stop all forms of dancing,
beer drinking and expressions of what they viewed as nudity and illicit sexual
behaviour. Male and female initiation rites, male polygamy and the exchange
of women against cattle (the *lobola* system), and especially the role of ancestors
in worship, were rejected as anti-Christian. They advocated strict separation of
the saved from the unsaved, the Christians from the non-Christians, and they
demanded a singular reading of biblical principles that would result in inter-
mittent purifications of the tiny Christian community to weed out backsliders
and malcontents.

The Africans themselves, however, were doing much of the foundation
work in communicating the good news, and the mission record contains references to their evangelical activities almost from the beginning of the mission
enterprise. They were key mediators in translation work, and they were the
teaching and preaching 'helpers' responsible for everyday activities in the congregations and schools. They also provided the labour to construct mission
buildings, plough mission land, cultivate mission gardens and clean missionary
houses.

By the end of the 1840s, African Christians had organised a loose-knit
group that was meeting once a year to discuss evangelical strategy. By the end
of the 1850s, they were ready to establish mission stations on their own: the
Native Home and Foreign Missionary Society, formed in 1860, was apparently a unique African organisation among mission groups in Natal at the time.[19]
While the missionaries would eventually gain some control over the society's
activities, it was composed entirely of Africans who collected money from the

congregations (often at special 'monthly concerts' organised on Sunday afternoons by various congregations) and paid for their own missionaries.

The Home and Foreign Missionary Society's first appointee was Mbiyana
Ngidi, who in 1861 founded a new mission station (initially at a site called
Inhlimbithi and then at a site called Newspaper or more popularly Noodsberg)
between Esidumbini and Mapumulo on location land leased from the Natal
Native Trust. Ngidi would work on his own, and with considerable success, at
Noodsberg for the next two decades. The second appointee was a teacher from
the mission's primary school at Umvoti named Benjamin Hawes (in common
with many African Christians of this era, Hawes had adopted a Western name,
presumably at baptism). He served the congregation at Itafamasi, which had
been without a resident white missionary since 1853. At least three of the mission's twelve evangelical 'helpers' were funded by the Home and Foreign
Missionary Society by 1869, when Nathaniel Clark, the American Board's foreign secretary at the time, finally ordered the mission to convert the congregations into churches and start ordaining African ministers.

The American Board was a world leader in promoting self-governing, self-
supporting, self-propagating churches in the foreign mission field, and the Natal
mission had been under pressure for years to implement this 'three-self formula'.[20] The AZM reluctantly agreed to recognise some congregations as churches. They were to be organised in the Congregational manner – with their own
church leaders, constitutions, by-laws and membership lists. Relations with
African clergy were formalised in a 'Native Annual Meeting' which would be
held each year immediately after the mission's annual meeting.

The first church was organised at Umzumbe in May 1870 with Nguzana
Mngadi as its ordained pastor (his Christian name was Rufus Anderson, the
name of the American Board's most famous foreign secretary). Other churches
were created within weeks at Imfume (under a man named Msingaphansi
Nyuswa, who had served the local congregation for 20 years) and Inanda
(under a man named James Dube, the long-time preaching 'helper' of missionary pioneer Daniel Lindley, who had established the station). The mission continued, however, to drag its feet on the issue of ordaining African pastors. Two
years later, Benjamin Hawes was ordained pastor of the church at Itafamasi, and
Ira Adams Nembula accepted ordination to head the church at Amanzimtoti.
In 1876 Ngidi was finally ordained pastor of his church at Noodsberg. Seven
years later, Nqumba Nyawose, who had received training as a preacher (along
with Dube and Hawes) at Esidumbini, was given the pastorate of another
church called Empusheni on adjacent location land.[21]

Meanwhile, the question of standardising procedures for acceptance into the
Christian community had become a major concern for the mission.[22] Several
mission resolutions directed against African cultural practices, for example, were
passed during the 1860s, including one in 1862 that tried to force persons

married under 'Native law' who were seeking admission to the church to be remarried under 'English law'.[23] Militants were particularly anxious to stop the exchange of gifts associated with the *lobola* system that accompanied the marriage of females, but missionaries of the older generation like Lindley and Aldin Grout disagreed. They did not regard all customary practices as insurmountable barriers to church membership, and they were supported by others like the Lloyds.

The divisions were so serious that the AZM asked the home board in Boston to issue a ruling. Secretary Clark's reply in 1868 is worth noting, because he expressed the board's official attitude on these matters for the generation to come:

> The proper work of missionaries is to introduce the new divine life, not the forms it shall assume … A morality enforced upon unwilling minds is of little value … Your work is not to make American but Zulu Christians … The great thing is to bring men to Christ, not to change their social customs, their natural usages, or to lead them to adopt all the practices of civilized nations in their domestic life.[24]

The Natal missionaries chose to ignore Clark's advice. Grout, whose own authority had been compromised in a sustained conflict with landowners at Umvoti, retired in 1870 and Lindley followed in 1873. There was apparently no one on the mission with enough influence to oppose those who were determined to purify all Africans previously certified as members of the Christian community.

Among the first to go were the pastors. Rufus Anderson was charged with adultery, suspended in 1876 and dropped from the pastor's roll a year later. Benjamin Hawes was temporarily relieved of his duties for 'insubordination'. Ira Nembula had to leave the Amanzimtoti church two years after ordination because of his family's poor health, while Msingaphansi Nyuswa and James Dube died within a few years of ordination and were not replaced. Organisations like the Native Annual Meeting that had been recognised only a few years earlier to maintain contact with church leaders became defunct, and by 1878 the mission only had one ordained pastor in active service. Between 1872 and 1893 two pastors were ordained – Mbiyana Ngidi and Nqumba Nyawose – but both were leaders of frontier churches beyond the confines of the station community. Ngidi's relationship with the AZM gradually deteriorated: he left Noodsberg station for Zululand with a majority of his congregation in the early 1880s to establish a new station near Rorke's Drift, where he formed his own Uhlanga (National) Church about 1885.[25] Nyawose was suspended about 1890 for being 'heady and unmanageable' and thereafter was associated with the separatist church movement.

The campaign to purify the Christian community between the 1870s and 1890s was without precedent. Its effects would be felt in every sphere of mission activity and, as one missionary noted in the 1960s, 'are still with us today'.[26] Excommunications soared – at least one church was purged of all its members – as the assault on 'heathen' customs gained momentum. The missionaries probably spent years in intense discussions with African Christians over these issues before the conditions for admission to the mission's churches were finally standardised with a set of binding rules – designated the Umsunduzi Rules, because they were drafted at Umsunduzi station – in June 1879.[27] More were added in later years, and a 20-page compilation of these regulations, aptly described at the time as a 'Mosaic code', was issued in 1900.[28] The Americans also sought alliances with other missionary societies, which would lead to the formation of the Natal Missionary Society (July 1883) and various other white missionary organisations interested in the moral 'welfare' of African Christians in colonial Natal.

While the new religious order was articulated largely by the mission patriarchy, it could not have been constructed without the active assistance of missionary wives and other women recruited as teachers. These activities are best illustrated in the temperance crusade, which was initiated by Laura Bridgman, who with her husband Henry resided at Umzumbe mission station.[29] While the temperance crusade was directed against all intoxicating beverages, in the mission's view the main problem at the time was beer drinking (especially a traditional brew called *utshwala*). Beer drinks were a custom accepted by all African Christians, even among the students at the mission's theological school, which was then located at Umzumbe. Mrs Bridgman gained her first temperance pledge from a student at the school in 1878, but he went back to beer when the Anglo–Zulu War intervened in 1879 and the Bridgmans sought a safer haven in Durban.

Mrs Bridgman redoubled her efforts when she returned. While she continued working with the theological students and their families, she concentrated her energies on 'the school-house full of children. Could we not work up a temperance sentiment among them; could we not kindle a flame in their young hearts, which they would take to their homes and start a fire ablaze among the people there and on the station?' If the children agreed to abstain from drinking beer, they were given 'a little bit of blue ribbon to pin on their dresses'. Mrs Bridgman would use the children to get to the men – the patriarchal pillars of the Christian community.

Then we planned a great picnic at the river and the children were to march around with music and flags and banners. This took with them like a charm, and enthusiasm was kindled. Then followed a series of meetings in the chapel, one every two months through the year. The boys and girls learned pieces, recitations and dialogues, the chapel was decorated in finest style with flowers, flags and banners. Much of the dramatics was employed with fine effect ... The people were amused, captivated and convinced. One by one they came forward to take the ribbon ... But all this was not accomplished by meetings alone. Many were the talks and arguments and prayers we had with those men in our little room on every suitable occasion. Those who were the hardest to yield were the strongest and the firmest to stand.

Thus was born what would be known for decades to come as the Blue Ribbon Army.

From Umzumbe, the Blue Ribbon Army marched to Amanzimtoti, where Mrs Addie Robbins was instrumental in the temperance campaign,[30] and on to Inanda, where Mary Edwards, mistress of Inanda Seminary, the AZM's prestigious girls boarding school, took over. The movement soon spread to other stations, where missionary women hoisted the temperance banner. An unknown number of African women and children were also involved in spreading the gospel of temperance (they are all but invisible in the mission record), especially when it spilled over into 'kraal' outstation schools and preaching places beyond the station community. The mission launched a vigorous pamphleteering campaign on temperance issues, and the crusade was taken up by other missionary societies as well. The war on drink spread to the settlers, and Mrs Bridgman became one of the founders of the Women's Christian Temperance Union in Natal and, later on, in South Africa.

The temperance movement opened the door to further efforts to purify the struggling African churches. The Bridgmans, working closely with those who wore the Blue Ribbon, convinced a majority of church members to approve a new church code in 1884. The Umzumbe Rules, a more detailed version of the rules drawn up at Umsunduzi, became a model for other congregations. New organisations like the Amavoluntiya (Volunteers), which consisted of lay men and women from the churches, were created to preach salvation and purity to relatives, friends and neighbours.[31] 'Bible women' were trained and sent into homes to read from scripture and pray with families.[32] Fervent prayer meetings, hymn-singing festivals,[33] and open-air healing services and revivals[34] were regular occurrences in the everyday lives of African Christians on the American mission in the last three decades or so of the nineteenth century.

The missionaries and their converts would remember this period as a turning point in the history of the church (it is still remembered in Congregational Church lore as the era of the 'Great Revivals'). As the AZM's official letter to the board put it in 1906:

The record of admissions, trials, suspensions, expulsions, made sad reading. There were few members down to 1881 who did not sooner or later come under discipline ... [Now] there is no longer any contest over the rules ... It is understood everywhere that these are the rules of all our churches, and that those who violate them are liable to be expelled or suspended from the church.[35]

And they were right. The mission, of course, was influenced profoundly by the actions it took in 'purifying' the church, but I have space only to consider how these actions affected the church itself and the broader African Christian community.

TOWARDS AN AUTONOMOUS CHURCH

The purge of the church was undertaken during a period of increasing pressure for autonomy from African community leaders. The first step towards this goal was taken when a 'Committee on Union and Co-operation with the Native Christians' presented a plan that was accepted on the occasion of the mission's jubilee celebration in December 1885. Six men – two missionaries, two laymen who apparently represented a militant group of 'young people' in the church,[36] and two African ministers from the Home and Foreign Missionary Society – were elected to a committee called the Abaisitupa.

The Abaisitupa (meaning 'The Six') would pool the financial resources of mission (meaning the 'native agency' fund, which was money allocated to help subsidise the salaries of African clergy) and church. It was only an advisory body at first, but the missionaries still demanded the post of treasurer and insisted they had the right to control all appointments. Nevertheless, the African members accepted their responsibilities with enthusiasm and the Abaisitupa would become the main catalyst in mediating relations between mission and church in the next generation.[37]

Pushed by the American Board, pulled by the Abaisitupa, threatened by dissident church leaders and a surging separatist movement, the missionaries would now try to orchestrate the structures needed for an autonomous church. They turned to the Home and Foreign Missionary Society for help. Sidelined by decades of purges, the HFMS was reorganised and rejuvenated in 1895 as an assembly composed of two delegates from each congregation, the 'approved' pastors and preachers still in active service, and the Abaisitupa. The Abaisitupa, then, was the executive committee for the society, which would meet formally at least twice a year. One of these meetings would be held at the same time as the mission's annual meeting, and the old Native Annual Meeting was resuscitated in 1896 for this purpose. The Pastors' Conference, as it would soon be called (because those in attendance were clergy in charge of churches), began 'to vote on matters which came within its scope' in 1902.[38] Missionary appointees on the Abaisitupa would still have some say in church matters, but African members had a majority vote and they would be the spokesmen for their people.

Nevertheless, self-governing churches in the Congregational tradition would not survive unless they could support themselves. The mission had lost credibility because the purges in part had been directed against wealthier church members.

> They have been cut off for various offences. So long as they hoped to be restored or to exercise control over the secular affairs of the church, they continued to contribute, but when it became evident that there could be no restoration without reformation and that they were altogether out-siders ... then contributions began to decrease and in some cases they have ceased entirely.[39]

African monetary contributions to churches and schools did decline rapidly in the 1880s – reaching a low of £230 in 1889.

Judson Smith, who replaced Clark as foreign secretary of the American Board, had warned the Zulu mission in 1888 that 'no man will ever become fit to be a pastor except by being made a pastor, and having his natural qualifica-tions drawn out by the pressure of responsibility ... A church that has a mis-sionary for its pastor can never come to the idea of self-support.'[40] The next step towards the creation of an autonomous church, then, was the restoration of the pastorate.

The term 'pastor' in the language of nineteenth-century missionaries nor-mally meant an ordained male minister. African pastors were men of power and privilege in the encounter between coloniser and colonised on the mission field. Ordained pastors were the only clergy who could perform the all-impor-tant rites of communion and baptism, and they had the legal right to solemnise Christian marriages. They were the spiritual leaders of their churches, and they were authorised to collect and control funds on behalf of the churches. They were recognised by the colonial government and accorded certain social and economic privileges (such as travelling on trains at a reduced fare), which brought them a measure of security and mobility in Natal's settler-dominated society. Above all, the rite of ordination gave African pastors ecclesiastical equal-ity with white missionaries.[41]

The Abaisitupa approved four men for ordination in 1896 – a move that immediately tripled the number of pastors from two to six. A host of factors blocked the appointment of more pastors and preachers to head churches, but the numbers do suggest a dramatic increase in the overall number of 'approved' African clergy serving AZM churches between 1885 and 1910.

African clergy serving the American mission, 1885–1910[42]

Year	Pastors	Preachers	Evangelists
1885	2	7	50
1890	2	16	85
1895	6 (1896)	22	160
1899	5	15	253
1903	10	19	414
1905	6–7	12	345
1910	8	25	489

The first African secretary on the Abaisitupa was appointed in the mid-1890s, and the key post of treasurer was handed over to Africans in 1901 (the first treasurer being Mvakwendlu Sivetye). The salaries of African clergy were now based entirely on contributions the churches made to the Home and Foreign Missionary Society: the mission's 'native agency' fund ceased when the American Board subsidy for that purpose was stopped in 1895. Church contributions to the HFMS dropped to a low of £46 in 1885–6 and rose gradually in the 1890s (from £237 in 1890–1, for example, to an average of £321 between 1895 and 1897). Contributions more than doubled, however, after Sivetye took office, averaging £850 to £1100 a year between 1903 and 1908. A minister's salary was not the only issue that had to be resolved in order to achieve financial autonomy, but it was the major one. Only 5 of the mission's 23 designated churches were not self-supporting by 1903, and the AZM noted that individual contributions as a proportion of total income exceeded 'wealthy American churches'.[43]

The increase in African clergy during these years is also associated with renewed efforts by the Abaisitupa and the Home and Foreign Missionary Society to evangelise rural Natal. Church workers – spearheaded largely by the evangelists – were now operating in hitherto inaccessible areas of mission reserves and locations, launching outreach programmes in southern Natal (beyond the borders of traditional American missionary activity) and in Zululand north of the Thukela River. Migrants from American mission churches were also establishing new congregations in Johannesburg and elsewhere in the Transvaal. African Congregationalists were active beyond South Africa in AZM-initiated efforts to launch branches in colonial Mozambique and Rhodesia.[44] Although membership in American mission churches remained small in comparison to missionary societies like the Methodists, the growth rate really was spectacular during this period: while there were 646 designated church members (and 13 churches) in 1880, for example, there were 5837 members (and 26 churches) in 1910.[45]

The AZM would now claim that self-governing, self-supporting, self-propagating churches were a reality. Mission reports in the last five years or so of the colonial era described relations with the Abaisitupa as 'most cordial. The meetings are invariably harmonious, and your [missionary] members consider service on this committee a real privilege.' As the mission's letter to the board in 1906 put it: 'The hopeful thing is that the church can be trusted ... to discipline a member. Our pastors and preachers can generally be trusted not only to set the right example, but to preach a right doctrine on these questions. There is no question that in number and character the leaders among the natives are in advance of those of 25 years ago.' The question posed in the waning years of colonial rule was 'not how soon may we go but rather how long can we stay? How long will the churches accept our co-operation? ... Despite the differences of the past ... not for years has our Mission enjoyed the confidence of the churches to such a gratifying degree as now.'[46]

TOWARDS AN AFRICAN CHRISTIAN COMMUNITY

In the Natal mission field, relations between believer and non-believer are memorialised in the distinction between the *amakholwa* (Christians who were card-carrying members of mission churches) and the *amabhinca* (non-Christian traditionalists). The distinction was fundamental to missionaries in the nineteenth century, because it helped them to define who they were, and who their converts might become, in relation to the 'other' – the heathen African. Religious discourse on the American mission field, however, was not limited to conversations between missionaries or even to conversations between missionaries and purified *amakholwa*, who might adhere to missionary notions of the Christian enterprise.

The *amakholwa* community was much, much larger than the group of Christians identified as Christians in American mission statistics. This community embraced Africans who had fled or been forced out of mission churches, Africans who had joined separatist churches or returned to a more traditional way of life. Mission Christians, moreover, regularly crossed denominational boundaries in the search for a more authentic religious experience. Even for certified *amakholwa* of the American mission, the debate over church regulations, for example, continued for decades and was never fully resolved.[47] The *amabhinca* are also impossible to reduce to an amorphous mass of unbelievers. They listened to the evangelists and attended schools, wore clothes and bought land, and were in daily contact with their Christian neighbours. African migrants of all religious persuasions, moreover, worked and lived together in town.

The religious conversation between missionary and African Christians on the American Zulu Mission can perhaps best be illustrated by examining briefly the history of the separatist movement. While resistance to missionary authority can be traced to at least the 1850s, there is no evidence that African Christians who left the American mission actually established churches independent of the mission before the 1880s. A combination of circumstances, however, made conditions more favourable for an independent church movement to flourish in American mission churches in the last generation of the colonial era.

The serious erosion in the economic fortunes of Africans living in rural Natal from the 1880s, a surge of new discriminatory laws under responsible government (from 1893) and the first significant migration of Africans from the countryside to town certainly had religious as well as political implications. The relationship between African independent churches and the early African nationalist movement in Natal should also be considered. For example, new ideas – such as those propagated by the missionary entrepreneur and visionary Joseph Booth, a radical fundamentalist who spent three months in Durban in 1896 extolling the virtues of an 'Africa for the Africans' to the educated African Christian elite – 'acted as a powerful stimulus to the schismatic spirit so prevalent at just that time'.[48]

The AZM lacked money and missionaries to monitor the activities of the churches except through the Abaisitupa, while the purges effectively fragmented the congregations and left large numbers of people outside the framework of mission Christianity. The new generation of African Christians was more dispersed among the non-Christian community, more distanced from station life, more alienated from the mission church and often more vocal about the need to retain certain customary practices.

The major separatist leaders between the 1880s and 1910s were the leaders of American mission churches. Mbiyana Ngidi, the ordained AZM pastor who established the Uhlanga Church in Zululand about 1885, has already been mentioned. He returned to Natal about 1890, and the pro-Ngidi faction gained temporary control of the church building at Noodsberg. Although little has been written about Ngidi or his church, these separatists undoubtedly influenced subsequent events at Table Mountain and Johannesburg that led to the founding of the Zulu Congregational Church (ZCC) – the most significant breakaway church from the AZM during the colonial era.

The story of the Zulu Congregational Church begins with two established and highly regarded preachers, standard bearers in the campaign to purify the Christian community, who were rewarded with churches of their own on the borders, as it were, of mission activity.[49] Table Mountain was the mission's only inland station, and the last resident missionary had left in 1860. It was isolated from the centres of mission activity on the coast, and the reserve (the mission only received the title-deed in 1875) was barely accessible to the outside world by wagon even in the 1880s. The area had long been coveted by white farmers and townsmen living in nearby Pietermaritzburg. They grazed their cattle on the land and paid the missionaries to cut down the trees for timber and fire-wood, which triggered numerous disputes with the local African population.

The mission finally placed a preacher named Daniel Njaleki at Table Mountain in 1873. He built a church, hired a teacher and started a primary school, and a small Christian community gradually re-emerged on the station. Njaleki and most of his parishioners left the station in the early 1880s and migrated to newly conquered Zululand in search of land. The move was moti-vated apparently by economic grievances triggered by the white farmers (whose cattle were tramping their gardens and making their own cattle sick), a two-year drought and crop failure. Njaleki hoped the AZM 'might consent to still regard him as belonging to us [the AZM] and would aid in his support'. But the mission refused, so Njaleki returned in 1884 and was allowed to go back to the church at Table Mountain.[50] When Njaleki, in ill health, left Table Mountain again in 1888, the congregation nominated a man named Simungu (or Usimungu) Bafazini Shibe to be their preacher.

Shibe had lived for many years at Umzumbe, where he worked as a brick-layer and road builder for the Bridgmans until he finished primary school. Shibe was then sent for further training to Amanzimtoti Seminary and the the-ological school, where he remained for about seven years before returning to the church at Umzumbe. The missionaries approved Shibe's move to Table Mountain, and they had nothing but praise for his activities as preacher-in-charge of this frontier church.

Table Mountain, however, had been a source of conflict in AZM dealings with colonial officials since the early 1870s. The Natal government had tried to annex the reserve in 1888 (the Native Lands Resumption Bill) and again after the settlers were granted responsible government.[51] The Americans were in contact with the Natal Congregational Union (representing white Congregational churches established by the British settler community in the Colony), and they clearly hoped its members could be persuaded to take up some of the burden of supervising African mission work. A contract was nego-tiated allowing the NCU to take over Table Mountain station for a trial peri-od of ten years. George Pugh, a former treasurer of the NCU, was placed in charge of Table Mountain in 1896. The Americans retained ultimate control, and the NCU agreed to provide yearly activity reports and 'accept our gener-al plans and rules for mission work'.[52]

In retrospect, the events that led to the creation of a separatist church at Table Mountain were predictable to all concerned. Shibe was fired soon after Pugh arrived (Shibe was actually away at the time on extended sick and study leave at Lovedale in the eastern Cape), despite protests from the mission and the Abaisitupa. But Shibe returned to Table Mountain with support from a major-ity of his former parishioners. They recognised the threat that Pugh posed and urged the mission to ordain Shibe in a vain bid to reassert the independence of the Table Mountain church. The NCU demanded that the Americans support Pugh and remove Shibe from the reserve, while Shibe's followers and African members of the Abaisitupa demanded that the Americans support the besieged preacher. In the end, the mission sided with its white trustee.

Meanwhile, a similar situation was developing in Johannesburg, where African migrants from the Natal mission had established a congregation of their own in the late 1880s. They hired a white businessman and ex-Congregational minister to lead the church in 1892, but his tenure was brief and disastrous. Accused of mishandling church funds, he left within a year, and church leaders asked the mission for an African minister to take charge of the work in Johannesburg. The Americans were, however, clearly intent on expanding their activities in the urban areas, so they sent a veteran missionary named Herbert Goodenough to Johannesburg to buy a building plot (in the suburb of Doornfontein) and erect a small chapel, which was formally opened in December 1893. Goodenough wanted to stay, and the mission agreed that he would be in charge of the Johannesburg mission. An African preacher – generally named in mission correspondence as Fokoti[53] – was chosen to head the church. Fokoti was born and raised at Amanzimtoti, trained at the theological school and, like Shibe, had passed the AZM moral litmus test with flying colours.

Under the leadership of Goodenough and Fokoti, the Johannesburg church expanded even more rapidly, and in new directions, than it had previously. A mine-compound ministry was launched, multi-racial, open-air evangelistic meetings were held regularly with other mission groups in the Market Square area (in the centre of Johannesburg), and special services were conducted for Cape coloureds working in the city. The church itself was flourishing with several hundred members, an evening school and preaching places in various parts of Johannesburg. Relations between mission and congregation began to unravel when the AZM agreed to a proposal from Goodenough's wife Carrie to use money she had inherited to buy land and build a large house next to the church. The Goodenoughs would live in the house, rent rooms to tenants and give a portion of the rent money to the mission to expand its work on the Witwatersrand.

This decision triggered a series of events that in retrospect were also predictable, and they led to the creation of a separatist church in Johannesburg. Goodenough apparently immersed himself more and more in administering his own property: the apartments, for example, were rented to poor white and Cape coloured families, and a kindergarten was opened for their children. Goodenough also retained a stranglehold over the financial affairs of the church, and at the same time he distanced himself personally and professionally from Fokoti, eventually removing him to a preaching place in Germiston. Fokoti's supporters started holding separate services and asked the mission to ordain their preacher and place him in control of the Johannesburg mission. A white supporter, who 'makes himself perfectly one with the natives',[54] tried to mediate on behalf of Fokoti and his parishioners, but the AZM again sided with its white trustee.

Mission correspondence at the time suggests the Americans knew they had placed themselves in an untenable position. Shibe and Fokoti had been friends for years, and they were in regular contact not only with each other but with other separatists[55] and with the leaders of mission churches in Natal. The ordained pastors and preachers – indeed, most of the church communicants – were in sympathy with the separatists, and the entire mission enterprise was in jeopardy. The Americans warned the pastors not to take matters into their own hands ('The organization of churches and the ordination of pastors can only be done with the approval and co-operation of the Mission itself'),[56] but they did nothing further to provoke the separatists. They appealed to all the participants to keep talking (and even sent evangelists to Table Mountain to conduct revival services) in the apparent belief that no decision was the right decision.

The years between 1898 and 1900 were a turning point in the history of the separatist movement as far as the AZM were concerned, and it was not the missionaries but African church leaders who actually averted a wholesale secession. Shibe's and Fokoti's followers had appealed separately to the American Board in March and November 1897, but the foreign secretary refused to intervene in either dispute. The dissidents finally decided to take matters into their own hands: in December, Shibe travelled to Johannesburg to meet with Fokoti, and in February 1898 the two congregations joined together and ordained the two men as ministers of a new organisation – the Zulu Congregational Church.[57]

Shibe returned to Table Mountain and with his congregation selected a plot of land in the reserve to build their church. Pugh's personal authority was apparently compromised not only in the Christian community but also among the non-Christian majority in the reserve. Table Mountain was more heavily populated than most other American reserves, and competition between chiefs over land and followers had become quite intense by the mid-1890s. The principal contenders for land in the reserve by this time were two chiefs, and land issues dividing the chiefdoms became inextricably linked with religious issues dividing the Christian community. Pugh sided with the chief (a man named Mgangezwe) who had the largest following and convinced the AZM to recognise him as the sole authority in the reserve in 1899. The other chief (a man named Mdepa) and his people sided with Shibe against Pugh and the American mission.

Access to land and property formed the key issues in the struggle for control over religious discourse. Pugh forced the American mission, for example, to initiate proceedings against Shibe to remove him from Table Mountain. The local magistrate sided with the AZM, but Shibe fought back, hired a white lawyer and won on appeal to the Supreme Court in September 1898. Pugh reported that 'news of our defeat has gone like wildfire over the country'.[58] Once it was realised that Africans could not be easily removed from mission reserves – especially over religious disputes – those who had stayed with Pugh and the mission church, along with non-Christian residents who were loyal to Chief Mdepa, sought to join the ZCC.

The mission then petitioned the governor to have Shibe removed, but again they were turned down because this separatist leader was one of the first African converts on the American mission to be 'exempted' from Native Law. While the few Africans who held this status were still subject to various forms of discrimination, in theory they had the same legal status as whites in the Colony and were even eligible to vote. Shibe's links with the early African nationalist movement in Natal are fairly clear. He participated in meetings of the Funamalungelo society, a forerunner of the Natal Native Congress, which was started in 1888 by exempted Africans in Natal as a forum to voice their interests and concerns. He read African protest newspapers like *Inkanyiso yase Natal*.[59] He was in contact with people like Harriette Colenso, a vigorous supporter of African civil rights, and especially with leaders of the *amakholwa* elite like John Langalibalele Dube, the founding father of African politics in the Colony.

Dube (1871–1946) – a son of the mission[60] – was the epitome of the AZM's vision of African Christian enterprise at the turn of the century. He had studied for years in the United States (initially at Oberlin College and later at Union Missionary Seminary in Brooklyn, New York) and was ordained there in 1899. He had helped in the revision of the Zulu Bible, taught at Amanzimtoti Seminary and was pastor of the station church at Inanda until 1908. But he was even more active during these years as an educator (the founder of Ohlange Industrial Institute in August 1901) and journalist (the founder of *Ilanga lase Natal* in April 1903).[61] Dube, and other individuals associated with the AZM like Martin Lutuli, would also play a critical role in the Natal Native Congress (the forerunner in Natal of the African National Congress), which was launched in 1899 as an umbrella political body for the modernising, educated African Christian elite.[62]

Dube had mastered the nuances of colonial discourse, and he lived by the codes and rituals of mission Christianity. And yet, the American missionaries never quite knew what to make of Dube, who was at the height of his influence as a leader of his people during the first two decades of the new century. He remained a loyal member of the mission, but he maintained contact with Shibe and at one stage was actually invited to lead the ZCC. *Ilanga* regularly carried news of the ZCC in its columns, and one of Dube's brothers was a leader in Shibe's church.[63]

Dube would voice the frustrations of African modernisers who were disillusioned with missionary indifference to their political and economic interests. Their grievances were enumerated on a leader page in *Ilanga*, for example, in 1908:

1. The missionaries keep themselves apart from the Natives, they no longer mix with the Natives to hear their spiritual and bodily needs. The Natives only see the missionary now at the Church.
2. … men of note who own property and businesses of their own … are regarded as the missionary's enemies.
3. The missionaries do nothing to assist the natives in becoming owners of businesses.
4. … This is why the old missionaries are constantly being referred to by the Natives.
5. The Natives whilst under the wearying rule of the Government, do not now often hear the word of the missionary spoken in their defence.

The commentary concluded with a Zulu proverb: 'Faithful are the wounds of a friend.'[64]

The immediate grievances of both the Johannesburg and Table Mountain separatists boiled down to personal differences with the resident missionary and questions of control over church funds, land and property. From the American mission's perspective, however, the attempt to assert (or reassert) white control over congregations that had been established essentially by Africans lay at the heart of the dispute. And the major issue was the impact the secessionists had on the AZM's core churches in Natal:

> The disorganization of the Johannesburg and Table Mountain work was far from being the most serious … In the questions at issue the seceders had the fullest sympathy and moral support of practically our entire constituency. It is probable, too, that the secession itself was not undertaken without the sanction of the American Mission churches in Natal. The peril of complete rupture between the Mission and its churches … was imminent.[65]

Indeed, both Shibe and Fokoti claimed their church was approved by the Natal mission churches at a meeting at Itafamasi in June 1897, when they were promised help in setting up churches apart from the resident missionaries at Table Mountain and in Johannesburg.

Fokoti died soon after his ordination, but he was replaced by one of the ordained pastors, a man named Sunguzwa Nyuswa, who left his congregation at Umtwalumi to join the separatists.[66] Although the mission was shocked, it proved to be a blessing in disguise, for Nyuswa was to play a key role in affecting a reconciliation between mission and church. Frederick Bridgman, a son of Henry and Laura Bridgman and himself a member of the AZM, later said the ordinations of Shibe and Fokoti 'saved the day' for the mission, and even Goodenough concluded: 'They [the dissidents] don't see it, but it is very clear to me ... They will alienate the sympathy which they have had hitherto among the Natal churches.'[67]

By 1900 branches of the ZCC had been started on several rural stations and outstations in Natal's mission reserves (including Umvoti, Amanzimtoti, Ifafa, Umtwalumi and Umzumbe) and locations. The ZCC had also established branches in three cities (Durban, Johannesburg and Pretoria) and claimed to have adherents living in Zululand and even in Mozambique (presumably, apostates from existing American Board programmes). The missionaries were divided on how to proceed, but African church leaders feared they could no longer contain their congregations, as more and more members were migrating to the ZCC. So they convinced the mission to open up reconciliation talks with the separatist churches.

Reconciliation was achieved in part because the ZCC was essentially in two factions led by Nyuswa in Johannesburg and Shibe in Natal, in part because Nyuswa took over the leadership role in negotiating a settlement, and in part because the leaders of Natal's mission churches, led by the Abaisitupa, were able to convince their communicants to accept the agreement. To the AZM's 'inexpressible joy,' Nyuswa and the Johannesburg church agreed to an amendment that retained the missionaries as 'consultants' in matters affecting the churches and stopped short of 'absolute independence'. After ten months of discussion, the agreement went into effect in September 1900. The autonomy of individual churches and the authority of the Abaisitupa and the Home and Foreign Missionary Society would be respected. And all American mission churches would now be members of a new body to be called the African Congregational Church.[68]

Shibe apparently rejected the agreement because the AZM would not accept the validity of his ordination – a vital link in the mission's tenuous authority over the churches. But Shibe was also motivated by the need of his followers for land – he was finally forced to leave Table Mountain in 1903 – and by a personal desire to improve his own economic status as the leader of an independent church. For example, he bought 300 acres of crown land next to Umzumbe to establish his headquarters: the money was contributed by parishioners, but the title-deed was registered in Shibe's name and it would remain the private property of his family. Shibe, of course, was convinced he had been 'sold out' by the AZM (a phrase Shibe used repeatedly in his letters), and he and his followers were being persecuted for their beliefs. Consequently, he protested against discriminatory acts of the missionaries and the Natal government in the pulpit and urged his people to maintain unity in the face of oppression.

The ZCC's impact on the American mission was essentially limited to the first two decades of the new century. Shibe's people were found on most American stations-cum-reserves by 1910, although the ZCC's stronghold was still at Table Mountain. The Natal Congregational Union withdrew from Table Mountain in 1904 before the end of its ten-year contract with the AZM, and Pugh had relatively little to show for his efforts. The Americans failed to evict the ZCC from the reserve, and Table Mountain was essentially abandoned to the separatists. Shibe's followers launched churches (some of them with primary schools) elsewhere in Natal outside the American sphere of influence, and in several towns outside the Johannesburg metropolitan area in the Transvaal.[69] Nevertheless, the ZCC suffered secessions in 1902, 1907, 1916 and 1918. When Shibe died in 1924, his church divided again into three opposing factions and apparently ceased functioning as a cohesive organisation.[70]

CONCLUSION

Settler furore over separatist churches like the ZCC and other expressions of the independent African at work in colonial Natal in the last decade or so of colonial rule severely tested the AZM's resolve to disengage itself from church affairs. Even a cursory reading of mission letters, reports and correspondence from various government officials (especially the Native Affairs Department) suggests that the AZM was targeted for surveillance.

Natal had by far the most repressive attitude towards African clergy and churches – especially those deemed to be separatists – in colonial South Africa. The white population in Natal was very small in relation to the African population, and the settlers had an 'almost pathological' fear of a 'Native uprising'. For many years the Americans, as historian Shula Marks points out, 'had borne the brunt of the attack on mission work in Natal', and they were not surprised that the government's case against 'Ethiopianism' (the label attached to all independent African church activity at the time) focused on Congregationalism and on the work of the AZM. The Americans – and perhaps especially the Americans – were in a vulnerable position, because they were a foreign mission group with no visible connection to a white settler church and no visible control over their African constituents.[71]

The missionaries, then, posed problems for a government that was aggressively expanding white control into all spheres of African life. When the event popularly known as Bambatha's 'rebellion' broke out in 1906, for example, government officials and settlers alike were convinced it had been prompted by African Christians inspired by the separatists. As Marks has suggested: 'what people believe to be true is frequently more important in determining the subsequent course of events, than the reality … the psychological reality of the "Ethiopian menace" played an important part in the government's reaction to the disturbances.' Autonomous black churches in colonial Natal would not be tolerated because they were believed to undermine white supremacy, and the Americans were singled out for attack. As S.O. Samuelson, Natal's permanent undersecretary for Native Affairs, put it: 'Ethiopian organisations no doubt owe their origin and parentage to some centrifugal force inherent in the American Zulu Mission … The African Congregational Church … [is] a separate and distinct native, black, or Ethiopian Church.'[72]

Natal's prime minister, Frederick Moor, finally instructed the AZM to draft a new constitution for the churches in 1907 that totally abrogated the rights given to them only seven years earlier. All bodies created to administer the churches – including the Abaisitupa, the Home and Foreign Missionary Society, and the Pastors' Conference – would now be 'purely advisory'. The missionaries would have veto power over all proposals made by churches and church leaders, no matter how trivial they might be, and Africans could not be 'present at' or have 'a voice in' any AZM meeting. The mission had exclusive rights to all church and school property outside as well as inside the glebes, and any church member who disagreed with a decision made by a missionary could be excommunicated. A new 'rule' was written into the *incwadi yabelusi* (pastors' handbook) that read: 'No Church or Pastor of the Churches … who rejects the counsel of the American missionaries, or engages in work other than that under them, or who works in opposition to them, can remain in fellowship with the American Congregational Churches.' Finally, the name of the church was changed to reflect the demand for white control-from the African Congregational Church to 'The Congregational Churches of the American Board'.[73]

The AZM celebrated its seventy-fifth anniversary in 1910 and reported that 'mutual relations' with the Natal government were 'restored'. While the Americans had been 'investigated as it is safe to say no mission outside Turkey or Russia had ever been before', the AZM had not 'departed in any particular from the methods and polity under which its work has been conducted'. Missionaries like Frederick Bridgman argued that the 'constitution' was only drawn up to satisfy the government: 'In actual practice, we are far more Congregational than this statement might lead one to suppose.'[74] But for those most concerned – the African clergy and their churches – this interpretation was inaccurate and ultimately unacceptable. Whereas the 1900 agreement was initiated largely by Africans to serve African needs, the 1907 'constitution' was created by white missionaries in response to the needs of the white settler community.[75]

Nevertheless, the American mission at the end of the colonial era was far different from the one that had been struggling for survival seventy years or so earlier. Despite their conflicts with Natal politicians, the Americans were well connected in the social and civic life of the white settler community and well respected as trustees of African interests in white missionary circles. Those Americans arriving in Natal at the turn of the century, moreover, were better educated, more convinced that mission should centre its activities in the cities and not really interested in duplicating the work of Africans in the churches. They would usher in the modern era.

This generation produced Frederick Bridgman (he arrived in 1897), who would become the expert in matters relating to African social welfare, James Dexter Taylor (he arrived in 1899), who would take charge of the theological school and later represent the mission in the church ecumenical movement, Dr James McCord (he arrived in 1899), who would transform the mission's medical programme,[76] and Albert LeRoy (he arrived in 1901), who would become the mission's main voice in African higher education. As Frederick Bunker, a contemporary, put it: 'In all the plans for [mission] reorganization they carry the balance of power and are fully fitted to do so.'[77]

Under their leadership, the AZM was moulded into a cohesive unit and its structures delineated as never before in its history. The intellectual and emotional transition from personal overseer to administrator-once-removed was completed, while the AZM itself was gradually transformed into an organisation of missionary specialists. Despite government demands that whites exercise total control of mission work, these were the missionaries who persuaded their older colleagues to relinquish control of the churches, abandon mission work that was not commensurate with resources expended (like the use of mission personnel for teaching in primary schools or the use of scarce funds for the Zulu literature programme), and concentrate on the urban mission and on post-primary education at the two main male and female boarding schools at Amanzimtoti and Inanda.

They were also representative of the new era of white liberals – dubbed 'liberal segregationists' by the historian Paul Rich and others – who would seek to moderate racial tensions in a rigidly segregated society by setting up parallel political, social and cultural organisations for Africans in town and countryside. LeRoy's friend and patron, for example, was Charles Loram, who was an inspector of schools at the time in Pietermaritzburg. Loram would become superintendent of education for Natal and a key player in advocating an educated African elite that would serve African needs (as mediated by whites) in designated African areas and would not pose a challenge to white supremacy. The men and women of the American mission would adapt this strategy to suit their own needs in the generation to come.[78]

NOTES

CHAPTER 2

1. Thanks to Mary-Lynn Suttie for bibliographical help, and to Greg Cuthbertson, Tilman Dedering, Johannes du Bruyn, Richard Elphick, Martin Legassick, Nigel Penn and Nicholas Southey for comment.

2. M.J. Cowie, *The London Missionary Society: A Bibliography* (Cape Town, 1969); E.C. Tait, *Dr John Philip, 1775–1851: A Selective Bibliography* (Johannesburg, 1972); J.W. Hofmeyr and K.E. Cross, *History of the Church in Southern Africa*, 3 vols. (Pretoria, 1986–93); D. Chidester et al., *Christianity in South Africa: An Annotated Bibliography* (London, 1997).

3. Some of the Wesleyan Methodist Missionary records were destroyed in the World War II bombing of London. The LMS records were incorporated in those of the Council for World Mission and rehoused in the library of the School of Oriental and African Studies, University of London. They were also microfilmed by Inter Documentation, Zug, Switzerland.

4. To call his book the first work of history produced in South Africa is to use a very broad definition of 'history'; Philip did not set out to write a history. A. Bank, 'The Great Debate and the Origins of South African Historiography', *Journal of African History*, 38(2), 1997 and 'History and the Political Mythology of Apartheid: The Genealogy of the Philip Myth', Unpublished seminar paper, University of Cape Town, 1998. John Campbell's *Travels in South Africa* (London, 1812) did not discuss the history of the LMS in South Africa.

5. E.g., John Mackenzie, *Ten Years North of the Orange River* (Edinburgh, 1871), and *Austral Africa: Losing it or Ruling it* (London, 1887).

6. 'South Africa is, in some respects,' said one LMS Report, 'the most trying field in which your missionaries have to labour ... their patience and faith are sorely tried by the combination of influences which tend to produce a mass of dull, inert, dead opposition to all spiritual influences. The uncertain nature of the seasons causes a constant anxiety about the things of this life which is not healthy; the frequent political complications produce a spirit of unrest and suspicion; the gross materialism of the native character is a difficult soil in which to plant the seeds of spiritual truth ...': *The Eighty-Eighth Report of the London Missionary Society for the year ending April 30th 1882* (London, n.d), pp.14–15.

7. Bank, 'Great Debate'; R. Ross, 'James Cropper, John Philip and the *Researches*', in H. Macmillan and S. Marks (eds.), *Africa and Empire* (London, 1989), and 'Donald Moodie and the Origins of South African Historiography', in R. Ross, *Beyond the Pale* (Johannesburg, 1993). The key response to Philip was D. Moodie, *The Record*, 3 parts (Cape Town, 1838–41). Moodie and others also wrote briefer, more polemic works.

8. G.M. Theal, *Compendium of South African History and Geography* (Lovedale, 1873).

9. Cf. C. Saunders, *The Making of the South African Past* (Cape Town, 1988), Part 2. George Cory wrote of the 'mania ... which possessed the London Missionary Society to extend its influence to regions beyond civilisation rather than to concern itself with work equally, if not more, necessary nearer home, but less likely to arrest public attention ...': *The Rise of South Africa*, I (London, 1910), p.299.

10. Saunders, *Making of the South African Past*, pp.64ff; W.M. Macmillan, *My South African Years* (Cape Town, 1975). Macmillan's books were *The Cape Colour Question* (London, 1927) and *Bantu, Boer, and Briton: The Making of the South African Native Problem* (London, 1929).

11. Something of what was lost can be gleaned from Macmillan's notes from the papers, now in Rhodes House Library, Oxford. There were, of course, other Philip papers, and the idea of publishing them was raised by Roger Beck but appears to have got nowhere. R.B. Beck, 'Editing and Publishing the John Philip Papers: Practical Considerations', *History in Africa*, 18, 1991.

12. C.S. Horne, *The Story of the LMS, 1795–1895* (London, 1894); Richard Lovett, *The History of the London Missionary Society, 1795–1895*, 2 vols. (London, 1899).

13. J. du Plessis, *A History of Christian Missions in South Africa* (London, 1911), pp.viii, 99. The chapters dealing with the LMS are 12–17 and 25–7. Of Philip he wrote: 'with all his faults, he must be set down as one of the greatest benefactors of the Hottentots and other natives that have lived in South Africa' (p.153).

14. Du Plessis presented Van der Kemp as a devout Reformed Christian led astray by Rousseau, a view which later scholarship showed to be wrong; see, esp., I.H. Enklaar, *Life and Work of Dr J. Th. van der Kemp* (Cape Town, 1988).

15. C.P. Groves, *The Planting of Christianity in Africa*, I (London, 1948), Chs. 10, 11.

16. D.R. Briggs and J. Wing, *The Harvest and the Hope* (Johannesburg, 1970). Briggs had completed a B.D. dissertation at Rhodes University in 1952 entitled 'An Historical Survey of Bethelsdorp Station of the LMS from its Inception until the Death of Doctor van der Kemp'.

17. B. Holt, *Joseph Williams and the Pioneer Mission to the South-Eastern Bantu* (Lovedale, 1954); C. Northcott, *Moffat* (London, 1961); Enklaar, *Van der Kemp*. For an excellent critical review of the Dutch missiologist's book on Van der Kemp see E. Elbourne, 'Concerning Missionaries: The Case of Van der Kemp', *Journal of Southern African Studies*, 17(1), 1991.

18. Edwin Smith, *The Blessed Missionaries: The Phelps-Stokes Lectures for 1949* (Cape Town, 1950).

19. N. Majeke [D. Taylor], *The Role of the Missionaries in Conquest*, new edn (Cape Town, n.d. [1988]); C. Saunders, 'Mnguni and Three Hundred Years Revisited', *Kronos: A Journal of Cape History*, 11, 1986. For a useful general discussion of different views on the role of missionaries, see C. Villa-Vicencio, 'The Missionaries', in M. Prozesky and J. de Gruchy (eds.), *Living Faiths in South Africa* (Cape Town, 1995), pp.64–8.

20. Philip assured the Governor that 'every portion of our [missionary] influence will be used to make the Griquas serviceable to the Colony': Majeke, *Role of the Missionaries*, p.79.

21. Ibid., pp.8, 20, 23 and Ch. 3.

22. J. Boas, 'The Activities of the London Missionary Society in South Africa, 1803–1836', *African Studies Review*, 16, 1973.

23. Saunders, *Making of the South African Past*, p.138.

24. M. Wilson, 'Missionaries: Conquerors or Servants of God?', *South African Outlook*, 1258 (March 1976): pp.40–2.

25. A. Sillery, *John Mackenzie of Bechuanaland 1835–1899: A Study in Missionary Imperialism* (Cape Town, 1970); A. Dachs, 'Missionary Imperialism: The Case of Bechuanaland', *Journal of African History*, 13(4), 1972. Cf. A. Dachs (ed.), *Papers of John Mackenzie* (Johannesburg, 1975).

26. 'The fundamental flaw in the Majeke-Taylor pamphlet', wrote Macmillan's son, 'was an essential racism which made no distinction between the views and interests of different mis-

sionaries …': H. Macmillan, 'Introduction', in H. Macmillan and S. Marks (eds.), *Africa and Empire: Macmillan, Historian and Social Critic* (London, 1989), pp.11–12.

27. D. Williams, 'The Missionaries on the Eastern Frontier of the Cape Colony, 1799–1853', Ph.D. thesis, University of the Witwatersrand, 1960. Williams's later writing includes 'Social and Economic Aspects of Christian Mission Stations in Caffraria, 1816–1854', *Historia*, 31(2), Sept. 1985, and 'The Missionary Personality in Caffraria, 1799–1853', *Historia*, 34(1), May 1989. The first doctoral thesis on the history of the LMS in South Africa was completed by Harry Gailey at University of California, Los Angeles, in 1957. Though Gailey went on to write a general *History of Africa*, 2 vols. (New York, 1970, 1972), his thesis remained largely old-fashioned in approach.

28. The lines often went across the page both horizontally and vertically, for the missionaries were concerned to save paper. This often made their script very difficult to read.

29. Martin Legassick, 'The Griqua, the Sotho-Tswana and the Missionaries', Ph.D. thesis, University of California, Los Angeles, 1969, and 'The Northern Frontier', in R. Elphick and H. Giliomee (eds.), *The Shaping of South African Society*, 2nd edn (Cape Town, 1989). Among others who worked in similar vein was Anthony Dachs, who considered the role of the LMS among the Tswana and how the Tswana had responded to the LMS presence: see, e.g., A. Dachs, 'Christian Missionary Enterprise and Sotho-Tswana Societies in the Nineteenth Century', in A. Dachs (ed.), *Christianity South of the Zambezi*, I (Gwelo, 1973).

30. E.g., Dachs, 'Missionary Imperialism'; K. Crehan, 'Khoi, Boer and Missionary: An Anthropological Study of the Role of Missionaries on the Cape Frontier, 1799–1850', M.A. dissertation, University of Manchester, 1978; C. Bundy, *The Rise and Fall of the South African Peasantry* (London, 1979), Ch. 2. On the role of missionaries as traders, a key article is R.B. Beck, 'Bibles and Beads: Missionaries as Traders in Southern Africa in the Early Nineteenth Century', *Journal of African History*, 30(2), 1989.

31. V.C. Malherbe, 'The Life and Times of Cupido Kakkerlak', *Journal of African History*, 20(3), 1979; J. Hodgson, 'Do we hear you Nyengana? Dr J.T. Vanderkemp and the First Mission to the Xhosa', *Religion in Southern Africa*, 5(1), 1984; D. Crafford (ed.), *Trail-Blazers of the Gospel: Black Pioneers in the History of Southern Africa* (Pretoria, 1991). The lay assistants at Bethelsdorp included Jochim Vogel, Kruisman, Boezak, Samson, Jocham, Abraham and Jacob.

32. J. Sales, *Mission Stations and the Coloured Communities of the Eastern Cape* (Cape Town, 1975).

33. B. le Cordeur and C. Saunders (eds.), *The Kitchingman Papers* (Johannesburg, 1976); and C. Saunders, 'James Read', *South African Outlook*, 1258 (March 1976) 'James Read: Towards a Reassessment', *Collected Seminar Papers* (University of London) 7, (1977); and 'Madolo: A Bushman Life', *African Studies*, 36, 1977.

34. T. Kirk, 'Progress and Decline in the Kat River Settlement', *Journal of African History*, 14, 1973; J. Visagie, 'Die Katriviernedersetting, 1829–1839', D.Phil. thesis, University of Pretoria, 1978.

35. G. Cuthbertson, 'Van der Kemp and Philip: The Missionary Debate Revisited', *Missionalia*, 17(2), 1989:77; A. Ross, *John Philip (1775–1851): Missions, Race and Politics in South Africa* (Aberdeen, 1986). Cuthbertson described Ross's book as a 'sanitised piece of biographical history in a doctrinaire liberal mould': 'Van der Kemp and Philip', p.90.

36. N. Etherington, ' Missionaries and the Intellectual History of Africa: A Historical Survey', *Itinerario*, 7, 1983, and 'Recent Trends in the Historiography of Christianity in Southern Africa', *Journal of Southern African Studies*, 22(2), June 1996.

37. T. Dedering, 'Khoikhoi and Missionaries in Early Nineteenth Century Southern Namibia: Social Change in a Frontier Zone', *Kleio*, 12, 1995; M.G. Aschaber, 'Sie zogen aus und predigten an allen Orten' [a thesis on the LMS missionary Michael Wimmer], University of Innsbruck, 1994; T. Dedering, *Hate the Old and Follow the New* (Stuttgart, 1997), Chs. 4, 5.

38. Nigel Penn, 'The Northern Cape Frontier Zone, 1700–c.1815', Ph.D. thesis, University of Cape Town, 1995, Chs. 12, 13.

39. K. Schoeman, *A Thorn Bush that Grows in the Path: The Missionary Career of Ann Hamilton, 1815–1823* (Cape Town, 1995), and *J.J. Kicherer en die Vroeë Sending, 1799–1806* (Cape Town, 1996). Schoeman's other writing on the LMS includes his edition of *The Missionary Letters of Gottlob Schreiner 1837–1846* (Cape Town, 1991), 'Die Londense Sendinggenootskap en die San: Die Stasies Ramah, Konnah en Philippolis, 1816–1828', and 'Die Londense Sendinggenootskap en die San: Die Stasie Boesmanskool en die Einde van die Sending, 1828–1833', both in *South African Historical Journal*, 29, 1993 and 30, 1994 respectively, and 'Bastiaan Tromp Writes "The Very Truth": A Letter to the London Missionary Society, 1812', *Quarterly Bulletin of the South African Library* 47(2), 1992.

40. J. Cobbing, 'The Mfecane as Alibi: Thoughts on Dithakong and Mbolompo', *Journal of African History*, 30, 1989; G. Hartley, 'The Battle of Dithakong and "Mfecane" Theory', in C. Hamilton (ed.), *The Mfecane Aftermath: Reconstructive Debates in Southern African History* (Johannesburg, 1995).

41. E. Elbourne, '"To Colonise the Mind": Evangelical Missionaries in Britain and the Eastern Cape 1790–1837', D.Phil. thesis, University of Oxford, 1991.

42. N. Mostert, *Frontiers: The Epic of South Africa's Creation and the Tragedy of the Xhosa People* (New York, 1992), pp.287ff. Mostert mentioned that Van der Kemp kept his firearm beside his bed 'ready primed', and described how Henry Calderwood alarmed even the British High Commissioner by his zeal to see the colonial troops go after Sandile, the Xhosa ruler, in 1847 (p.921).

43. Mary Cravens, 'The New Culture Brokers: Women in the 19th Century Protestant Missions to South Africa, 1799–1914', B.A. dissertation, Princeton University, 1993; N. Erlank, 'Missionary Wives and Perceptions of Race in the Early Nineteenth Century Cape Colony', South African Historical Society conference, Rhodes University, 1995, and 'Writing Women in(to) Early Nineteenth Century Cape Town', *Kronos: A Journal of Cape History*, 23, Nov. 1996; W. Woodward, 'The Petticoat and the Kaross: Missionary Bodies and the Feminine in the London Missionary Society 1816–1828', *Kronos: A Journal of Cape History*, 23, Nov. 1996; G. Cuthbertson and L. Kretzschmar, 'Gender and Mission Christianity', *Missionalia*, 24(3), Nov. 1996.

44. E.W. Said, *Culture and Imperialism* (London, 1993); A. Porter, 'Africa, Christian Missions and "Cultural Imperialism,"' in M.G. Aschaber (ed.), *Aspects of African History* (Vienna, 1998).

45. E.g., J. Hodgson, 'Do we hear you Nyengana?' and *The God of the Xhosa* (Cape Town, 1982). Cf. S. Kaplan (ed.), *Indigenous Responses to Western Christianity* (New York, 1995).

46. E.g., W. Mills, 'Missionaries, Xhosa Clergy and the Suppression of Traditional Customs', in H. Bredekamp and R. Ross (eds.), *Missions and Christianity* (Johannesburg, 1995).

47. N. Etherington, 'Gender Issues in South-East African Missions', in Bredekamp and Ross, *Missions and Christianity*, p.150. Cf. N. Erlank, 'Reinterpreting the Writing of Missionary History: The Case of Mrs Jane Philip (Wife of the More Famous John)', Conference on Gender and Colonialism, University of the Western Cape, 1997; K. McKenzie, '"My Own Mind Dying Within Me": Eliza Fairbairn and the Reinvention of Colonial Middle-Class Domesticity in Cape Town', *South African Historical Journal*, 36, May 1997.

48. D. Stuart, '"Of Savages and Heroes": Discourses of Race, Nation and Gender in the Evangelical Missions to Southern Africa in the Early Nineteenth Century', Ph.D. thesis, University of London, 1994; P. Landau, 'Explaining Surgical Evangelism in Colonial Southern Africa: Teeth, Pain and Faith', *Journal of African History*, 37(2), 1996. Van der Kemp was now seen as the first 'medical missionary' in Africa: C. Allwood, 'Mission as Healing the Sick: Christian Medical Missionaries in South Africa', *Missionalia*, 17(2), 1989.

49. L. de Kock, *Civilising Barbarians: Missionary Narrative and African Textual Response in Nineteenth-Century South Africa* (Johannesburg, 1996); Stuart, '"Of Savages and Heroes."'

50. A. Hastings, *The Church in Africa, 1450–1950* (Oxford, 1994).

51. An earlier study of the beginnings of LMS work among the Tswana was the thesis by J. du

Bruyn, 'Die Aanvangsjare van die Christelike Sending onder die Tlhaping 1800–1825', *Archives Yearbook for South African History*, 1989, no. 2 (Pretoria). An important subsequent study is P. Landau, *The Realm of the Word: Language, Gender and Christianity in a Southern African Kingdom* (London, 1995), the focus of which was 'how African Christians constructed a political realm of power' (p.xvii).

52. J. Comaroff and J. Comaroff, *Of Revelation and Revolution: The Dialectics of Modernity on a South African Frontier*, 2 vols. (Chicago, 1991, 1997), quotation from I, p.xi. For an excellent critical review of vol. I, see J. du Bruyn, 'Of Muffled Southern Tswana and Overwhelming Missionaries: The Comaroffs and the Colonial Encounter', *South African Historical Journal*, 31, 1994.

53. R. Elphick, 'South African Christianity and the Historian's Vision', *South African Historical Journal*, 26, 1992. In answering their critics in the Introduction to their second volume, the Comaroffs did not respond to this key point.

54. Questions asked by Elbourne in 'Concerning Missionaries'.

55. E. Elbourne, 'Early Khoisan Uses of Mission Christianity', *Kronos: A Journal of Cape History*, 19, Nov. 1992:24. Cf. E. Elbourne, 'A Question of Identity: Evangelical Culture and Khoisan Politics in the Early Nineteenth-Century Eastern Cape', *Collected Seminar Papers on the Societies of Southern Africa in the 19th and 20th Centuries*, University of London, 18, 1992.

56. R. Ross, 'The Social and Political Theology of Western Cape Missions', in Bredekamp and Ross, *Missions and Christianity*, esp. p.197. Ross differentiated what he called the 'Bethelsdorp tendency' from others within the LMS.

57. Bredekamp and Ross, *Missions and Christianity*, p.4, and E. Elbourne, 'Early Khoisan Uses of Mission Christianity'. Cf. also the chapter by R. Ross and E. Elbourne in the other major collection on Christianity to be published recently: R. Elphick and R. Davenport (eds.), *Christianity in South Africa* (Cape Town, 1997). It was only after the major war of the 1850s and the disaster of the 'cattle-killing' that there was large-scale conversion among the Xhosa.

58. Etherington, 'Historiography of Christianity', p.207.

59. Even putting together a map of the LMS stations for *The Kitchingman Papers* (ed. Le Cordeur and Saunders) proved a difficult task. But cf. F. Frescura, *Index of the Names of Mission Stations* (Johannesburg, 1982), and the map in Elphick and Davenport, *Christianity*, which shows the extent of LMS work compared to other mission societies.

60. E.H. Ludlow, 'The Work of the LMS in Cape Town, 1812–1841', Honours essay, University of Cape Town, 1981.

61. A. Appel, *Bethelsdorp, 1828–1945: Van Sendingstasie tot Stadsperiferie* (Port Elizabeth, 1994).

62. G. Cuthbertson, 'Missionary Imperialism and Colonial Warfare: London Missionary Society Attitudes to the South African War, 1899–1902', *South African Historical Journal*, 19, 1987. Etherington attributes the paucity of studies on twentieth-century European missionaries to the ebbing of the missionary impulse: Etherington, 'Historiography of Christianity', p.209. We need to know more about African ordinations in the LMS mission. Les Switzer mentions the first in 1873 and nine others by 1910: L. Switzer, *Power and Resistance in an African Society* (Madison, 1993), p.125.

63. Cf. A.C. George, 'The London Missionary Society and Education: A Study of the Eastern Cape to 1852', M.Ed. dissertation, Rhodes University, 1983; J.G. George, 'Education and London Missionary Society Policy in their Cape and Bechuana Missions from 1800 to 1925', Ph.D. thesis, University of Kent, 1987.

64. Le Cordeur and Saunders (eds.), *Kitchingman Papers*, for example, reveals the extensive links from Bethelsdorp to numerous other missionary societies. Many LMS missionaries went on to work for other societies.

65. Roland Oliver, *The Missionary Factor in East Africa* (London, 1952), p.42. He added: 'In missionary work it [the LMS] was predisposed to favour intensive methods, since, renouncing so much of the control and discipline which other Churches exercised over their professed

adherents, it had farther to lead them before they made the formal profession by baptism.'

66. Richard Elphick called for this in 'Writing Religion into History', in Bredekamp and Ross, *Missions and Christianity*, and in his Introduction to Elphick and Davenport, *Christianity*, pp.1ff. One recent attempt to do this is T. Keegan, *Colonial South Africa and the Origins of the Racial Order* (Cape Town, 1996).

67. J. Lazerson, *Against the Tide* (Boulder, 1994), pp.6–7.

68. P. Kapp, 'Dr John Philip: Die Grondlegger van Liberalisme in Suid-Afrika', *Archives Yearbook for South African History*, 1985, no. 2.

69. A. Bank, 'John Philip and Humanitarian Liberalism at the Cape', *Journal of Southern African Studies* Conference, University of York, 1994, and 'Liberals and their Enemies', Ph.D. thesis, University of Cambridge, 1995. Bank's ideas are incorporated in Keegan, *Colonial South Africa and the Origins of the Racial Order*.

70. R. Vigne, *Liberals against Apartheid* (London, 1997).

71. Etherington, 'Historiography of Christianity', p.217.

CHAPTER 3

1. The author holds a D.Th. in political theology from the University of the Western Cape and is the Director of the Kuruman Moffat Mission Trust. This work forms part of research towards a contemporary biography of Robert Moffat.

2. A. Ross, *John Philip*, pp.218ff.

3. Ibid., p.220

4. Cobbing, 'Mfecane as Alibi', pp.487–519.

5. E. Eldredge, 'Sources of Conflict in Southern Africa c.1800–1830', in Hamilton, *Mfecane Aftermath*, pp.123–61.

6. Hartley, 'Battle of Dithakong', pp.395–416.

7. Comaroff and Comaroff, *Of Revelation and Revolution*, I, see pp.32ff.

8. See, e.g., Charles Villa-Vicencio, *Theology of Reconstruction: Nation-building and Human Rights* (Cambridge, 1992).

9. Moffat was asked to identify the body of Livingstone when it arrived back in England, and was a pallbearer at Livingstone's funeral and burial at Westminster Abbey.

10. John Smith Moffat, *The Lives of Robert and Mary Moffat* (London, 1886), popular edn 1889, from which subsequent references are made.

11. Edwin W. Smith, *Robert Moffat: One of God's Gardeners* (London, 1925).

12. Cecil Northcott, *Robert Moffat: Pioneer in Africa* (London, 1961).

13. The library at the Kuruman Mission has the following: *Rivers of Water in a Dry Place: The Introduction of Christianity into South Africa and of Mr Moffat's Missionary Labours designed for the Young* (London, c.1865); W. Walters, *Life and Labours of Robert Moffat, D.D.* (London, 1883); J. Marrat, *Robert Moffat, African Missionary* (London, 1895); David J. Deane, *Robert Moffat of Kuruman* (London, c.1900); H. Williams, *Robert Moffat: The Story of a Long Life in the South African Mission Field* (London, c.1900); J.J. Ellis, *Robert Moffat: The South African Pioneer* (London, c.1910); I. Clinton, *Friend of the Chiefs: The Story of Robert Moffat* (London, 1958).

14. Robert Moffat, *Missionary Labours and Scenes in Southern Africa* (London, 1842).

15. I. Schapera (ed.), *Apprenticeship at Kuruman* (London, 1951).

16. J.P.R. Wallis (ed.), *The Matabele Journals of Robert Moffat, 1829–1860*, I and II (London, 1945).

17. A. Ross, *John Philip*, p.1.

18. It is important to note that I have no quarrel with the substance of Ross's work. Indeed, I feel that we are all in his debt for his critical work on John Philip. However, quite why he saw the need to deflate Moffat in order to inflate Philip continues to mystify me, for in the act of rescuing one LMS missionary from misunderstanding he has contributed to the mis-

understanding of another one.

19. 'As I verily believe that you will find a close application to study as hard an undertaking as anything you have hitherto engaged in': quoted in J.S. Moffat, *Lives*, p.16.

20. See the reference in the *Matabele Journals*, II, p.92. Later Wallis laments the fact that Moffat's third journey could have been 'more eminent' if Moffat had 'just so much more of his son-in-law Livingstone's spirit as would have reconciled him to a longer absence from his wife'. The patriarchal assumptions of this comment do unintended credit to Moffat!

21. Wallis, 'Introduction' in the *Matabele Journals*, I, p.x.

22. See Nancy Jacobs, 'The Flowering Eye: Water Management in the Upper Kuruman Valley, South Africa, c.1800–1962', *Journal of African History*, 37, 1996:237–60.

23. It is worth noting that Moffat was attached to the Tswana mission in 1820 and arrived there in that year at the end of his 'honeymoon' with Mary and John Campbell, a director of the LMS, who was exploring the possibilities for future mission work. He did not receive permission from the Cape Colony to live beyond the borders until 1821. It was during this wait at Griquatown that their first child, Mary, was born. She married David Livingstone in Kuruman in January 1845.

24. This village still exists today.

25. He learnt Dutch whilst in Stellenbosch in 1817, waiting for permission to undertake a missionary journey to Namaqualand, and it served him all his life, particularly in communicating with the Griqua, Koranna and Bergenaar inhabitants of the Orange River. Furthermore, it enabled him to converse with Chief Mzilikazi through the help of 'William', a Griqua man who had been captured by the Ndebele and who could speak both Dutch and Ndebele. Like many of the Ndebele captives, William had risen to prominence in Mzilikazi's army.

26. F.R. Bradlow, *Printing for Africa* (Kuruman, 1987).

27. His son John even suggests that he was more devoted to the Bible Society. 'Loyal and devoted as he ever was to his own society, the tie of affection to the kindred institution [the Bible Society] was even stronger and deeper': *Lives*, p.155.

28. This is alongside other great translators such as William Tyndale, Jerome, Martin Luther and William Carey. See Smith, *Moffat*, p.245.

29. For the first three journeys see Wallis, *Matabele Journals*, I.

30. For the fourth and fifth journeys see ibid., II.

31. Ibid., I, p.20.

32. Ibid., pp.321, 324, 328, 330.

33. See Wallis, 'Introduction', in ibid., II, pp.2ff.

34. Quoted in J.S. Moffat, *Lives*, p.220.

35. David Livingstone, quoted in Northcott, *Moffat*, p.181.

36. Thus Moffat tells Mzilikazi, 'missionaries could have no objections to fulfil his orders, so far as writing was concerned, but he must look to traders, who might be induced to come thus far, and on no account to missionaries, whose duty it was to supply him and his people with the knowledge of Divine things; that while they would ever feel willing to render every assistance in their power, they would on no account engage to supply him with anything in the way of trade'. *Matabele Journals*, II, p.134.

37. Ibid., pp.265ff.

38. See, for example, his refusal to represent the British government to Mzilikazi when asked to do so by Dr Andrew Smith on the 1835 trip. 'The Doctor had, on the road, more than once requested me to take a part in impressing on Moselekatse's mind, and getting him to understand, the nature and importance of the messages he had from Government to deliver to him. Though I would at any time cheerfully interpret, I felt at the same that it was my duty to steer clear of subjects relative to Government, as I had ever declared our non-connection, as missionaries': *Matabele Journals*, I, p.78.

39. See J.S. Moffat's comments in *Lives*, pp.64ff.

40. See *Missionary Labours*, pp.206ff. for Moffat's discussion on the conflicting roles of missionary and government agent. This quotation is from p.207.

41. Ibid., pp.207ff.

42. Comaroff and Comaroff, *Of Revelation and Revolution*, I, p.273.

43. This was a major responsibility Moffat took upon himself on his fourth journey to Mzilikazi. See *Matabele Journals*, II, and Northcott, *Moffat*, pp.250ff.

44. Andrew F. Walls, *The Missionary Movement in Christian History* (Maryknoll, 1996), pp.28ff.

45. Although I have searched in vain for a reference as to why Moffat translated Luke's Gospel first, my own hunch is that Moffat had a resonance with its incarnational concerns, it having long been recognised that Luke is the gospel of the poor, women and aliens.

46. J.S. Moffat, *Lives*, p.133.

47. Ibid., p.197.

48. Moffat, *Missionary Labours*, p.vi.

49. J.S. Moffat, *Lives*, p.167.

50. Ibid., p.242.

51. Comaroff and Comaroff, *Of Revelation and Revolution*, I, p.11.

52. Ibid., p.235

53. Seemingly aware of this, they do offer something of a narrative of the 'curious case' of the Methodist missionary Joseph Ludorf. Nevertheless, his responses are taken to represent certain options of an ideal type rather than to indicate a dialectic between social experience and political theology in the life of a missionary. See ibid., pp.279ff.

54. J.S. Moffat, *Lives*; Smith, *Moffat*; Northcott, *Moffat*.

55. Into this dynamic was introduced a personal tension between Moffat and Philip to do with the governance, not of the Colony, but of the missions belonging to the LMS. Thus it was that Moffat distanced himself from Philip in the area of politics as a way of asserting his independence from him, subconsciously identifying the vastly different political circumstances of the individual LMS missions as a reason for missionary independence. Moffat's son John, writing soon after Moffat's death in 1883, notes that Moffat and Philip 'could not be far away from each other in personal brotherly feeling'. He goes on to say that at the heart of their tension was Moffat's 'stout Nonconformist objection to the principle of a superintendency': *Lives*, p.44.

56. Almost all quotations from and references to Moffat and politics are drawn from *Apprenticeship at Kuruman (1820–28)* and *Missionary Labours and Scenes* (1842). Both these sources belong to the first period, and both reflect Moffat's early thoughts (and in the case of the former, his very early thoughts!), his ecclesiastical tension with Philip, and his relative isolation from the politics of the Colony. To make matters worse, two-fifths of the only other published source on Moffat, the *Matabele Journals* also focus on this first period (the journeys of 1829–30, and 1835).

57. Schapera, 'Introduction' to *Apprenticeship*, p.xxvii.

58. See J.S. Moffat, *Lives*, pp.147ff.

59. Comaroff and Comaroff, *Of Revelation and Revolution*, I, p.274.

60. Northcott, *Moffat*, p.208.

61. As quoted in ibid., pp.210ff.

62. As quoted in J.S. Moffat, *Lives*, pp.196ff.

63. 'Extracts from Transcripts from Robert Moffat's Journal, with Additions from Memory and Note Books; Made for the Information of the London Missionary Society', in *Matabele Journals*, I, pp.372ff.

64. Ibid., pp.380ff.

65. Extract from a letter by F.W. Chesson in *Lives*, p.296.

66. Jane Moffat's recollections in J.S. Moffat, *Lives*, p.276.

67. Letter to Mr Dickson, reproduced in ibid., p.282.

68. Comaroff and Comaroff, *Of Revelation and Revolution*, I, p.269.

69. Ibid., p.273.

70. Moffat's 'perfect disinterestedness' has been noted by a number of people. See the report of the funeral sermon by Rev. J.C. Harrison in J.S. Moffat, *Lives*, p.287, and a recollection by R. Robinson, Home Secretary of the LMS in ibid., p.299. See also Smith, *Moffat*, p.247. Northcott comments: 'It was this unromantic, objective view of his immediate neighbours [Boer and black] which saved Moffat from the miseries of disappointments and frustrated hopes, and also from the expectation of miracles. He lived and worked in an African world of hard facts, and, while he could lament the weakness and frailty of human nature, he never strayed into cynicism': *Moffat*, p.211.

71. Comaroff and Comaroff, *Of Revelation and Revolution*, I, p.273. Perhaps this is the correct place to note the disquiet that I have generally with the rather naïve and stereotyped recourse to theological themes and phrases such as 'saving souls' in the work of the Comaroffs. This essay being about Moffat and not about the Comaroffs, space prevents a deeper critique of the (non-)theological presuppositions that underpin their work.

72. 'But it must be realised that his missionary career was for many years spent outside the borders of the Colony, among tribes who had not yet become subject to the rule of the Europeans and seen their land seized and parcelled out amongst colonists. The missionaries who worked in the Cape Colony itself could not possibly avoid noticing the social and political discriminations imposed upon the people whose souls they sought to save': Schapera, 'Introduction' to *Apprenticeship*, p.269. 'Of course, while Philip spent most of his time at Cape Town, the hub of the small South African world, Moffat remained steadfastly at the evangelical workface': Comaroff and Comaroff, *Of Revelation and Revolution*, p.269.

CHAPTER 4

1. William Monk (ed.), *Dr Livingstone's Cambridge Lectures* (London, 1860), pp.227–8.

2. *Speeches, Letters and Selections from Important Papers of the late John Mitford Bowker*, facsimile reprint (Cape Town, 1962), pp.116–25.

3. H. Smith, R.T. Handy and L.A. Loetscher (eds.), *American Christianity: Interpretation and Documents* (New York, 1963), pp.186–9.

4. Robert Knox, *The Races of Men* (London, 1860), pp.23–24.

5. Edward Hume, *David Livingstone* (London, 1910), p.viii.

6. I. Schapera (ed.), *David Livingstone: Family Letters*, 2 vols. (London, 1959), Letter 68.

7. I. Schapera (ed.), *Livingstone's Missionary Correspondence* (London, 1961), Letter 58.

8. David Livingstone, *Missionary Travels and Researches in South Africa* (London, 1857), pp.9–10.

9. Schapera (ed.), *Livingstone's Missionary Correspondence*, Letter 43.

10. Horace Waller (ed.), *Livingstone's Last Journals*, II (London, 1874), p.118.

11. George Seaver, *David Livingstone: His Life and Letters* (London, 1957).

12. Schapera (ed.), *Livingstone's Missionary Correspondence*, Letter 45.

13. Ibid., Letter 42.

14. Ibid., Letter 44.

15. Timothy Holmes, *Journey to Livingstone* (Edinburgh, 1993), p.66.

16. Livingstone to Agnes Livingstone, Sept. 1869, National Library of Scotland, MS 10780.

17. Schapera (ed.), *Livingstone: Family Letters*, Letter 5.

18. I. Schapera (ed.), *Livingstone's African Journal*, 2 vols. (London, 1962), II, p.359.

19. Schapera (ed.), *Livingstone: Family Letters*, Letter 1.

20. Ibid., Letter 7.

21. Ibid., Letter 37.

22. Waller (ed.), *Livingstone's Last Journals*, II, Ch.3 passim.

23. Timothy Holmes (ed.), *David Livingstone: Letters and Documents* (London, 1990), p.50.

24. Frank Debenham, *The Way to Ilala* (London, 1955).

25. Holmes, *Journey to Livingstone*, pp.146–7.

26. Schapera (ed.), *Livingstone: Family Letters*, Letter 38.

27. Holmes, *Journey to Livingstone*, pp.41–2.

28. R. Foskett (ed.), *The Zambesi Journal and Letters of Dr John Kirk*, 2 vols. (London, 1965), p.602.

29. Holmes (ed.), *Livingstone: Letters and Documents*, p.47.

30. Sir Harry Johnston, *Livingstone* (London, 1891), p.301.

31. Livingstone, *Missionary Travels*, p.516.

32. Wainwright was a liberated slave, a Christian educated at Nassik Government School, Bombay. He was one of the groups sent up by Stanley to serve Livingstone. He said prayers over the burial of Livingstone's heart and viscera at Chitambo's and was a pallbearer at Westminster Abbey.

33. Johnston, *Livingstone*, p.300.

34. Tim Jeal, *Livingstone* (London, 1973), Ch.1 passim.

35. Bertram Wyatt-Brown, *Southern Honor* (New York, 1982) is a brilliant study of the similar phenomenon among whites of the Southern States and its important influence on their history.

36. Oliver Ransford, *Livingstone: The Dark Interior* (London, 1976).

CHAPTER 5

This essay is an abridged and amended version of Chapter 3 of Comaroff and Comaroff, *Of Revelation and Revolution*, II. We are grateful to Hylton White for undertaking the task of editing the chapter down to less than half its original size; it is from his draft that the present version has been produced.

1. This epigraph comes from Schapera (ed.), *Apprenticeship*, p.188.

2. See D. Chamberlin (ed.), *Some Letters from Livingstone 1840–1872* (London, 1940), p.115, on the 'daily labours' of an LMS evangelist in southern Africa c.1848.

3. For comparison of the daily labours of LMS evangelists with the everyday routines of nearby Wesleyan missionaries during the same period, see W.C. Holden (ed.), *Reminiscences of the Early Life and Missionary Labours of the Reverend John Edwards* (Grahamstown, 1886), p.93.

4. Schapera (ed.), *Apprenticeship*, p.116

5. W.C. Willoughby, *Race Problems in the New Africa: A Study of the Relation of Bantu and Britons in those parts of Bantu Africa which are under British Control* (Oxford, 1923), p.255.

6. See Philip, *Researches*, I, pp.204f.

7. Schapera (ed.), *Apprenticeship*, p.188.

8. J. Campbell, *Travels in South Africa: Being a Narrative of a Second Journey*, II (New York and London, 1822), p.60.

9. T. Pringle, in London Missionary Society, *Missionary Sketches*, [October 1828] no. 43: South African Library, Cape Town; South African Bound Pamphlets, no. 54.

10. Comaroff and Comaroff, *Of Revelation and Revolution*, I, p.80.

11. Moffat, *Missionary Labours*, pp.500, 588.

12. R. Delavignette, *Christianity and Colonialism* (London, 1964), p.8

13. Moffat, *Missionary Labours*, pp.616–17.

14. Dachs (ed.), *John Mackenzie*, p.72.

15. I. Schapera (ed.), *David Livingstone: South African Papers, 1849–1853* (Cape Town, 1974), p.76.

16. Willoughby, *Race Problems*, p.181.

17. J. Muldoon, 'The Indian as Irishman', *Essex Institute Historical Collections*, 3(267–89), 1975:275. Ironically, by 1815, says Halévy, Irish pastoralists were wealthier than those who tenanted 'tillage farms'. But the graziers were despised, both by their compatriots and by

Halévy, for their uncouth ways: among other things, they allowed animals to run free in the kitchens of their 'absurdly luxurious' homes. See E. Halévy, *England in 1815* (New York, 1961), p.208.

18. Schapera (ed.), *Livingstone: South African Papers*, pp.75–6.

19. E. Spenser, 'A Veue of the Present State of Ireland' (1596), in A.B. Grosart, *The Complete Works in Verse and Prose of Edmund Spenser*, IX (London, 1882–4), p.235.

20. Macmillan, *Bantu, Boer and Briton*, p.76.

21. Dachs, *John Mackenzie*, p.72; Bundy, *Rise and Fall*, p.39.

22. S. Broadbent, *A Narrative of the First Introduction of Christianity amongst the Barolong Tribe of Bechuanas, South Africa* (London, 1865), p.204.

23. Moffat, *Missionary Labours*, p.613.

24. Ibid.; Comaroff and Comaroff, *Of Revelation and Revolution*, I, Ch. 3.

25. Ibid., pp.42ff.

26. Philip, *Researches*, II, p.146; Holden, *Reminiscences*, pp.83ff.; Moffat, *Missionary Labours*, p.435.

27. Broadbent, *Narrative*, p.71.

28. Ibid., p.98.

29. Moffat, *Missionary Labours*, p.613.

30. Comaroff and Comaroff, *Of Revelation and Revolution*, I, Plates 4a and 4b.

31. For a comment on the connection between consumer goods and ideological signs, with special reference to bread as a religious symbol in Christian sacrament, see V.N. Volosinov, *Marxism and the Philosophy of Language* (New York, 1973), p.10.

32. Campbell, *Travels in South Africa*, I, pp.139ff.

33. Ibid., p.178; Schapera, *Apprenticeship*, pp.187–8.

34. Moffat, *Missionary Labours*, p.285.

35. Livingstone, *Missionary Travels*, pp.215ff.; W. Crisp, *The Bechuana of South Africa* (London, 1896), p.16.

36. Campbell, *Travels in South Africa*, II, p.150; Holden, *Reminiscences*, p.87.

37. Moffat, *Missionary Labours*, p.330.

38. Broadbent, *Narrative*, p.63.

39. Philip, *Researches*, II, p.121.

40. J. Mackenzie, *Ten Years North of the Orange River: A Story of Everyday Life and Work among the South African Tribes* (Edinburgh, 1871), p.92.

41. Rev. Willoughby, no date, p.28.

42. T. Hardy, *The Return of the Native* (London, 1963), p.181.

43. Philip, *Researches*, II, pp.114–15.

44. Halévy, *England in 1815*, p.210.

45. Comaroff and Comaroff, *Of Revelation and Revolution*, I, pp.146ff.

46. J. Brown, Taung, 1900, 'Report for 1900: Ten Years Review'. CWM, LMS South Africa Reports, 3–1.

47. Rev. Willoughby, no date, [b].

48. J. Mackenzie in A.J. Dachs, 'Missionary Imperialism: The Case of the Bechuanaland', *Journal of African History*, 13, 1972:652.

49. Moffat, *Missionary Labours*, p.254.

50. Mackenzie, *Ten Years North*, p.402.

51. Livingstone, *Missionary Travels*, p.21.

52. R.L. Cope, *The Journals of the Reverend T.L. Hodgson: Missionary to the Seleka-Rolong and the Griquas, 1821–1831* (Johannesburg, 1977), p.157.

53. Philip, *Researches*, II, p.356.

54. Ibid., p.116.

55. Mackenzie, *Ten Years North*, pp.385ff.

56. Philip, *Researches*, II, p.116.

57. Ibid., p.118.

58. O.H. Spohr (ed.), *Foundation of the Cape (1811) and About the Bechuanas (1807)* (Cape Town, 1973), p.77.

59. Crisp, *The Bechuana*, p.16.

60. Moffat, *Missionary Labours*, p.505.

61. M. Kinsman, '"Beasts of Burden": The Subordination of Southern Tswana Women, ca.1800–1840', *Journal of Southern African Studies*, 10, 1983:46. The use of 'scratching' to describe African hoe agriculture – with all its faunal resonance – was not uncommon in contemporary European writings, hence the title of M.L. Pratt's essay, 'Scratches on the Face of the Country', *Critical Inquiry*, 12, 1985:119–43. As far as we are aware, it appears, for the first time, in connection with the South African interior, in Somerville's diary entry for 1 Dec. 1801 in E. Bradlow and F. Bradlow (eds.), *William Somerville's Narrative of his Journey to the Eastern Cape Frontier and to Lattakoe 1799–1802* (Cape Town, 1979), p.139.

62. Philip, 1828, *Researches*, II, p.139.

63. A.J. Wookey, Kuruman, 24 Sept. 1873. CWM, LMS South Africa Reports, 3–1.

64. Bradlow and Bradlow, *William Somerville's Narrative*, p.143.

65. Broadbent, *Narrative*, p.105.

66. Campbell, *Travels in South Africa*, I, p.177.

67. Moffat, *Missionary Labours*, p.285.

68. Chamberlin, *Letters from Livingstone*, p.203.

69. For a statement of the LMS vision of agrarian transformation in Africa written with a century of hindsight, see Willoughby, *Race Problems*, p.181. Although part of an essay on 'native education', this passage captures the missionary perspective on material improvement among 'a race whose feet are on the lower rungs of progress'.

70. R.E. Prothero (Lord Ernle), *English Farming Past and Present* (London, 1912), p.312.

71. E.L. Jones, *The Development of English Agriculture, 1815–1873* (London, 1968), pp.10ff.

72. See, for example, Halévy, *England in 1815*, pp.220ff.

73. Ibid., p.224.

74. See J. Caird, *High Farming, under Liberal Covenants, the Best Substitute for Protection*, 4th edn (Edinburgh and London, 1849).

75. O. Goldsmith, *The Deserted Village*, 1st edn (New York: D. Appleton, 1857), p.13.

76. Comaroff and Comaroff, *Of Revelation and Revolution*, I, p.75.

77. G.S.R. Kitson Clark, *Churchmen and the Condition of England 1832–1885: A Study in the Development of Social Ideas and Practice from the Old Regime to the Modern State* (London, 1973), pp.168ff.

78. Much has been written on the symbolic centrality of the domesticated landscape in nineteenth-century European self-imaginings; although, as Darian-Smith reminds us, 'the garden is a complex concept with a constantly changing meaning', one that defies 'stable figural representation': E. Darian-Smith, 'Legal Imagery in the "Garden of England,"' *Indiana Journal of Global Legal Studies*, 2, 1995:397; see also 'Introduction', in W.J.T. Mitchell (ed.), *Landscape and Power* (Chicago, 1994). Our concerns here, however, are less with its conceptual archaeology 'at home' than with its transposition to Africa.

79. A.J. Wookey, *Chronicle of the LMS*, p.303.

80. M. Alloula, *The Colonial Harem*, trans. M. Godzich and W. Godzich (Minneapolis, 1986), p.21.

81. For an account of the development of the LMS mission garden at Kuruman, see Schapera (ed.), *Apprenticeship*. Broadbent, *Narrative*, pp.104ff., gives a parallel description of the first Wesleyan station among Tswana.

82. Schapera (ed.), *Apprenticeship*, p.111.

83. Livingstone, *Missionary Travels*, p.21.

84. J. Archbell, Platberg, 2 Sept. 1833. WMMS, South Africa Correspondence (Albany), 303.

85. R.U. Moffat, *John Smith Moffat C.M.G., Missionary: A Memoir* (London, 1921), p.14.

86. Smith, *Moffat*.

87. V.S. Forbes (ed.), *Travels and Adventures in Southern Africa*, I (Cape Town, 1967), pp.96–7.

88. Broadbent, *Narrative*, pp.104–5.

89. Livingstone, *Missionary Travels*, pp.215ff; Crisp, *The Bechuana*, p.16.

90. See, e.g., J. Archbell, Cradock, 23 May 1831. WMMS, South Africa Correspondence (Albany), 303.

91. Volosinov, *Marxism*, p.10.

92. S.M. Molema, *The Bantu, Past and Present* (Edinburgh, 1920), p.119

93. Broadbent, *Narrative*, pp.104–5.

94. Northcott, *Moffat*, p.148.

95. A. Huxley, *Point Counter Point* (London: Flamingo, 1994), p.217.

96. Schapera (ed.), *Apprenticeship*, p.113.

97. T. Hodgson, Matlwassie, 12 Jan. 1824. WMMS, South Africa Correspondence, 300.

98. See, e.g., Schapera (ed.), *Apprenticeship*, pp.52, 71ff.

99. Comaroff and Comaroff, *Of Revelation and Revolution*, I, pp.144ff.

100. Schapera (ed.), *Apprenticeship*, p.23.

101. Philip, *Researches*, II, pp.118, 113–14.

102. Cope, *Reverend Hodgson*, p.206.

103. Schapera (ed.), *Apprenticeship*, p.292.

104. Ibid., p.290.

105. J. Cameron, Platberg, 26 Sept. 1842. WMMS, South Africa Correspondence (Bechuana), 315–121.

106. K. Shillington, *The Colonisation of the Southern Tswana, 1870–1900* (Johannesburg, 1985), p.18.

107. Dachs, *John Mackenzie*, p.110.

108. A. Wyatt Tilby, 'Some Missionary Pioneers in South Africa', in A.R. Colquhoun, *United Empire: The Royal Colonial Institute Journal* (London, 1967), pp.190–5; Shillington, *Colonisation*, p.17; Broadbent, *Narrative*, p.105.

109. Mackenzie, *Austral Africa*, II, p.341.

110. I. Schapera and J.L. Comaroff, *The Tswana*, rev. edn (London, 1976); Shillington, *Colonisation*, p.92.

111. Northcott, *Moffat*, p.148.

112. Moffat, *Missionary Labours*, p.605.

113. Broadbent, *Narrative*, p.106.

114. Mackenzie, *Austral Africa*, II, p.168.

115. Ibid.

116. Mackenzie, *Ten Years North*, p.70.

117. Ibid., pp.90, 131.

118. Ibid., pp.70ff.

119. N. Parsons, 'The Economic History of Khama's Country in Botswana, 1844–1930', in R. Palmer and N. Parsons (eds.), *The Roots of Rural Poverty in Central and Southern Africa* (London, 1977), p.128.

120. Shillington, *Colonisation*, pp.66ff.

121. See A.J. Wookey, Kuruman, 23 May 1884. CWM, LMS Incoming Letters (South Africa), 42–3–C.

122. Mackenzie, in *Ten Years North*, among others, notes that mission land was only given to monogamous men, p.70.

123. E. Holub, *Seven Years in South Africa: Travels, Researches and Hunting Adventures, Between the Diamond-Fields and the Zambesi*, I (Boston, 1881), pp.125, 120.

124. See J. Mackenzie, Kuruman, 17 Feb. 1882. CWM, LMS South Africa Reports, 2–1.

125. Comaroff and Comaroff, *Of Revelation and Revolution*, I, pp.140ff.

126. Kinsman, "'Beasts of Burden,'" p.39.

127. Shillington, *Colonisation*, pp.63ff.

128. Ibid., pp.99ff.

129. Mackenzie, *Austral Africa*, II, p.341.

130. Holub, *Seven Years*, II, p.22.

131. Ibid., I, pp.278–82; II, p.22.

132. Ibid., II, p.13.

133. Shillington, *Colonisation*, p.129.

134. Z.K. Matthews, 'A Short History of the Tshidi Barolong', *Fort Hare Papers*, 1, 1945:20.

135. A. Anderson, *Twenty-five Years in a Waggon: Sport and Travel in South Africa* (London, 1888), p.117.

136. Wookey, *Chronicle of the LMS*, pp.303f, 306.

137. Crisp, *The Bechuana*, p.17; See also J. Brown, Taung, 1900, 'Report for 1900: Ten Years Review'. CWM, LMS South Africa Reports, 3–1.

138. I. Schapera, 'Economic Conditions in a Bechuanaland Native Reserve', *South African Journal of Science*, 30, 1933:647.

139. Wookey, *Chronicle of the LMS*, pp.304–5.

140. See, e.g., A.J. Gould, Kuruman, 16 Feb. 1891. CWM, LMS Incoming Letters (South Africa), 48–1–B.

141. J. Brown, Kuruman, 28 May 1898. CWM, LMS Incoming Letters (South Africa), 55–1–C.

142. An anonymous letter to the *Diamond Fields Advertiser*, 23 Feb. 1897, objected to the government regulations. See also J. Brown, Kuruman, 5 Jan. 1899, 'Report for 1898, Kuruman'. CWM, LMS South Africa Reports, 3–1.

143. J. Parson, *Botswana: Liberal Democracy and the Labor Reserve in Southern Africa* (Boulder, 1984).

144. Bundy, *Rise and Fall*.

145. V.I. Lenin, 'The Development of Capitalism in Russia' (selections), in H.M. Christman (ed.), *Essential Works of Lenin* (New York, 1971), pp.14ff.; D.F. Ferguson, 'Rural/Urban Relations and Present Radicalism: A Preliminary Statement', *Comparative Studies in Society and History*, 18, 1976:106–18; F.G. Snyder, *Capitalism and Legal Change: An African Transformation* (London, 1981), pp.282ff.

146. Volosinov, *Marxism*, p.23.

147. Comaroff and Comaroff, *Of Revelation and Revolution*, I, Ch.4.

148. Z.K. Matthews, as South African readers will know, was a black scholar and political figure of great stature. The author of *Freedom for My People* (Cape Town and London, 1981), he did fieldwork among the Rolong – under the informal supervision of Schapera and the International African Institute – in the late 1930s. His notes are housed in the Botswana National Archives. The data for this paragraph are drawn largely from handwritten fieldnotes entitled 'Agriculture'.

149. The data for the following paragraphs are composed from (i) Matthews's notes; (ii) our own agrarian histories collected in the Mafikeng District (1969–1970) and Barolong, southern Botswana (1974–5 and 1976–7); and (iii) sources already quoted in this paper.

150. See, e.g., Mackenzie, in *Austral Africa*, I, p.76, who says that, though severely weakened by events on the frontier, Southern Tswana chiefs and other leaders 'tried to rally their people … for the old life in the large native town'. In fact, these rulers were not all as impotent as he made out; some did sustain centralised polities.

151. J. Comaroff, *Body of Power, Spirit and Resistance: The Culture and History of a South African People* (Chicago, 1985), pp.187ff; B.A. Pauw, *Religion in a Tswana Chiefdom* (London, 1960), pp.221ff.

152. Schapera, 'Economic Conditions', p.638.

153. Comaroff and Comaroff, *Of Revelation and Revolution*; J. Comaroff and J. Comaroff,

Ethnography and the Historical Imagination (Boulder, 1992).

154. See Matthews, 'Second Field Work Report', p.2.

155. We base this statement on records of 'tribal' meetings kept, from early this century, at the Tshidi-Rolong Community Offices, and on the oral accounts of older informants, which we sought in response to missionary reports (e.g., Campbell, *Travels in South Africa*, II, pp.156ff.; Philip, *Researches*, II, p.133) about Tlhaping and Rolong public assemblies.

156. The evidentiary basis for our portrayal of this class-in-formation is once again composed from several sources, including B. Willan (ed.), *Sol Plaatje: Selected Writings* (Johannesburg, 1997); S.T. Plaatje, *Native Life in South Africa* (New York, n.d.); Matthews's fieldnotes, missionary records, and our own agrarian histories.

157. G.M. Setiloane, *The Image of God among the Sotho-Tswana* (Rotterdam, 1976), pp.174ff.

158. Willan, *Plaatje: Selected Writings*; Setiloane, *The Image of God*, pp.168, 173.

159. Both Mhengwa Lecholo and Chief Kebalepile told us of cases in which this had happened among Tshidi-Rolong. It can be confirmed by correlating the dates at which new wards were created with biographies of their founding heads.

160. Shillington, *Colonisation*, p.69.

161. Ibid., p.20.

162. Mackenzie, *Austral Africa*, II, pp.76–7.

163. For further analysis see, e.g., Comaroff and Comaroff, *Ethnography*, pp.95–125; J.L. Comaroff, 'Tswana Transformations, 1953–1975', Supplementary Chapter in I. Schapera (ed.), *The Tswana* (London, 1976), pp.71–5.

164. Mackenzie, *Austral Africa*, II, p.77.

165. S.M. Molema, *Chief Moroka: His Life, his Times, his Country and his People* (Cape Town, 1951), pp.191–2.

CHAPTER 6

Thanks to Kirsten McKenzie and Harriet Deacon for comments on an earlier version of this chapter, and to Damien Browne for comments on the current chapter. Some of the material here may also be found in N. Erlank, 'Writing Women In(to) Early Nineteenth Century Cape Town', *Kronos: A Journal of Cape History*, 23, Nov. 1996:75–90.

1. G. Theal, *History of South Africa* (London, 1908); G.E. Cory, *The Rise of South Africa* (London, 1913), and other references in this chapter. See also Keegan, *Colonial South Africa and the Origins of the Racial Order*, p.88 and footnote 47 for a brief discussion of this.

2. A. Ross, *John Philip*; Bank, 'Great Debate'. In addition, Philip features in articles by Andrew Ross and Robert Ross in Hugh Macmillan and Shula Marks's volume, *Africa and Empire*.

3. Bank, 'Great Debate'.

4. There is one exception to this. Wendy Woodward's 'The Petticoat and the Kaross: Missionary Bodies and the Feminine in the London Missionary Society, 1816–1828', *Kronos: A Journal of Cape History*, 23, 1996:91–107, discusses the nature of missionary desire, the representation of indigenous women, the disruptive sexuality of male missionaries, and the construction of female missionaries as lacking sexuality, all as portrayed in a number of missionary narratives, one of whose authors was Dr Philip (p.92).

5. A. Ross, 'John Philip: Towards a Reassessment', in Macmillan and Marks, *Africa and Empire*, p.126.

6. Writing as Nosipho Majeke in *The Role of Missionaries in Conquest* (n.p., 1952).

7. C. Pateman, 'Introduction', in *The Disorder of Women: Democracy, Feminism and Political Theory* (Cambridge, 1989), p.3. See also C. Pateman, *The Sexual Contract* (Cambridge, 1988) for a fuller discussion of the exclusion of women and the private domestic sphere from modern civil society and from political theory which researches modern civil society.

8. Andrew Ross's work on Philip pays more attention than most to his background, specifi-

cally his exposure to both the late eighteenth-century evangelical revivals in Scotland and the Scottish Enlightenment. Ross also criticises other work on Philip for ignoring this background. Ross, 'John Philip', in Macmillan and Marks, *Africa and Empire*, p.126.

9. On this subject see E. Fox-Genovese, 'Placing Women's History in History', *New Left Review*, 133, 1982:5–29, esp. p.7; J. Scott, 'Gender: A Useful Category of Historical Analysis', in J. Scott, *Gender and the Politics of History* (Columbia, 1988), esp. pp.42–5. For the South African case, see L. Manicom, 'Ruling Relations: Rethinking State and Gender in South African History', *Journal of African History*, 33, 1992:441–65.

10. Manicom, 'Ruling Relations', p.444.

11. C. Smith-Rosenberg, 'Hearing Women's Words: A Feminist Reconstruction of History', in C. Smith-Rosenberg, *Disorderly Conduct: Visions of Gender in Victorian America* (Oxford, 1985), p.19.

12. University of Cape Town, Centre for African Studies (hereafter CAS), BC742/E (all letters in this collection are between John Philip and Jane Ross unless otherwise specified).

13. CAS, BC742/E, 20 April 1808

14. CAS, BC742/E, 23 June 1808 and 15 July 1808.

15. Rhodes House, Oxford, Philip Papers, MSS Afr.s.216, John Philip to 'respected Brother and Father', 4 May 1825. The quotations in these references are from the notes taken by Macmillan and his students on the Philip papers prior to the fire at the University of the Witwatersrand which destroyed much of the Philip material. On the suggestion of Hugh Macmillan I followed up a possibility that more transcripts of the destroyed material might be found in the papers of the estate of Dame Lucy Sutherland, a former student of Macmillan's. The archivist at Lady Margaret Hall, Oxford, where Dame Lucy had been principal, informed me that there was no material of this kind in the papers she left.

16. Ibid., 19 Jan. 1837.

17. Ibid., 2 May 1837.

18. Historical Papers Department, University of the Witwatersrand Library, Johannesburg (hereafter Wits) A85, 1 April 1837.

19. L. Davidoff and C. Hall, *Family Fortunes: Men and Women of the English Middle Class 1780–1850* (London, 1987), p.179. Also M. Jeanne Peterson, *Family, Love and Work in the Lives of Victorian Gentlewomen* (Bloomington, 1989).

20. A. Duff, 'Female Education in India', in *Missionary Addresses Delivered before the General Assembly of the Church of Scotland in the Years 1835, 1837, 1839* (Edinburgh, 1850), pp.217–18; J. Burgh, 'The Dignity of Human Nature', in H. Poston (ed.), *A Vindication of the Rights of Woman* (New York, 1975), p.197.

21. Authorised King James Version.

22. John Philip to Eliza Philip, quoted in U. Long, *An Index to Authors of Unofficial Privately Owned Manuscripts Relating to the History of South Africa: 1812–1920* (Cape Town, 1946), pp.149–50.

23. The rise of industrial capitalism that precipitated this development occurred alongside the political development of modern civil society – the public and private being mirrored in both. This is a rather crude description of a more complex process. See L. Davidoff, 'Regarding Some "Old Husbands' Tales": Public and Private in Feminist History', in J.B. Landes (ed.), *Feminism, the Public and the Private* (Oxford, 1998), pp.164–94 for a discussion of the historiography of this concept. The entire volume, as the title indicates, is useful on the construction of the categories of public and private, and the dynamics involved in the various constructions.

24. Davidoff and Hall, *Family Fortunes*. For a discussion of the ideology and practices of the European middle class in Cape Town for this period, see K. McKenzie, 'Gender and Honour in Middle-Class Cape Town: The Making of Colonial Identities 1828–1850', D.Phil. thesis, Oxford University, 1997; N. Erlank, 'Letters Home: The Experiences and Perceptions of

Middle Class British Women at the Cape 1820–1850', M.A. dissertation, University of Cape Town, 1995. McKenzie's thesis is particularly useful on the significance and symbolism, if not reality, of separate spheres (pp.12–16).

25. McKenzie, 'Gender and Honour', p.132.

26. Ibid., p.132.

27. For Elizabeth Lyndall see K. Schoeman (ed.), *The Recollections of Elizabeth Rolland (1803–1901)* (Cape Town and Pretoria, 1987).

28. Long, *Index*, p.150.

29. J. Philip, *Researches*, I, p.185; II, p.107. He devoted an entire book to the subject of Mrs Smith: *Memoir of Mrs. Matilda Smith* (London, 1824).

30. Schoeman, '*A Thorn Bush that Grows in the Path': The Missionary Career of Ann Hamilton, 1815–1823*, esp. pp.39, 59–61; Woodward, 'The Petticoat and the Kaross', pp.99–100.

31. Rhodes House, Philip Papers, MSS Afr.s.218, private notes of Dr Philip.

32. Ross, *John Philip*, p.6.

33. Wits A85, Mrs Philip to Miss Wills, 31 May 1838. Unless otherwise indicated, all Mrs Philip's letters are addressed to Miss Wills.

34. Ibid., 10 Sept. 1831.

35. Ibid., 27 Aug. 1835, 31 May 1838.

36. H. Ludlow, 'The London Missionary Society in Cape Town', B.A. Honours essay, University of Cape Town, 1981, p.45.

37. Wits A85, 16 March 1830. This was obviously one of those times when Dr Philip was in favour at Government House.

38. Ibid., 2 July 1830, 30 June 1831.

39. For a discussion of the LMS's work in this area see Ludlow, 'The LMS in Cape Town', pp.44–58.

40. Ibid., pp.50–1.

41. School of Oriental and African Studies, London, Council for World Mission Archives, SA Incoming, Mrs Philip to the Directors, 17 Feb. 1835.

42. References to her work in this area can be found in Wits A85, 26 Jan. 1832, 1 April 1837, 31 May 1838, 23 Sept. 1841, 24 April 1843, 30 Oct. 1843 and 9 Jan. 1844.

43. Wits A85, 28 March 1834.

44. Ibid., 30 Oct. 1843.

45. Davidoff and Hall, *Family Fortunes*, Ch. 6, '"The Hidden Investment": Women and the Enterprise'.

46. Particularly in Cape Town in the early nineteenth century; see Appendix 2 on women's work in Erlank, 'Letters Home'.

47. School of Oriental and African Studies, University of London, CWM, SA Incoming, Mrs Philip to the Directors, 11 Feb. 1834, and also 24 Aug. 1836.

48. Ibid., Mrs Philip to Mr Baillie, 2 Nov. 1833. It is clear, too, that the missionaries sometimes resented Mrs Philip's methods, as is evident from a protest against her in 1845. Rhodes House, Philip Collection, MSS Afr.s.218, Richard Birt to Mrs Philip, 12 Dec. 1845.

49. Wits, A85, 31 May 1838, 1 April 1837.

50. Ibid., 1833.

51. Ibid., 1 April 1837.

52. Ibid., 11 Dec. 1838.

53. Ibid., 30 June 1831.

54. Ibid., 2 June 1830, 9 July 1839; Cory Library for Historical Research, Rhodes University, Grahamstown (hereafter Cory), MS 6164, Jane Philip to Eliza Fairbairn and Wilberforce Philip, 1 Nov. 1838.

55. Wits A85, 30 June 1831, 24 April 1843.

56. Ibid., 2 July 1830, 30 June 1831, 10 Sept. 1831, 27 Aug. 1835, 11 Dec. 1838, 9 July 1839, 24

April 1843, 30 Oct. 1843.

57. The following are very useful on this subject: R. Anstey, *The Atlantic Slave Trade and British Abolition 1760–1810* (London, 1975), Ch.7, 'The Evangelical Worldview'; C. Hall, 'The Early Formation of Victorian Domestic Ideology', in S. Burman (ed.), *Fit Work for Women* (London, 1979); B. Hilton, *The Age of Atonement* (Oxford, 1987), Ch.1; F. Prochaska, *The Voluntary Impulse: Philanthropy in Modern Britain* (London, 1988).

58. Comaroff and Comaroff, *Of Revelation and Revolution*, I, p.62.

59. Prochaska, *The Voluntary Impulse*, p.24.

60. Anstey, *The Atlantic Slave Trade*, p.164.

61. This is the thesis of Prochaska's book, though the situation in Cape Town was rather different; see McKenzie, 'Gender and Honour', p.133.

62. Wits A85, 9 July 1839.

63. Ibid., 31 May 1838.

64. CAS, BC742/E, 23 June 1808.

65. Ibid., 26 Feb. 1808.

66. Or, in late-twentieth-century speak, he was a sexy man.

67. Ross, *John Philip*, p.6.

68. Cory, MS 6097, Mary Anne Foulger to Eliza Philip, 23 July 1829.

69. Cory, MS 6150, Mary Anne Foulger to Eliza Fairbairn, 11 Sept. 1837.

70. N. Erlank, 'Circulating in Cape Town: Material Culture and Social Relations in the Life of Lady Margaret Herschel', B.A. Honours essay, University of Cape Town, 1993, p.77. Mrs Philip did not accompany Dr Philip on these visits. In 1837, in a letter from England, he complimented Mrs Philip on the Herschels seeking her out for her own sake. Rhodes House, Philip Papers, MSS Afr.s.217, 17 Feb. 1837.

71. He was certainly kinder to Mary Anne Foulger, in his letters to her, than he was to his daughter, Eliza. Davidoff and Hall, *Family Fortunes*, pp.346–8.

72. Rhodes House, MSS Afr.s.217, Mrs Philip to Dr Philip, 23 Sept. 1836.

73. Ibid., Mrs Philip to Dr Philip, 19 Jan. 1837. The dates between the two letters indicate that the January letter might indeed have been a direct reply to a direct reply of Philip's.

74. CAS, BC742/E, 26 Feb. 1808. Philip is quoting a 'celebrated author' who, if not St Augustine himself, must surely have been paraphrasing him.

75. This is definitely evocative of St Augustine of Hippo. H. Chadwick (trans.), *Saint Augustine, The Confessions* (Oxford, 1991).

76. S. Mills, *Discourses of Difference: An Analysis of Women's Travel Writing and Colonialism* (London and New York, 1991), p.58. Also, Jane Miller, *Seductions* (Cambridge, Mass., 1991).

77. Mills, *Discourses of Difference*, p.59.

78. Woodward, 'The Petticoat and the Kaross', p.94.

79. L.A. Stoler, 'Carnal Knowledge and Imperial Power', in M. di Leonardo (ed.), *Gender at the Crossroads of Knowledge* (California, 1991), p.52. Another article by Stoler ('Making Empire Respectable: The Politics of Race and Sexual Morality in 20th Century Colonial Cultures', *American Ethnologist*, 16, 1989:634–60) discusses in more detail the tendency of post-colonial writing to treat sex as a metaphor for colonial penetration and subjugation rather than sex itself.

80. Philip, *Researches*, II, p.225.

81. P. Scully, *Liberating the Family? Gender and the British Slave Emancipation in the Rural Western Cape, South Africa, 1823–1853* (Portsmouth, NH, 1997), pp.34, 38, Ch. 2, 'Gender, Sexuality and Amelioration', passim.

82. *South African Historical Journal*, 36, 1997.

CHAPTER 7

1. V. Bickford-Smith, 'Meanings of Freedom: Social Position and Identity among Ex-slaves and their Descendants in Cape Town, 1875–1910', in N. Worden and C. Crais (eds.), *Breaking the Chains: Slavery and its Legacy in the Nineteenth-Century Cape Colony* (Johannesburg, 1994), p.297.
2. Report for 1841, Vogelgezang to Directors, LMS 18/2/D.
3. Philip to Burder, 28 Dec. 1821, LMS 8/2/E.
4. *Missionary Chronicle*, May 1820, p.215.
5. L. Meltzer, 'Emancipation, Commerce and the Role of John Fairbairn's *Advertiser*', in Worden and Crais (eds.), *Breaking the Chains*, p.169.
6. *Missionary Chronicle*, May 1820, p.215.
7. R. Watson, *The Slave Question* (Hanover and London, 1990), p.130.
8. Worden and Crais (eds.), *Breaking the Chains*, p.4.
9. J.B. Peires, 'The British and the Cape, 1814–1834', in R. Elphick and H. Giliomee (eds.), *The Shaping of South African Society, 1652–1840*, 2nd edn (Cape Town, 1989), pp.477–99.
10. F. Quinn and G. Cuthbertson, *Presbyterianism in Cape Town: A History of St Andrew's Church, 1829–1929* (Cape Town, 1979), p.5.
11. *The Report of the Directors to the Members of the Missionary Society*, May 1820, p.77 (hereafter DR).
12. Ibid., May 1821, p.77.
13. Philip to Burder, 19 May 1820, LMS 8/2/B.
14. Philip to Burder, 28 Dec. 1820, LMS 8/2/E.
15. DR, May 1821, pp.75–6.
16. The name Union Chapel commemorated the uniting of Presbyterians and Congregationalists in 1820 but it was in fact a Congregational chapel: Quinn and Cuthbertson, *Presbyterianism*, p.6.; Miles to Directors, 27 Oct. 1830, LMS 12/3/B; DR, May 1823, p.91; J. Thomas, in Le Cordeur and Saunders (eds.), *The Kitchingman Papers*, p.66.
17. Davidoff and Hall, *Family Fortunes*, Part I.
18. Philip to Directors, 23 Oct. 1823, LMS 9/1/D.
19. See committee listed in 'Report of Cape Town Auxiliary Missionary Society for 1841', LMS 19/3/B.
20. N. Worden, E. van Heyningen and V. Bickford-Smith, *Cape Town: The Making of a City*, (Cape Town, 1998), p.129.
21. Davidoff and Hall, *Family Fortunes*, p.143.
22. Jones, *The Charity School Movement* (London, 1938), p.7.
23. Ibid., p.14.
24. Miles to Hankey, 10 March 1826, LMS 10/1/B; Kitchingman to Directors, 6 March 1826, LMS 10/1/B.
25. 'Report of the South African Missions', 1830, LMS 12/2/A.
26. Miles to Directors, 14 Feb. 1827, LMS 10/2/B.
27. Miles to Directors, 27 Oct. 1830, LMS 12/3/D.
28. Worden et al., *Cape Town*, p.121.
29. Ibid., p.120.
30. Ibid., pp.120–2. Life expectancy at birth of coloured people was 23 years.
31. Address to Governor … from Miles and 54 merchants of Cape Town, 16 Feb. 1830, LMS 11/4/C.
32. Miles to Orme, 17 July 1829, LMS 11/3/E.
33. Elliott to Directors, 14 Jan. 1829, LMS 11/3/A; 12 June 1829, LMS 11/3/C; 17 July 1829, LMS 11/3/E.
34. Macmillan, *Cape Colour Question*, pp.221–30.

35. Philip to Clayton, 25 Dec. 1830, LMS 12/1/D.
36. Accession 1415, box 32, Cape Archives; Philip Family Letters, Mrs Philip to Mrs Reed, 11 July 1833. Mrs Philip took over control of the LMS accounts from Miles, kept the books of the Paris Missionary Society in Basutoland, and was on a number of committees including that of the Ladies Benevolent Society.
37. Philip to Directors, 13 Nov. 1829, LMS 11/4/B; 29 Nov. 1829, LMS 11/4/C.
38. 'Report of the South African Mission', 1830, LMS 12/2/A; DR, May 1831, p.76.
39. *The Cape of Good Hope Almanac*, 1843, p.272.
40. 'Report of the South African Missions', 1830, LMS 12/2/A; 'Report of the Cape Town Auxiliary Missionary Society for 1832', LMS 13/2/A.
41. DR, May 1833, pp.72–3; DR, May 1834, p.82; J. Sibree (comp.), *London Missionary Society: Register of Missionaries, Deputations etc. from 1796–1923* (London, 1923), p.30.
42. Lovett, *The London Missionary Society*, I (London, 1899), pp.677ff.
43. DR, May 1832, p.80; DR, 1833, pp.72–3.
44. Canham to Ellis, March and April 1836, LMS 15/1/C.
45. Ross, *John Philip*, p.94.
46. Philip to Directors, 14 Jan. 1831, LMS 12/4/B.
47. Foster to Directors, 2 Nov. 1830, LMS 12/2/A.
48. Ibid.; Philip to Directors, 14 Jan. 1831.
49. Macmillan, *Cape Colour Question*, pp.56–57, 103–4.
50. 'Report of the South African Missions, 1830', LMS 12/2/A.
51. He and his ten-year-old half-brother, David, stopped at Cape Town en route to New Zealand and were persuaded to stay and establish a school according to their father's system. *Dictionary of South African Biography*, I, p.132.
52. T. Raymont, *A History of the Education of Young Children* (London, 1937), pp.78ff.
53. H. Silver, *Education as History* (London, 1983), pp.60–9.
54. Raymont, *History of Education*, p.93.
55. Theal, *History of South Africa*, II, p.213; Worden et al., *Cape Town*, p.125.
56. F.R. Bradlow, *Baron von Ludwig and the Ludwig's-burg Garden: A Chronicle of the Cape from 1806 to 1848* (Cape Town, 1965), p.12; *Cape of Good Hope Almanac*, 1832.
57. Bradlow, *Baron von Ludwig*, pp.12–13.
58. Philip to Ellis, 4 July 1833, LMS 13/3/C.
59. Philip to Directors, 6 Oct. 1837, LMS 15/3/C.
60. R. Shell, *Children of Bondage: A Social History of the Slave Society at the Cape of Good Hope, 1652–1838* (Johannesburg, 1994), pp.356–7.
61. Elliott to Directors, 24 July 1828, LMS 11/1/C.
62. Philip's lengthy discussion of Islam and slavery is in Philip to Directors, 14 Jan. 1831, LMS 12/4/B.
63. For Elliott's views on Islam and slavery, see Elliott to Directors, 24 July 1828; 12 June 1829, LMS 11/3/C; 2 Oct. 1829, LMS 11/3/E; 19 Jan. 1831, LMS 12/4/C.
64. 'Report of the Cape Town Auxiliary Missionary Society for 1832', LMS 13/4/C.
65. 'Report of the Cape Town Auxiliary Missionary Society for 1833', LMS 13/4/C.
66. Philip to Directors, 6 Oct. 1837, LMS 15/3/C.
67. *South African Directory and Almanac, 1834*, p.136.
68. Philip to Directors, 6 Oct. 1837, LMS 15/3/C.
69. To Kitchingman, 7 Jan. 1836, in Le Cordeur and Saunders (eds), *Kitchingman Papers*, p.162.
70. Freeman to Ellis, 14 Feb. 1836, LMS 15/1/B; 3 June 1836, LMS 15/1/C; DR, May 1837, p.93; DR, May 1838, p.82.
71. Sibree, *London Missionary Society*, p.43.
72. Ibid., p.81.
73. Freeman to Ellis, 3 June 1836, LMS 15/1/C; Williams to Ellis, 6 March 1837, LMS 15/3/B.

74. DR, May, 1837, p.935.
75. Williams to Ellis, 6 March 1837, LMS 15/3/B; Mrs Philip to Ellis, 18 Jan. 1838, LMS 16/1/A; Philip to Governor, 21 Aug. 1839, LMS 16/4/B; 'Report of the Cape Town Auxiliary Missionary Society for 1841', LMS 19/3/B.
76. Calderwood to Ellis, Dec. 1838, LMS 16/2/B.
77. Jones, *Charity School Movement*, pp.142 ff.
78. K. McKenzie, 'The *South African Commercial Advertiser* and the Making of Middle Class Identity in Early Nineteenth-Century Cape Town', M.A. dissertation, University of Cape Town, 1993, pp.94–5.
79. Philip to Directors, 6 Oct. 1837, LMS 15/3/C.
80. Raymont, *History of Education*, p.54.
81. *South African Commercial Advertiser (SACA)*, 6 April 1836.
82. Mrs Philip to Directors, 20 Dec. 1841, LMS 18/2/B; to Ellis, 5 Oct. 1837, LMS 15/3/C; Philip to Ellis, 29 July 1838, LMS 16/1/C.
83. Philip to Governor, 21 Aug. 1839, LMS 16/4/B.
84. Mrs Philip to Ellis, 19 Feb. 1838, LMS 16/1/A; to Tidman, 25 Feb. 1841, LMS 17/2/D; to Directors, 20 Dec. 1841, LMS 18/2/B; 31 July 1843 and 3 Aug. 1843, LMS 19/2/C.
85. Philip to Ellis, 6 Oct. 1837, LMS 15/3/C.
86. M. Sanderson, *Education, Economic Change and Society in England, 1780–1870* (London, 1983), pp.54–5.
87. Davidoff and Hall, *Family Fortunes*, p.293.
88. Ibid., p.295.
89. Comaroff and Comaroff, *Of Revelation and Revolution*, I, p.81.
90. *Cape of Good Hope Annual Register, Directory and Almanac for 1837*, p.46; Mrs Philip to Ellis, 6 March 1837, LMS 15/1/A; to Directors, 19 July 1837, LMS 15/3/B.
91. Philip to Directors, 6 Oct. 1837, LMS 15/3/C; Calderwood to Ellis, Dec. 1838, LMS 16/2/B; 'Report of the Cape Town Auxiliary Missionary Society for 1838'.
92. Williams to Ellis, 6 March 1837, LMS 15/3/C.
93. Mrs Philip to Directors, 19 July 1837, LMS 15/3/B.
94. Ibid.; Mrs Philip to Ellis, 5 Oct. 1837, LMS 15/3/C; 29 Aug. 1838, LMS 16/1/C; to Directors, 20 Dec. 1841, LMS 18/2/B; Philip to Ellis, 29 July 1838, LMS 16/1/C.
95. Mrs Philip to Ellis, 5 Oct. 1837; 18 Jan. 1838, LMS 16/1/A; 29 Aug. 1838, LMS 16/1/C.
96. Philip to Governor, 21 Aug. 1839, LMS 16/4/B.
97. Vogelgezang to Directors, Report for 1841, LMS 18/2/D; Report for 1842, LMS 18/5/B.
98. Mrs Philip to Ellis, 5 Oct. 1837.
99. Mrs Philip to Ellis, 18 Jan. 1838.
100. Mrs Philip to Ellis, 5 Oct. 1837.
101. Philip to Directors, 6 Oct. 1837, LMS 15/3/C.
102. M. Legassick, 'The Griqua, the Sotho-Tswana, and the Missionaries', Ph.D. thesis, University of California, Los Angeles, 1969, p.664.
103. *Dictionary of South African Biography*, I, p.397.
104. Philip to Directors, 28 Jan. 1840, LMS 17/1/A.
105. Mrs Philip to Directors, 20 Dec. 1842, LMS 18/2/B.
106. *Dictionary of South African Biography*, I, p.398.
107. DR May 1840, pp.72–3; Sibree, *London Missionary Society*, p.45.
108. Philip to Directors, 6 Oct. 1837, LMS 15/3/C; Philip to Ellis, 29 July 1838, LMS 16/1/C.
109. Calderwood to Ellis, Dec. 1838, LMS 16/2/B; 'Report of the Cape Town Auxiliary Missionary Society for 1838', LMS 16/4/D.
110. *Cape of Good Hope Almanac and Annual Register, 1842*.
111. *SACA*, 4 Sept. 1839.
112. R. Shell, 'Between Christ and Mohammed: Conversion, Slavery, and Gender in the Urban

Western Cape', in R. Elphick and R. Davenport (eds.), *Christianity in South Africa: A Political, Social and Cultural History* (Oxford and Cape Town, 1997), p.272.

113. DR, May 1840, p.74.
114. Vogelgezang to Directors, Report for 1841, LMS 18/2/D.
115. Vogelgezang to Directors, Report for 1842, LMS 18/5/B.
116. Vogelgezang, Report for 1841.
117. DR, May 1843, p.84.
118. Mrs Philip to Directors, 9 Feb. 1843, LMS 19/1/C.
119. Philip to Directors, 18 Aug. 1841, LMS 18/2/A.
120. Macmillan, *Bantu, Boer and Briton*, p.192, n.1; p.214, n.2.
121. Philip to Directors, 11 June 1842, LMS 18/3/C.
122. Merrington to Directors, 29 May 1843, LMS 19/2/A.
123. Rutherfoord and Cameron to Freeman and Tidman, 15 June 1843, LMS 19/2/B.
124. Macmillan, *Bantu, Boer and Briton*, p.192, n.1.
125. Philip to Directors, 26 June 1843, LMS 19/2/B.
126. Vogelgezang to Directors, 1 March 1844, LMS 20/1/C.
127. Bickford-Smith, 'Meanings of Freedom', pp.289–90.
128. Ibid., pp.290–7.
129. Mrs Philip, 20 Dec. 1841, LMS 18/2/B.
130. Bickford-Smith, 'Meanings of Freedom', pp.297ff.
131. Vogelgezang, Report for 1842.

CHAPTER 8

1. James Read, jun., *Annual Report 1856*, LMS-SA 30/2/B.
2. James Read, sen. to Kitchingman, 17 July 1843, in Le Cordeur and Saunders (eds.), *Kitchingman Papers*, p.236. Two decades earlier Read had been demoted from his position as missionary at Bethelsdorp by the congregation in consequence of his adultery. This, though, was very much at the instigation of other missionaries of the LMS, and seems to have been against the wishes of many, perhaps most, of the congregation.
3. Doug Stuart, '"Of Savages and Heroes": Discourses of Race, Nation and Gender in the Evangelical Missions to Southern Africa in the Early Nineteenth Century', Ph.D. thesis, University of London, 1994, Ch. 8.
4. Minutes of the Eastern District Committee, June 1843, LMS-SA 19/2/B.
5. Philip to LMS, 26 June 1843, CWM SA–19/2/B.
6. Read to Kitchingman, 22 Jan. 1844, in Le Cordeur and Saunders (eds.), *Kitchingman Papers*, pp.242–3; see also Martin Legassick, 'The Griqua, the Sotho-Tswana and the Missionaries, 1780–1840: The Politics of a Frontier Zone', Ph.D. thesis, University of California, Los Angeles, 1969, esp. Ch.11.
7. Campbell to Directors, 7 April 1813, LMS-SA 7/4/B.
8. Read to Kitchingman, 2 Dec. 1840, in Le Cordeur and Saunders (eds.), *Kitchingman Papers*, p.218.
9. Ibid. A Socinian, it will be remembered, denied the divinity of Christ.
10. Patricia E. Scott, 'An Approach to the Urban History of Early Victorian Grahamstown, 1832–1853, with particular reference to the Interiors and Material Culture of Domestic Dwellings', M.A. dissertation, Rhodes University, Grahamstown, 1987, p.114.
11. V.C. Malherbe, 'The Cape Khoisan in the Eastern Districts of the Colony before and after Ordinance 50 of 1828', Ph.D. thesis, University of Cape Town, 1997, pp.211–12, 261.
12. Fuller and others to Miles, 25 April 1827, LMS-SA 10/2/B; Malherbe, 'Cape Khoisan', p.268.
13. Monro to Burder, 3 July 1827, LMS-SA 10/2/C.

14. Keith S. Hunt, 'The Development of Municipal Government in the Eastern Province of the Cape of Good Hope, with special reference to Grahamstown, 1827–1862', *Archives Year Book for South African History*, 24, 1961:156.

15. B.A. le Cordeur, 'Robert Godlonton as Architect of Frontier Opinion, 1850–1857', *Archives Year Book for South African History*, 22(2), 1959:35–44; Tony Kirk, 'Progress and Decline in the Kat River Settlement, 1829–1854', *Journal of African History*, 14, 1973:411–28, and 'The Cape Economy and the Expropriation of the Kat River Settlement, 1846–1853', in Shula Marks and Anthony Atmore (eds.), *Economy and Society in Pre-Industrial South Africa* (London, 1980); Clifton C. Crais, *White Supremacy and Black Resistance in Pre-industrial South Africa: The Making of the Colonial Order in the Eastern Cape, 1770–1865* (Cambridge, 1992).

16. Read, sen. to Kitchingman, 11 April 1837, in Le Cordeur and Saunders (eds.), *Kitchingman Papers*, p.176.

17. Read, jun. to Philip, 17 July 1843, LMS–SA 19/3/A.

18. *Graham's Town Journal*, 23 April 1840; 15 Dec. 1840.

19. Smit to Philip, 25 Nov. 1842, LMS–SA 19/3/A.

20. Read, jun. to Philip, 17 July 1843, LMS–SA 18/3/C.

21. Read to Directors, 15 Aug. 1843, LMS–SA 19/2/C.

22. Address to the Ministers assembled in Grahamstown, 14 April 1842, in Standen to Philip, 4 May 1842, LMS–SA 18/3/C.

23. Smit to Philip, 13 Jan. 1843, LMS–SA 19/3/A.

24. Locke to Philip, 30 March 1843, LMS–SA 19/1/C.

25. Long Bush is probably 'Lange Vlakte', a farm in the lower Bushman's River veldcornetcy granted to Paul Keteldas, a Khoi from Bethelsdorp in the early 1830s. See Malherbe, 'Cape Khoisan', pp.249–56.

26. Smit to Philip, 16 Dec. 1842, LMS–SA 19/3/A.

27. Smit to Directors, 30 Aug. 1844, LMS–SA 20/2/C.

28. Marriage Book, Union Chapel, Cory MS 17067. In 1834 a DRC minister had to be reminded by the government that the fact that a couple had been living together was no grounds for refusing them the right to marry. See Malherbe, 'Cape Khoisan', p.302. For analogous cases in the Dutch Reformed Church in Cape Town, see McKenzie, 'Gender and Honour', pp.261–6.

29. Read to Kitchingman, 17 July 1843, in Le Cordeur and Saunders (eds.), *Kitchingman Papers*, p.236.

30. Locke to Philip, 30 March 1843, LMS–SA 19/1/C.

31. Arian et al. to Directors, 17 July 1844, LMS–SA 20/2/A.

32. I have retained the inconsistent spelling of personal names in direct quotations.

33. Deacons and Subscribers, Graham's Town, to Directors, undated, LMS–SA 19/1/C. None of the signatories to this letter turn up in J.C. Chase's directory of Grahamstown for 1842, and only one, possibly, in the *Cape Almanac*'s directory for 1853. This was one of the subscribers, Adam Vandervoort, there named as Van der Vent, who was then a carrier living in the location. This is of course primarily a comment on the racial bias of the directories. See Scott, 'Approach', Appendices A1 and 2.

34. Read to Directors, 15 Aug. 1843, LMS–SA 19/2/C.

35. Read to Philip, 21 Aug. 1843, LMS–SA 19/3/A.

36. James Kitchingman, John Monro and Adam Robson to Directors, 28 Aug. 1844, LMS–SA 20/2/C.

37. Minutes of the Eastern District Committee, June 1843, LMS–SA 19/2/B.

38. The allegation of racism made here is based on the private comments of James Read, notably Read to Kitchingman, 17 July 1843, in Le Cordeur and Saunders (eds.), *Kitchingman Papers*, p.236.

39. Locke to Philip, 8 July 1843, LMS–SA 19/3/A.

40. Read, jun. to Philip, 17 July 1843, LMS-SA 19/3/A.

41. Schreiner to Philip, 4 May 1846 in Karel Schoeman (ed.), *The Missionary Letters of Gottlob Schreiner, 1837–1846* (Cape Town and Johannesburg, 1991), pp.134–5. See also Read to Directors, 15 Aug. 1843, LMS-SA 19/2/C. The description of Schreiner's action in this letter does not name him, but I concur with the editors of the *Kitchingman Papers* (p.227) in assuming that Read's comments apply to him. In general, see Robert Ross, *Adam Kok's Griquas: A Study in the Development of Stratification in South Africa* (Cambridge, 1976), pp.43–5.

42. Read to Kitchingman, 11 Dec. 1843, in Le Cordeur and Saunders (eds.), *Kitchingman Papers*, p.240.

43. Read to Kitchingman, 22 Jan. 1844, in Le Cordeur and Saunders (eds.), *Kitchingman Papers*, pp.243–4.

44. Elders and Deacons of the Church at Philipton to Philip, no date, enclosed in Philip to Directors, 26 June 1843, LMS-SA 19/2/B.

45. Philip to Directors, 19 Sept. 1846, LMS-SA 22/2/B.

46. See Andrew George Brooks-Neil, 'A Constitutional History of Trinity Church, Grahamstown, 1877–1980', B.D. dissertation, Rhodes University, Grahamstown, 1992.

47. T. Durant Philip, cited in Macmillan, *Cape Colour Question*, p.275; William Elliot, 'Letter', in *Evangelical Christendom*, II, June 1848:106; John Philip, *Letter to the Directors of the London Missionary Society on the Present State of their Institutions in the Colony of the Cape of Good Hope* (Cape Town, 1848); David Livingstone, 'Missions in South Africa', in Schapera (ed.), *Livingstone: South African Papers*, pp.103–7; David Livingstone and Robert Moffat, cited in Richard Lovett, *The London Missionary Society*, 2 vols. (London, 1899), I, pp.574–9; William Ellis, *Three Visits to Madagascar during the years 1853, 1854, 1856* (London, 1858), pp.241–3; Andries Appel, 'Bethelsdorp: Van politieke Simbool tot alledaagse Werklikheid', *South African Historical Journal*, 18, 1986, 166–8; John Marincowitz, 'Rural Production and Labour in the Western Cape, 1838 to 1888, with special reference to the Wheat Growing Districts', Ph.D. thesis, University of London, 1985, pp.180–7; R. Ross, *Adam Kok's Griquas*, p.78.

48. Robert Ross, 'The Kat River, Rebellion and Khoikhoi Nationalism: The Fate of an Ethnic Identification', *Kronos: A Journal of Cape History*, 24, 1997; Stanley Trapido, 'The Emergence of Liberalism and the Making of "Hottentot Nationalism," 1815–1834', *Collected Seminar Papers of the Institute of Commonwealth Studies, London: The Societies of Southern Africa in the Nineteenth and Twentieth Centuries*, 17, 1992; Edna Bradlow, 'The Khoi and the Proposed Vagrancy Legislation of 1834', *Quarterly Bulletin of the South African Library*, 39, 1985.

49. Elizabeth Elbourne and Robert Ross, 'Combating Spiritual and Social Bondage: Early Missions in the Cape Colony', in Elphick and Davenport (eds.), *Christianity in South Africa*, p.46.

50. See Cape of Good Hope, Legislative Council, *Master and Servant: Addenda to the Documents on the Working of the Order in Council of the 21st July 1846* (Cape Town, 1849), p.13. (This at least is according to the table of contents; the only copy of this rare volume which I have been able to locate, that at Rhodes House, Oxford, does not include pages 1–27. I have not yet managed to locate a copy in the Cape Archives, either of the original memorial or of the printed version, but no doubt they could be found.)

51. Smit to Freeman, 6 Aug. 1851, LMS-SA 25/2/A. See also Andries Lynx to Keviet Piqueur, printed in Robert Godlonton, *Narrative of the Kafir War of 1850–51* (Grahamstown, 1851), pp.283–4.

52. W.A. Maxwell and R.T. McGeogh (eds.), *The Reminiscences of Thomas Stubbs* (Cape Town, 1978), pp.144–5, 273.

53. Mostert, *Frontiers*, p.1158.

54. R. Ross, 'Kat River'.

CHAPTER 9

1. Robert Ross, 'Congregations, Missionaries and the Grahamstown Schism of 1842–3', else-where in this volume; my warm thanks to Robert Ross for showing me an advance copy of this essay.

2. Stewart J. Brown, 'The Ten Years' Conflict and the Disruption of 1843', in Stewart J. Brown and Michael Fry (eds.), *Scotland in the Age of the Disruption* (Edinburgh, 1993), pp.1–27.

3. Le Cordeur and Saunders (eds.), *Kitchingman Papers*, pp.191–2; Ross, *John Philip*, p.178.

4. As the infamous battle of Dithakong demonstrates, whatever else it may or may not prove about the so-called *mfecane*. See Hamilton (ed..), *Mfecane Aftermath*; Cobbing, 'Mfecane as Alibi', pp.487–519.

5. Ross, *Adam Kok's Griquas*, pp.44–5.

6. 'Moffat did not know how to get the Griequa out-stations under him but by a majority in that committee and by shutting out native teachers': Read, sen. to Kitchingman, Bethelsdorp, 22 Jan. 1844, in Le Cordeur and Saunders (eds.), *Kitchingman Papers*, p.242.

7. As argued in Brownlee, Kayser, Merrington, Locke, Birt, Calderwood and Gill to LMS directors, Umxelo, 10 Oct. 1844, LMS-SA 20/3/A.

8. Many of the pertinent documents are reproduced in Schapera (ed.), *Apprenticeship*; on Moffat as an authoritarian, cf. also Schoeman, 'A Thorn Bush', for Moffat's treatment of Ann Hamilton; Comaroff and Comaroff, *Of Revelation and Revolution*, I. On Read and the Tswana mission: J.T. du Bruyn, 'James Read en die Tlhaping, 1816–1820', *Historia*, 35, 1990:23–38. Doug Stuart, in '"Of savages and heroes,"' disagrees with me on the role of Khoikhoi evan-gelists at Moffat's station in Kuruman.

9. Saunders, 'James Read', pp.19–25.

10. Calderwood and Birt to LMS directors, Umxelo, 26 Sept. 1844, LMS-SA 20/2/D; this let-ter was signed on behalf of Brownlee, Kayser, Locke, Calderwood, Merrington, Gill and Birt, who had attended the meeting that gave rise to these sentiments.

11. Read, jun. to Philip, 13 May 1844, enclosed in Philip to Tidman, Cape Town, 10 Oct. 1844, LMS-SA 20/3/A.

12. Donovan Williams, *When Races Meet: The Life and Times of William Ritchie Thomson, Glasgow Society Missionary, Government Agent and Dutch Reformed Church Minister, 1794–1891* (Johannesburg, 1967), p.137.

13. Brown, 'The Ten Years' Conflict', pp.4–5; Williams, *When Races Meet*, pp.136–7.

14. Charles Lennox Stretch [presumably to Philip], 24 June 1844: copy enclosed in Philip to Tidman, 10 Oct. 1844, LMS-SA 20/3/A.

15. Stretch [presumably to Philip], 'Caffraria', 24 June 1844, enclosed in Philip to Tidman, 10 Oct. 1844, LMS-SA 20/3/A. Richard Paver, who stayed for nine months at Glen Thorn, probably in 1844 and early 1845, later recorded, 'Mr. Pringle had established a school on the farm for the education of his own children and those of his neighbours ... ably conducted by the Revd. P. Wither, who also officiated at a church which was a short distance from the homestead and built at Mr. Pringle's own cost'. John Pringle's sister Isabella Pringle ran an 'infant, or rather preparatory, school'. One might speculate that the white children went to Mr Wither's school and the black to Miss Pringle's, although this is not clear; there is no mention of 'Notishe'. A.H. Duminy (ed.), *The Reminiscences of Richard Paver* (Cape Town, 1979), p.52.

16. Stretch [presumably to Philip], 'Caffraria', 24 June 1844, enclosed in Philip to Tidman, 10 Oct. 1844, LMS-SA 20/3/A,.

17. Read, jun. to Philip, 13 May 1844, enclosed in Philip to Tidman, Cape Town, 10 Oct. 1844, LMS-SA 20/3/A.

18. Read, jun. to Philip, 13 May 1844, and Read, sen. to Rev. Struthers, Kat River, 22 Feb. 1844, both enclosed in Philip to Tidman, Cape Town, 10 Oct. 1844, LMS-SA 20/3/A; Read, sen.

to Kitchingman, Philipton, 1 July 1844, in Le Cordeur and Saunders (eds.), *Kitchingman Papers*, pp.249–51.

19. Read, sen. to Rev. Struthers, Kat River, 22 Feb. 1844, in Philip to Tidman, Cape Town, 10 Oct. 1844, LMS-SA 20/3/A.

20. Stretch [presumably to Philip], 'Caffraria', 24 June 1844, enclosed in Philip to Tidman, 10 Oct. 1844, LMS-SA 20/3/A. Stretch was John Pringle's brother-in-law.

21. 'Duplicate – Copy of a document signed by the Missionaries' [dated on internal evidence 1 May 1844], enclosed in Philip to Tidman, 10 Oct. 1844, LMS-SA 20/3/A. The other missionaries who signed were Brownlee, Kayser, Ross, McDiarmid, Govan, Thomson, Bennie, Laing and Weir.

22. Niven to Stretch, n.d., enclosed in Philip to Tidman, 10 Oct. 1844, LMS-SA 20/3/A.

23. Read, sen. to Kitchingman, Philipton, 1 July 1844, in Le Cordeur and Saunders (eds.), *Kitchingman Papers*, p.249.

24. For example, Cumming to Read, sen., 11 May 1844, and Campbell to Read, sen., 30 May 1844, both enclosed in Philip to Tidman, 10 Oct. 1844, LMS-SA 20/3/A.

25. Govan to Cumming, Lovedale, 10 Dec. 1844, enclosed in Philip to LMS Directors, 10 Feb. 1845, LMS-SA 21/1/C.

26. Cumming to Govan, Iggibigha, 10 Dec. 1844, enclosed in Philip to LMS Directors, 10 Feb. 1845, LMS-SA 21/1/C.

27. Another GMS missionary, William Chalmers, later swore in the presence of all the missionaries who had signed the letter which the Reads would not sign that Cumming had told Chalmers that when he (Cumming) had visited Philipton after the Block Drift meeting, Read sen. asked for Struthers's address because he was 'much dissatisfied with what was done at said meeting and he meant to write his own explanation or account'. 'Statement of the Messrs Read relative to the case pending between themselves and the Caffre land Brethren', enclosed in Philip to LMS, 28 Feb. 1845, 21/2/A.

28. 'Notes on Revd J. Read's letter to his of Mr. Calderwood's people and the Reads' explanations', in Calderwood and Birt to LMS board, 26 Sept. 1844, LMS-SA 20/2/D.

29. Read, jun. to Arie van Rooyen and Valentyn Jacobs, 'Mr. Read's letter', enclosed in Calderwood and Birt to LMS board, 26 Sept. 1844, LMS-SA 20/2/D.

30. Govan to Cumming, Lovedale, 14 Dec. 1844, enclosed in Philip to LMS Directors, 10 Feb. 1845, LMS-SA 21/1/C.

31. Read, sen. and others to LMS Directors, Uitenhage, 24 Sept. 1844, enclosed in Elliot to Tidman and Freeman, LMS-SA 20/2/D.

32. Brownlee, Kayser, Merrington, Locke, Birt, Calderwood, and Gill to LMS, Umxelo, 10 Oct. 1844, LMS-SA 20/3/A.

33. Read, sen. to Kitchingman, Philipton, 22 Jan. 1844, in Le Cordeur and Saunders (eds.), *Kitchingman Papers*, pp.242–3.

34. Brown and Fry (eds.), *Scotland in the Age of the Disruption*.

35. The final dispute arose when the British government supported the Court of Sessions rejection through a series of court cases of the 1834 Veto Act (in itself a political compromise), which had given male heads of families the right to veto the choice of minister imposed upon a congregation by the patronage of the member of the landed gentry, or the burgh, in whose gift the parish was. Brown, 'The Ten Years' Conflict'.

36. Read, sen. to Kitchingman, Philipton, 22 Jan. 1844, in Le Cordeur and Saunders (eds.), *Kitchingman Papers*, p.243.

37. Ultimately bequeathing, so Andrew Ross argues, a more conservative version of evangelicalism to the Dutch Reformed Church and to some at least of the Scottish mission stations than that of Wilberforce, Philip and Read. A.C. Ross, 'The Dutch Reformed Church of South Africa: A Product of the Disruption?', in Brown and Fry (eds.), *Scotland in the Age of the Disruption*.

38. Donald C. Smith, *Passive Obedience and Prophetic Protest: Social Criticism in the Scottish Church 1830–1945* (New York, 1987), pp.52–3.

39. Ibid., pp.93–186.

40. James Read, jun., *The Kat River Settlement in 1851* (Cape Town, 1851); R. Ross, *Adam Kok's Griquas*; A. Ross, *John Philip*, pp.159–84.

41. 'Notes on Revd J. Read's letter to his and to Mr. Calderwood's people and the Reads' explanations …', Calderwood and Birt to LMS Directors, 26 Sept. 1844, LMS-SA 20/2/D.

42. Read, jun. to Calderwood, Philipton, 17 Sept. 1844, enclosed in Calderwood and Birt to LMS Directors, 26 Sept. 1844, LMS-SA, 20/2/D.

43. Kayser, Merrington, Locke, Birt, Calderwood, Gill to LMS, 10 Oct. 1844, LMS-SA 20/3/A.

44. Locke to LMS Directors, Graham's Town, 25 Sept. 1844, LMS-SA 20/2/D.

45. Calderwood and Birt to LMS Directors, Umxelo, 26 Sept. 1844, LMS-SA 20/2/D.

46. Read, sen. to Tidman, Philipton, 2 Oct. 1844, LMS-SA 20/3/A.

47. James McKay, *Reminiscences of the Last Kafir War, Illustrated with Numerous Anecdotes* (Grahamstown 1871; this edn, Cape Town, 1970), p.206. McKay considered that the slovenly wives of sergeants in the British army were not ladies either, nor indeed were the majority of white colonial wives; the instinctive laughter of the troops at the idea of Khoikhoi ladies is none the less revealing.

48. Robert Ross, 'The Etiquette of Race', in Ross, *Beyond the Pale*, pp.111–21. Pos continued, 'whoever does not want to be considered impolite must always have his hand ready to extend it to every white whom he meets': cited on p.119.

49. 'Let me beseech of you, Mr. Calderwood, just to reach back to an incident in your history at Blinkwater which happened a few years ago on Sunday morning, and think seriously of the injurious [influence?] which that single circumstance was calculated to exert over the minds of the people – Perhaps you are not aware that we (who are now charged with having attempted more than once to injure you in the dark) exerted ourselves in your behalf, and did all we could to counteract that influence': Read, jun. to Calderwood, Philipton, 17 Sept. 1844, enclosed in Calderwood and Birt to LMS Directors, Umxelo, 26 Sept. 1844, LMS-SA 20/2/D.

50. This of course implied that there was a 'native character' and that the Reads were familiar with it. 'Statement of the Messrs Read relative to the case pending between themselves and the Caffre land Brethren', enclosed in Philip to LMS Directors, 28 Feb. 1845, LMS-SA 21/2/A.

51. Janet Hodgson, 'A Battle for Sacred Power: Christian Beginnings among the Xhosa', in Elphick and Davenport (eds.), *Christianity in South Africa*, pp.68–88; Williams, *When Races Meet*; David Chidester, *Religions of South Africa* (London and New York, 1992); J.B. Peires, *The Dead Will Arise* (Johannesburg, 1989).

52. Robert Hunter, *History of the Missions of the Free Church of Scotland in India and Africa* (London, Edinburgh and New York, 1873), p.347.

53. A. Ross, *John Philip*, pp.185–6.

54. Philip to Tidman, 11 March 1845, LMS-SA 21/2; cited in A. Ross, *John Philip*, p.185.

55. Including lengthy discussions of Maqoma's drinking, and (in a key debate over the control of women) of the fact that the chief had compelled one of his wives to put to death the child born of an adulterous affair. Rev. Henry Calderwood, *Caffres and Caffre Missions; With Preliminary Chapters on the Cape Colony as a Field for Emigration and Basis of Missionary Operation* (London, 1858), pp.65–75.

56. Ibid., pp.17–30.

57. Deryck Lovegrove, 'Idealism and Association in Early Nineteenth-Century Dissent', in W.J. Sheils and Diana Wood (eds.), *Voluntary Religion* (Oxford, 1986), pp.303–18. Read itinerated in Essex and London with LMS founder Thomas Haweis; later in life he recalled that his reception by the Xhosa compared favourably with that at Ponders End, where 'a Man with

a Fiddle came and played before us, and the others with old kettles shaking full of Stones'. Cape Archives, A50: Read to Philip, 7 March 1846.

58. Calderwood, *Caffres and Caffre Missions*, pp.114–16.

59. Read, sen. to Kitchingman, Philipton, 25 March 1844, in Le Cordeur and Saunders (eds.), *Kitchingman Papers*, p.245.

60. Read, sen. to Kitchingman, Philipton, 11 March 1839, in Le Cordeur and Saunders (eds.), *Kitchingman Papers*, p.206. Just before referring to this figure, Read commented '[w]e have our own plans and we execute them. If the Doctor [Philip] will give us any assistance we take it, otherwise we get on without it as well as we can, but we cannot be waiting the decisions of Church Square. I would rather, as Matthew Wilks said, sell my shirt than the work should stand still, but my visit to England has assisted.'

61. Read, sen. to Kitchingman, Philipton, 25 March 1844, in Le Cordeur and Saunders (eds.), *Kitchingman Papers*, p.245.

62. 'Account of the Labours and of Native Teachers supported by private Individuals and churches in England in connection with Philipton Congregation Kat River'. Read, sen., Philipton, 17 April 1844, LMS-SA 20/1/C.

63. Ibid.

64. Ibid.

65. For a summary: Le Cordeur and Saunders (eds.), *Kitchingman Papers*, pp.189–91.

66. For a more extensive discussion, see my 'Early Khoisan Uses of Mission Christianity', in Bredekamp and Ross (eds.), *Missions and Christianity*.

67. Paul Landau, *The Realm of the Word: Language, Gender, and Christianity in a Southern African Kingdom* (Portsmouth, NH, 1995), p.xxviii.

68. All quotations from Read to LMS Directors, Philipton, 3 June 1843, LMS-SA 19/2/A.

69. Ibid.

70. Read, jun., *Kat River Settlement*, p.47.

CHAPTER 10

1. The most comprehensive recent biographical study is Enklaar, *Van der Kemp*.

2. W.F. Lye (ed.), *Andrew Smith's Journal of his Expedition into the Interior of South Africa: 1834–36* (Cape Town, 1975), p.40.

3. Legassick, 'The Griqua', pp.443–4.

4. Grout to Anderson, 1 July 1852; Archives of the American Board of Commissioners for Foreign Missions, Houghton Library, Harvard University (hereafter ABC). See also ABC 15.4, Grout to Rufus Anderson, 11 Feb. 1849 in which Grout predicts that the Natal government will not pay much attention to Schreuder: 'He is a good scholar, particularly in the language, but while here before, he … became very filthy in his habits, and manner of living, and his influence in civilization was worse than nothing, a point of high importance with English gentlemen.'

5. Note by Harriet Colenso on Colenso to Shepstone, 29 Jan. 1873; Colenso Papers, Killie Campbell Africana Library of the University of Natal, Durban.

6. Halfdan E. Sommerfelt, *Den Norske Zulu Mission* (Christiana, 1865), pp.166–7n.

7. O.G. Myklebust, *Den Norske Misjonsselskaps Historie: Sør-Afrika, China, Sudan*, III (Stavanger, 1949), p.34.

8. James Green, in a letter to a woman of Cape Town, extracted in Gray to Hawkins, 7 Sept. 1849, folio D7, Archives of the United Society for the Propagation of the Gospel in Foreign Parts, Rhodes House, Oxford (hereafter SPG).

9. SPG D7, Bishop Gray to Hawkins, 5 Feb. 1850.

10. SPG D8, Colenso to Secretaries, 9 Nov. 1855.

11. As explained by Robert Robertson in a letter to Mackenzie's sister; *The Net*, 3, 1868:172–3.

12. Myklebust, *Den Norske Misjonsselskaps Historie*, II, pp.67–9.
13. Ibid., p.33.
14. However, as Boston-based Secretary Rufus Anderson explained to Philip, democratic organisation was not incompatible with the principle that only college graduates should be employed; ABC 2.0, 16 July 1834.
15. ABC 15.4, Venable to Hill, 23 Sept. 1837.
16. N. Etherington, *Christianity in South Africa: A Political, Social and Cultural History* (Oxford, 1997), p.93.
17. Robert Robertson, writing in *The Net*, 3, 1868:172–3.
18. SPG D25, Robertson to Alice Mackenzie, enclosed in Alice Mackenzie to Hawkins, 2 Nov. 1863.
19. ABC 15.4, Mellen to RA, 10 Aug. 1855. This report by an American Congregational missionary may, of course, be coloured by a suspicion of all claims to episcopal authority.
20. SPG D8, Colenso to Secretary of SPG, 9 Nov. 1855
21. Myklebust, *Den Norske Misjonsselskaps Historie*, III, pp.50–1. However, the Norwegian clergy were allowed the privilege of trading, which was denied to the agents of most other societies; see SPG D44, Cree to Bullock, 25 Jan. 1876.
22. ABC 2.1.1 R., Anderson to the Brethren of the South African Mission, 14 Nov. 1849; ABC 15.4, Joint mission letter to Anderson, 24 April 1850. In 1875 child allowances put Bridgman at the top of the scale with an annual wage of £245; see AZM Case 1, 1/1/4a, Minutes of Mission Meeting, Durban, 19 June 1875.
23. ABC 15.4, Lindley and Wilder to Anderson, 7 March 1864. The American missionary Lewis Grout, on the other hand, noted in 1849 that his brethren lived in roomier houses than most of their contemporaries in the United States: ABC 15.4, Grout to Anderson, 28 June, 1849.
24. *Natal Independent*, 24 March 1853.
25. SPG D25, Callaway to the Secretaries, 22 June 1862.
26. SPG D8, Walton to Colenso, 4 Mar. 1859.
27. SPG D44, Cree to Bullock, 25 Jan. 1876. When a Norwegian missionary, S.M. Samuelson, defected to the Church of England, he continued trading, arguing that in Zululand the missionary must 'either buy things from the natives, or live alone and starve': SPG D44, Samuelson to Bullock, 3 Oct. 1876. The complaint which specifically aroused protests from private traders was sparked by Samuelson's sale of 300 animal skins to raise money to send one of his sons to Europe.
28. SPG D25, Application of Dean Green to SPG, 1865.
29. See, for example, ABC 15.4, Wilder to RA, 18 Nov. 1850.
30. ABC 15.4, Ireland to RA, 1 Nov. 1850.
31. *Missions-Berichte* (Berlin, 1853).
32. SPG E7, Callaway journal, 1 July to 30 Sept. 1860.
33. SPG D25, Callaway to Hawkins, 6 Feb. 1863.
34. ABC 15.4, Vol. 8, Wilder to Clark, 1 March 1872.
35. SPG E33, Samuelson to Secretaries, 24 Jan. 1878.
36. Brendan Carmody, quoting T.O. Beidelman in 'Conversion and School at Chikuni, 1905–39', *Africa*, 58, 1988:203.
37. SPG E33, Samuelson to Secretaries, St Paul's, 24 Jan. 1878.
38. ABC 15.4, Tyler to Clark, 12 Aug. 1878.
39. Ibid., Pinkerton to Clark, 3 March 1879.
40. Ibid., Abraham to Clark, 7 June 1869.
41. SPG D37, Green to Bullock, 3 June 1874.
42. Ibid., Table of salaries, 1867.
43. ABC 15.4, Bridgman to Clark, 12 June 1871.
44. Ibid., Pinkerton to Clark, 18 April 1876.

45. N. Etherington, *Preachers, Peasants and Politics in Southeast Africa* (London, 1978), pp.117–27, 148–9.

46. ABC 15.4, Ireland to Clark, 1 Nov. 1877, 6 June 1878.

47. Ibid., Ireland and Robbins to Clark, 6 Nov. 1878.

48. See W.R. Shenk, 'Henry Venn's Instructions to Missionaries', *Missiology*, 5, 1977:467–83, and 'Rufus Anderson and Henry Venn: A Special Relationship?', *International Bulletin of Missionary Research*, 5, 1981:168–72; Max Warren (ed.), *To Apply the Gospel: Selections from the Writings of Henry Venn* (Grand Rapids, 1971).

49. ABC 2.1.1, Clark to Grout, 14 May 1867.

50. Ibid., Clark to Grout, 17 Feb. 1867.

51. Ibid., Clark to Rood, 30 Dec. 1876.

52. ABC 15.4, Grout to Anderson, 16 Sept. 1861.

53. SPG E33, Jenkinson, Quarterly Report, 24 June 1878. Although the man concerned is unnamed, as he is said to have been both the brother and the son of missionaries, he is most likely to have been either the son of Ralph Stott or Joseph Jackson.

54. See, for example, SPG D25, Ferreira to Secretaries, April 1860; *The Net*, 4, 1869:36–7; *Missions-Berichte* (Berlin, 1859), pp.357–61.

CHAPTER 11

My thanks to the University of Houston's African American Studies Program for providing a grant to cover the costs associated with this study.

1. The American Board of Commissioners for Foreign Missions, or more popularly the American Board, was launched in 1810 in Boston, Mass., as a non-denominational Protestant missionary society. New England's Congregational churches, however, provided the earliest and strongest support for the American Board – the first foreign mission body in the United States – and in practice most missionaries were Congregationalists.

2. In most cases, I have retained the Zulu orthography in use at the time for the spelling of Zulu place names, organisations and personalities.

3. L. Switzer, 'The Problems of an African Mission in a White-dominated, Multi-racial Society: The American Zulu Mission in South Africa 1885–1910', Ph.D. thesis, University of Natal, 1971, p.10 (citing AZM report for 1850).

4. Comaroff and Comaroff, *Of Revelation and Revolution*, II, p.26.

5. The eastern Cape – especially the area between the Kei and Fish rivers known as the Ciskei – vied with Natal as the most concentrated area of missionary activity in the subcontinent during the nineteenth century. The Red–School argument is summarised in Switzer, *Power and Resistance*, pp.10–12.

6. E.g., N. Etherington, 'Christianity and African Society in Nineteenth Century Natal', in A. Duminy and B. Guest (eds.), *Natal and Zululand from Earliest Times to 1910: A New History* (Pietermaritzburg, 1989), pp.280–2; Hildegarde Fast, '"In at one Ear and out at the Other": African Response to the Wesleyan Message in Xosaland 1825–1835', *Journal of Religion in Africa*, 23, 1993:147–74. For a critique of the construction of African religion in religious studies, see R. Shaw, 'The Invention of "African Traditional Religion"', *Religion*, 20, 1990:339–53.

7. E.g., N. Etherington, 'Missionary Doctors and African Healers in Mid-Victorian South Africa', *South African Historical Journal*, 19, 1987:77–91; S. Feierman, 'Healing as Social Criticism in the Time of Colonial Conquest', *African Studies*, 54(1), 1995:73–88; R. Werbner, 'The Suffering Body: Passion and Ritual Allegory in Christian Encounters', *Journal of Southern African Studies*, 23(2), June 1997:311–24.

8. My understanding of these issues has been enriched by e-mail exchanges with Michael Mahoney (22 Nov., 5 Dec. 1997), who is examining religious discourses in a Ph.D. that

focuses on the Mapumulo–Lower Tugela region in Natal (a centre of American mission activity) between 1879 and 1906. The ideas of Richard Gray and Lamin Sanneh were also useful in helping me to conceptualise the topic: R. Gray, *Black Christians and White Missionaries* (New Haven and London, 1990); L. Sanneh, *Encountering the West. Christianity and the Global Cultural Process: The African Dimension* (Maryknoll, 1993).

9. African-American missionaries sponsored by the American Board were not sent to Natal, but they were sent to the Board's missions in colonial Mozambique and Rhodesia in the 1880s and 1890s. See, e.g., S.M. Jacobs, 'African-American Women Missionaries and European Imperialism in Southern Africa, 1880–1920', *Women's Studies International Forum*, 13(4), 1990:381–94.

10. The historian Jeff Guy suggests that the narratives of power characterising the Shepstone era in Natal were essentially patriarchal narratives that Shepstone constructed with 'leading African men, many of them soon to be known as chiefs'. These conversations linked coloniser and colonised in a system that was essentially built on compromise: the dynamics of male power and privilege within the chiefdoms ('in its most fundamental aspects, male control of female lives and labour') would be sustained by Shepstone and his chiefs in the new colonial order. J. Guy, 'An Accommodation of Patriarchs: Theophilus Shepstone and the System of Native Administration in Natal', Unpublished paper, History and African Studies Seminar Series, University of Natal, 1997. See also, J. Guy, 'Gender Oppression in Southern Africa's Precapitalist Societies', in C. Walker (ed.), *Women and Gender in Southern Africa to 1945* (Cape Town and London, 1990), pp.33–47.

11. M. Dinnerstein, 'The American Board Mission to the Zulu, 1835–1900', Ph.D. thesis, Columbia University, 1971, pp.195–8.

12. N. Etherington, 'Gender Issues', pp.137–9.

13. M. Dinnerstein, 'The American Zulu Mission in the Nineteenth Century: Clash over Customs', *Church History*, 45(2), 1976:243–4, 246 (as cited); Etherington, 'Gender Issues', pp.141–2.

14. Etherington culled the archives of several missionary societies in Natal between 1835 and 1885 and found 177 individuals whose reasons for coming to the mission station were recorded. Only 12 per cent claimed they were there for religious reasons, while 33 per cent were refugees, 26 per cent were seeking employment, 15 per cent had relatives on the station, and 14 per cent were converted elsewhere and had accompanied their missionary to the station. N. Etherington, 'Mission Station Melting Pots as a Factor in the Rise of South African Black Nationalism', *International Journal of African Historical Studies*, 9, 1976:592–605. The refugees were much the same in all missionary societies. They were women who had refused arranged marriages, women who were barren or past the age of child-bearing who had been abandoned by their husbands, widows who rejected customary marriages with their brothers-in-law, diviners who would not follow their vocation, outcasts accused of the crime of witchcraft; they were ambitious young men who could no longer find a place for themselves in the old order; and they were displaced persons – the aged, the disabled, the physically disfigured, the casualties of war.

15. Dinnerstein, 'American Board Mission', pp.43–52, and 'American Zulu Mission', p.236.

16. Switzer, 'Problems of an African Mission', pp.20, 41 (citing ABCFM, AZM reports).

17. Ibid., p.409, n.23 (citing two letters written in the 1890s).

18. John W. Colenso, the first Anglican Bishop of Natal, was a significant exception. But the man 'who denied the doctrine of eternal punishment, who permitted the baptism of polygynists and who supported hereditary Chiefs', as Etherington puts it, 'made fewer converts than did the American missionaries who preached hell-fire, temperance and monogamy'. Etherington, 'Christianity and African Society', p.282.

19. The Native Home and Foreign Missionary Society was initially called the Native Home Missionary Society. In later years it was also called the Zulu Home and Foreign Mission

Work and the Zulu Missionary Society.

20. The 'three-self formula' was the brainchild of the American Board foreign secretary Rufus Anderson (1796–1880) and his counterpart in Britain, the Anglican Henry Venn (1796–1873). While this strategy was not really implemented by the American Board until after the American Civil War (Anderson retired in 1866), it would have an enormous impact on the domestic and foreign mission field thereafter.

21. AZM, *Jubilee of the American Mission in Natal, 1835–1886* (Pietermaritzburg, 1886), pp.39–43; Switzer, 'Problems of an African Mission', pp.23–25.

22. Dinnerstein, for example, cites examples from the 1860s and 1870s of young men raised in the mission who wanted to retain the custom of *lobola* because they now had daughters or were responsible for sisters of marriageable age. Older men whose wives were no longer of child-bearing age were taking younger concubines, while the wives went to live with their eldest sons as custom dictated. Many *amakholwa*, moreover, were literate in Zulu and could see that the Bible did not support the mission's demand that Christians reject traditional African practices. Dinnerstein, 'American Board Mission', pp.165–7.

23. A.F. Christofersen, *Adventuring with God: The Story of the American Board Mission in South Africa*, ed. Richard Sales (Durban, n.d. [c.1967]), p.46 (citing minutes of mission meeting in Jan. 1862).

24. E.W. Smith, *The Life and Times of Daniel Lindley (1801–80)* (London, 1949), pp.392–3.

25. Ngidi had two cousins, William Ngidi and his brother Jonathan, and all three were converted to Christianity by Samuel Marsh, the American missionary at Table Mountain. Marsh left in 1851 due to ill health (he died in 1853), and he was replaced by Jacob Döhne, who had been with the Berlin Missionary Society before joining the Americans. Döhne was a Zulu linguist, but apparently he mistreated his African parishioners. The Ngidi brothers seem to have left Table Mountain shortly after Marsh withdrew and attached themselves to Bishop Colenso at his station, Ekukanyeni. William Ngidi had a decided influence on Colenso's theological outlook and mission activities, but he left the church in 1867 and returned to customary practices prohibited by the mission. William's brother Jonathan, an artisan and trader, later joined Mbiyana in Zululand.

26. Interview with the American Congregational missionary Richard Sales, Dec. 1964. See also Christofersen, *Adventuring with God*, pp.67–8 (editor's note).

27. Delegations of lay people from the churches, as well as their preachers and evangelists, were assembled at Umsunduzi, where they debated and finally voted in favour of the Umsunduzi Rules. Polygamy ('Remark – Any man living with more than one wife, shall be regarded as a polygamist') and *lobola* ('Remarks – 1. The demanding of cattle, or money, or goods of any kind for a daughter, or sister or female friend, as a condition of marriage … 2. The calling of cattle, or money or goods, by the mother of a girl or anyone standing in the place of the mother shall be regarded as *ukulobolisa*') were prohibited. No African male could live with a woman and no African female could live with a man until they were married 'in a Christian way'. No church member could drink beer or participate in beer drinks, drink any other intoxicating beverage or smoke the equivalent of marijuana or *dagga* (*insangu* in Zulu). Switzer, 'Problems of an African Mission', pp.33–4.

28. J.D. Taylor, *The American Board Mission in South Africa: A Sketch of Seventy-five Years* (Durban, 1911), p.21.

29. The following comments on the temperance crusade are taken from an unpublished memoir by Mrs Bridgman ('The Beginnings of the Temperance Movement at Umzumbe Mission Station, Natal, South Africa'), and additional reminiscences by her daughter, Amy Bridgman Cowles ('Beginnings of the Temperance Movement at Umzumbe'), in a file marked 'Umzumbe Church Records, 1860–1896'. I located the manuscripts initially at Inanda and was later permitted to transfer these and other unclassified documents from Inanda to the Natal Archives, Pietermaritzburg, for permanent deposit.

30. Her husband, Elijah, was in charge of the theological school at Amanzimtoti from 1875 to his death in 1889. They were the first missionaries to live at Umzumbe when the station was founded in 1861.

31. The Volunteers had 'their own constitution and uniform', and eventually became the strongest lay organisation, with branches 'in almost all the churches'. Christofersen, *Adventuring with God*, p.129. The AZM claimed in 1900 that 'volunteer' workers exceeded those of any other mission society 'regardless of size' associated with the American Board. Switzer, 'Problems of an African Mission', p.280, n.17 (citing 1900 AZM report).

32. The missionary responsible for much of this work was a teacher by the name of Gertrude Hance. See her reminiscences in *The Zulu Yesterday and To-day* (New York, 1916), esp. Chs. 5–7. African women seem to have played a prominent role in church evangelism during these years – so much so that they comprised a majority of the church membership by the late 1890s. More than 80 per cent of the church was female by the 1960s. Christofersen, *Adventuring with God*, p.126.

33. The importance of singing in the daily lives of African Christians raised in Nonconformist Protestant mission settings cannot be overestimated. See R.J. Slough, '"Let Every Tongue, by Art Refined, Mingle its Softest Notes with Mine": An Exploration of Hymn-singing Events and Dimensions of Knowing', in M.B. Aune and V. de Marinis (eds.), *Religious and Social Ritual: Interdisciplinary Explorations* (Albany, NY, 1996), pp.175–206.

34. There were visits by evangelists from South Africa, Britain and the United States to American mission stations – the most notable being the revivals conducted in 1896–7 and apparently in 1901 by a charismatic preacher named Elder Weavers, who operated a Bible school in Iowa.

35. Switzer, 'Problems of an African Mission', pp.43–4.

36. The mission used the phrase 'young people' when referring to young men (mainly students from the boarding schools and others associated with groups like the Blue Ribbon Army), who favoured separatist leaders like Mbiyana Ngidi and allegedly tried to buy land with money they collected for the evangelism programme.

37. The Abaisitupa would function as the church's executive body until 1919.

38. Switzer, 'Problems of an African Mission', p.424 (citing AZM report in 1902).

39. Ibid., p.41 (citing AZM report for 1886).

40. Ibid., p.362.

41. The pastors were at the top of a three-tiered hierarchy in church government. Below them were the preachers, who were also allowed a voice in ecclesiastical affairs and were sometimes appointed ministers of churches with the power to control church funds. Below the preachers were the evangelists – the largest in number but with no corresponding power. They were not allowed to supervise churches, and received little financial support. Evangelists were really laymen and laywomen from local congregations who devoted a specific portion of their time to missionary work in the vicinity of their parishes.

42. Compiled from ABCFM, AZM reports.

43. Switzer, 'Problems of an African Mission', pp.392, 426; AZM, *South African Deputation Papers*, privately printed 'for the information of the Deputation of 1903' in 1904, pp.14–15. Church membership pledges were fixed at a minimum of 8 shillings a year for adult males and 4 shillings a year for adult females.

44. Not much has been written on the efforts of the AZM's African churches in Natal to establish missions outside the colony. Most recruits sent to the Mozambique field (the main stations were at Inhambane and Beira), launched by the American Board in the 1880s, were Africans from Natal, and they came to regard Mozambique as their mission field. African Congregationalists continued to provide pastors and financial support to the church at Inhambane, for example, until the 1960s. Christofersen, *Adventuring with God*, pp.116–24. African Congregationalists were also recruited to work in south-eastern Rhodesia – essen-

tially an extension of the Mozambique mission – when mission stations were established there at the invitation of Cecil Rhodes beginning in the 1890s (the main stations were at Mount Silinda, Chikore and Melsetter). The American Board also established the West Central African Mission, as it was called, in Angola in 1886.

45. Switzer, 'Problems of an African Mission', p.40 (for 1880), p.460 (for 1910). Nine of the 26 designated churches in 1910 required financial aid from the Home and Foreign Missionary Society. Christofersen noted that the growth rate between 1885 and 1915 (when church membership reached 7322) was the high point in the expansion of the church: 'Thereafter growth has been steady but unspectacular in the churches founded by the American Board missionaries': Christofersen, *Adventuring with God*, p.95.

46. Switzer, 'Problems of an African Mission', pp.44, 427 (citing AZM reports in 1904 and 1906).

47. Author's interviews with the late Gideon Sivetye (the son of Mvakwendlu Sivetye, one of the prominent African pastors of this period, and himself an ordained minister) and Richard Sales (an American Board missionary stationed at Inanda during the mid-1960s), and discussions with church members at Umzumbe, Inanda and Groutville (Umvoti) between 1964 and 1967.

48. The quote is from the American missionary Frederick Bridgman. See Switzer, 'Problems of an African Mission', p.373, citing a paper on the 'Ethiopian Movement' prepared for the 1903 American Board deputation to Natal. The biographer Harry Langworthy suggests that Booth was both a pacifist and a radical fundamentalist. His interpretation of biblical precepts was literal, his view of a new millennium for Africa total. Booth advocated 'complete racial equality' and the unity of all 'Christians of the African race'. He called on African-Americans to return to Africa and assist Africans in Christianising, educating and industrialising the peoples of the continent. Booth's ideas were spelled out initially in a scheme called the African Christian Union (1896), which received decidedly mixed reviews from educated Africans in Natal and was condemned in African newspapers outside Natal like *Imvo Zabantsundu*. Booth himself believed he had unwittingly triggered an emotional 'avalanche' of bitterness among the 120 or so Africans who attended the all-night inaugural meeting of the ACU: 'Their many-sided indictments, summed up, amounted to this, there was no white man known to the Zulu people worthy of absolute trust, no missionary, no legislator, no civilian, NO, NOT ONE.' See H.W. Langworthy, *'Africa for the African': The Life of Joseph Booth* (Blantyre, 1996), esp. Chs. 4, 11.

49. On the Zulu Congregational Church (ZCC), cf. D.P. Collins, 'The Origins and Formation of the Zulu Congregational Church, 1896–1908', M.A. dissertation, University of Natal (Durban), 1978, esp. Chs. 3–5; Switzer, 'Problems of an African Mission', Ch.7. In addition to the archival record, both authors interviewed members of Shibe's family who had known Simungu and were actively involved in the ZCC.

50. Switzer, 'Problems of an African Mission', pp.101, 126, n.86 (citing AZM letters in 1886).

51. The 1888 Bill targeted the Table Mountain reserve and two Anglican reserves, Nonoti and Umlazi.

52. Collins, 'Zulu Congregational Church', p.66 (citing AZM report in 1893).

53. The name Fokoti is also spelled Fakoti and Fokati, and he is also referred to by several first and last names in the mission record, including Fokoti Makanya, Ndeya Makanya and Fokoti Tyotyo.

54. Switzer, 'Problems of an African Mission', p.380 (citing 1896 report).

55. Shibe knew several separatist leaders, including Pambini Mzimba, who left the Presbyterian mission in the eastern Cape after 35 years to establish the highly successful Presbyterian Church of Africa in 1898. Shibe and Fokoti were probably also acquainted with Edward Tsewu, who helped launch the Independent Presbyterian Church in Johannesburg in 1897, and Mangena (Moses) Mokone, who founded the Ethiopian Church in Pretoria in 1892.

56. Switzer, 'Problems of an African Mission', p.387 (citing 1897 mission report).

57. A white lawyer was consulted to provide a legal justification for the ordination service, and a black Wesleyan Methodist preacher sought (unsuccessfully) to gain recognition for the Johannesburg church from the Transvaal authorities. The ZCC had an executive council similar to the Abaisitupa, and its ecclesiastical procedures, church services, schools and so forth were patterned almost exactly on the mission church (they even used the same school primers and hymn books). As Shibe told the 1902 Lands Commission: 'if you wish to know what our church is like, I should say it was like the American Church as far as its laws are concerned.' Switzer, 'Problems of an African Mission', pp.417–18, n.73; Collins, 'Zulu Congregational Church', pp.116–17.

58. Collins, 'Zulu Congregational Church', p.87 (citing AZM letter in 1898).

59. *Inkanyiso yase Natal* (Natal Light) was launched in April 1889 by the Anglicans in Pietermaritzburg. The newspaper was turned over to its African editors in January 1895, and it survived for about 18 months as the first independent organ of African political opinon in Natal. L. Switzer (ed.), *South Africa's Alternative Press: Voices of Protest and Resistance, 1880–1960* (Cambridge, 1997), p.25.

60. His grandmother was one of Daniel Lindley's earliest converts, and his father, James Dube, was one of the first ordained pastors. His uncle, Mqawe, was the chief most sympathetic to the Christian community in the Inanda reserve.

61. Ohlange, a boys' secondary school, was established at Phoenix, a rural settlement outside Durban. For *Ilanga lase Natal* (Natal Sun), see R.H. Davis, '"Qude maniki!": John L. Dube, Pioneer Editor of *Ilanga lase Natal*', in Switzer, *South Africa's Alternative Press*, Ch. 2.

62. Dube was the first president of the South African Native National Congress when it was launched in 1912 (the name was changed to the African National Congress in 1923). Martin Lutuli, a founding member of the Natal Native Congress, was a prominent landowner from Umvoti, where he was elected chief of the local Christian community in 1908. His nephew and successor was Albert Lutuli (or Luthuli), the future Nobel prizewinner and ANC president (1952–67).

63. According to Mrs John M. Shibe, a daughter-in-law of Simungu Shibe, it was John Dube who suggested the name Zulu Congregational Church. Collins, 'Zulu Congregational Church', p.107. But Dube did not take up the offer to lead the ZCC: 'he [Dube] had come to the conclusion that the best of the people would not follow him away from the mission, and that he saw that his greatest influence lay in working in unison with us [the AZM]'. Switzer, 'Problems of an African Mission', p.398 (citing letter in 1900).

64. *Ilanga lase Natal*, 20 March 1908 (originally translated for the author by the late journalist, critic and writer R.R.R. Dhlomo).

65. Switzer, 'Problems of an African Mission', pp.403–4 (citing 'Ethiopian Movement', a paper prepared for the 1903 American Board deputation to Natal).

66. Nyuswa had spent 13 years as a student at the Amanzimtoti Seminary and the theological school and was sent to Umtwalumi in 1892. Under his tutelage, Umtwalumi had become the largest rural church in the American mission by 1896.

67. Switzer, 'Problems of an African Mission', pp.390–1 (citing AZM correspondence in 1898 and the 1903 'Ethiopian Movement' paper).

68. Collins, 'Zulu Congregational Church', pp.92–4. The mission noted: 'To the surprise of your committee not one vote was cast for "the Zulu Congregational Church" ... it was too tribal, sectional, limited – "African" having a wider meaning than "Zulu."' Switzer, 'Problems of an African Mission', p.405 (citing AZM report in 1901).

69. Goodenough returned to Johannesburg after the South African War and re-established a mine compound ministry, but his relations with African church members remained poor. African Christians from Natal were launching programmes of their own in the Transvaal, and operating largely outside Goodenough's authority. Separatist pressures could not be con-

tained, and the Transvaal mission was mired in controversy even after Goodenough was finally removed from the field in 1913.

70. Collins, 'Zulu Congregational Church', pp.131–3. The 1902 schism was generated by a dispute over land rights at Umzumbe, and those of 1907 and 1916 by quarrels between Shibe and his lieutenants. The 1918 schism was apparently the first to adopt doctrinal and ritual practices associated with Zionist churches.

71. The quotes are taken from E.H. Brookes and C. de B. Webb, *A History of Natal* (Pietermaritzburg, 1965), p.114; S. Marks, *Reluctant Rebellion: The 1906–8 Disturbances in Natal* (Oxford, 1970), p.331.

72. S. Marks, 'Christian African Participation in the 1906 Zulu Rebellion', *Bulletin of the Society for African Church History*, 2, 1965:61; Switzer, 'Problems of an African Mission', pp.451–2 (citing NAD report in 1907).

73. Switzer, 'Problems of an African Mission', pp.454–6.

74. Taylor, *American Board Mission*, pp.56–7; Switzer, 'Problems of an African Mission', pp.459–60 (citing AZM letter in 1907).

75. The African church would eventually weigh in with its own verdict. Once again, a focus of agitation was the church in Johannesburg, where a new minister – a man named Gardiner Mvuyana – was ordained in 1908. His home was the Ifafa mission station in Natal; he had been in contact with Shibe's followers and was in sympathy with the work of the ZCC. In Johannesburg he had built up a cadre of 60 lay preachers and evangelists, all but one of whom joined him in seceding from the American mission. The new church, launched in 1917, was named, appropriately enough, the African Congregational Church (ACC), and it proved to be a much more significant threat to the Americans than the ZCC. The churches were well organised and generously supported, and the ACC would claim more than 100 000 members – most of them in Natal and the Transvaal – by the 1960s. A brief description of the 1917 schism is given in Christofersen, *Adventuring with God*, p.113.

76. McCord moved the medical department from Adams, where it was a marginal activity, to Durban, pioneered an urban hospital for Africans in Natal (the McCord Zulu Hospital in Durban), established the first nursing course (lasting three years) for Africans, and the first class of trainee African nurses in South Africa.

77. Switzer, 'Problems of an African Mission', p.542 (citing letter in 1903).

78. On LeRoy and Loram, see S.M. du Rand, 'From Mission School to Bantu Education: A History of Adams College', M.A. dissertation, University of Natal, Durban, 1990, pp.50–60; R.H. Davis, jun., 'Charles T. Loram and the American Model for African Education in South Africa', in P. Kallaway (ed.), *Apartheid and Education: The Education of Black South Africans* (Johannesburg, 1984), pp.108–26. On the liberal segregationists, see S. Dubow, *Racial Segregation and the Origins of Apartheid in South Africa, 1919–36* (New York, 1989), esp. Ch.1; P.B. Rich, *Hope and Despair: English-Speaking Intellectuals and South African Politics, 1896–1976* (London and New York, 1993), esp. Chs.1–3.

INDEX

225